RARE BIRD PRESENTS

ALONG COMES...THE ASSOCIATION

Beyond Folk Rock and Three-Piece Suits

RARE BIRD PRESENTS

ALONG COMES...THE ASSOCIATION

Beyond Folk Rock and Three-Piece Suits

RUSS GIGUERE AND ASHLEY WREN COLLINS
FOREWORD BY DAVID GEFFEN

RARE BIRD BOOKS
LOS ANGELES, CALIF.

THIS IS A GENUINE RARE BIRD BOOK

Rare Bird Books
6044 North Figueroa Street
Los Angeles, California 90042
rarebirdbooks.com

For more information, address:
Rare Bird Books Subsidiary Rights Department
6044 North Figueroa Street
Los Angeles, California 90042

Set in Minion
Printed in the United States

Photos provided from Russ Giguere's personal archives unless otherwise noted.

© 1968 Paul McCartney / Photographer: Linda McCartney. All rights reserved.

Los Angeles Times Photographic Archive, Library Special Collections,
Charles E. Young Research Library, UCLA

10 9 8 7 6 5 4 3 2 1

Publisher's Cataloging-in-Publication Data

Names: Giguere, Russ, author. | Collins, Ashley Wren, author.
Title: Along Comes the Association: Beyond Folk Rock and Three-Piece Suits /
Russ Giguere and Ashley Wren Collins.
Description: Includes bibliographical references and index. |
First Hardcover Edition | A Genuine Rare Bird Book | New York, NY;
Los Angeles, CA: Rare Bird Books, 2020.
Identifiers: ISBN 9781644280270
Subjects: LCSH Giguere, Russ. | Association (Musical group). | Folk mu-
sic—United States. | Folk-rock music. | Popular music—1961-1970. | Rock
music—1961-1970. | Folk musicians—United States—Biography. | Rock musi-
cians—United States—Biography. | BISAC BIOGRAPHY &
AUTOBIOGRAPHY / Music | MUSIC / Genres & Styles /
Folk & Traditional | MUSIC / Genres & Styles / Rock
Classification: LCC ML421.A83 G54 2020 | DDC 784/.092/2—dc23

Contents

Along Comes The Association:
Beyond Folk-Rock and Three-Piece Suits
Acknowledgments

A GREAT WOMAN GOES a long way toward helping a man accomplish more than he ever could were he left to his own devices. To that end, I'd like to acknowledge three women without whom this book would still be a pipe dream. (And by that, I mean a dream I'd still be having while taking a toke on a pipe.)

First and foremost, I'd like to thank my wife, researcher/fact finder/truth seeker extraordinaire Valerie Yaros[1], for her invaluable, indispensable, and indefatigable scholarly efforts hunting down impossible facts and figures, recreating long forgotten timelines, sourcing and organizing pictures, and too many other things to list that made this book possible. If you had to rely on my memory alone, we'd be in trouble. Thank you, Valerie, from the bottom of my heart.

To my cowriter, Ashley Wren Collins, for putting up with me—I told her many stories, and she researched and dug deeper (nearly six feet under to an early grave!) to help me get my experiences on the page and give them a historical perspective to boot! Thanks, kid, for helping me make this dream come true.

And to my agent, Charlotte Gusay, for her perseverance, unflagging enthusiasm, and belief in me and this book.

---

1   Valerie Yaros has been a historian/archivist for Screen Actors Guild-American Federation of Television and Radio Artists since 1996. Historic sleuthing and fact-checking is her specialty and passion, and she has assisted numerous authors in the quest for historical knowledge. Valerie first recalls hearing The Association singing "Goodbye, Columbus" as a child on the car radio en route to Montgomery Mall in Bethesda, Maryland, with her mom. She then thought Columbus referred to the man who discovered America, but now knows better.

(Wait, there's a fourth woman!) Last but not least, to my daughter, Jill—I love you.

And now I turn to the men and mixed company:

To Tyson Cornell, Hailie Johnson, and the wonderful team at Rare Bird—thank you for being delightful, patient, and a joy to work with.

To Brian Cole, Larry Ramos, and Pat Colecchio—none of you are with us any longer, and Brian, you left far too soon, but I hope my version of our story would make you proud.

And last but not least, I thank the following people for their contributions to this book. Depending on my memory alone was not enough. Others' perceptions and recollections were very helpful in putting the pieces of the old memories puzzle together. So to Terry Kirkman, Ted Bluechel, Jim Yester, Jules Alexander, Jordan Cole, Del Ramos, Bruce Pictor, Henry Diltz, Danny Hutton, Bob Stane, J. D. Souther, Marty Nicosia, Elaine "Spanky" McFarlane, Paul Holland, Jayne Zinsmaster McKay, Joe Lamanno, Rick Colecchio, Paul Stanley, Mason Williams, Guy Pohlman, Ray Staar, Chrystal Starr Russell Klabunde, Barry DeVorzon, Donni Gougeon, Bob Werner, and David Jackson—thank you for your time, your talent, the memories, and the laughs we've shared together over the decades.

Foreword

By David Geffen

IN 1967, OUR COUNTRY was at war and rock and roll music was the anthem of the antiwar protesters. I had dropped out of college and fudged a document to make it look as though I had *indeed* graduated from UCLA, all to keep my job at the William Morris Agency, and I was interested in advancing my career in the music industry by working with the best rock and roll talent.

I was representing Janis Ian at the time and she was on a split bill with The Association at the Village Theatre (later the Fillmore East) in New York City. The concert promoter, Bill Graham, had accidentally put both Janis and The Association down as headliners. Well, you can't have two headliners. There were afternoon and evening concerts lined up, but I walked into the theater to find Lee Liebman, The Association's road manager, and Janis's manager arguing over who should headline. For me, the solution was simple. "She headlines one," I said, pointing to Janis, "and they," I nodded in the direction of six twenty-something men, "headline the other."

If anyone ever tries to use words to describe what happens when you hear beautiful music live—incredible, rich, complex vocal harmonies—it can't be done; you just can't do that feeling justice. No group sounded like The Association. They were the real deal. Eager and ambitious to make my mark in music, I was determined to sign them.

Pat Colecchio, The Association's manager, rang me up to thank me for handling the headliner incident. Colecchio got the group out of their contract (with an agency that was thought to have mob connections), and I signed them to William Morris.

The rest, as they say, is rock history. In this book, Russ Giguere has gone back in time—over fifty years now—to chronicle the experience of what it was like to be in the music scene in 1960s LA, where everyone knew everyone, played and sang with one another in various bands at all the clubs, and forever changed music—how we hear it, how we feel it, and what it means to us. His memoir is candid, frank, and, at times, laugh-out-loud funny. If you know Russ, you certainly wouldn't expect anything less from the man who used to call my office and answer my assistant's question, "Who shall I say is calling?" with a dramatic pause followed by, "The Phantom." My assistant would patch Russ straight through to me without missing a beat.

The Phantom days are long gone. The music business ain't what it used to be, that's for sure. But music made by The Association, well, there's a reason it's still living on in the airwaves today.

Turn the page, and *cherish*.

David Geffen
May 2018
Los Angeles, CA

Disclaimer #1

IF YOU'RE SITTING THERE, passing this book back and forth between your hands and wondering, "What the hell is The Association?" or maybe even, "Who does this Russ Giguere guy think he is, and what kind of a last name is Giguere?"—heck, maybe you're even asking *both* of these things—well, you might think I'd just mouth off at you. After all, I work in rock and roll, and those of us in the entertainment business sometimes get a reputation for being difficult. But no! You couldn't be further from the truth. Oh, sure—I'm the kind of guy who doesn't make a habit of caring about what people think, but since your curiosity is piqued, I'm patient and more than happy to explain.

First of all, my last name is pronounced "jig-air." If I had a dime for every time someone mispronounced it, I could buy the Taj Mahal. Second, The Association was a beloved (my literary agent told me to use that word and I'm not going to object) 1960s rock band (yes, I came of age in the early 1960s—I'm that old), probably best known for our chart-topping hits "Cherish," "Along Comes Mary," "Windy," "Never My Love," and "Everything That Touches You." In fact, "Never My Love," "Cherish," and "Windy" are three of BMI's one hundred most played songs (No. 2, No. 21, and No. 61, respectively) of the twentieth century. We have one double platinum record and six gold records, and we've sold more than seventy million records and had seven Top 40 hits. The original band consisted of six members, and I'm one of them.

We have played stadiums, amphitheaters, concert halls, opera houses, historic vaudeville halls, movie theaters, the steps of city halls, high school auditoriums, colleges, universities, pop festivals, jazz festivals, Riverfests, racetracks, night clubs, ski lodges, armories, zoos, parks, parking ramps, blocked-off streets, cornfields, private concerts, beaches on both the Pacific and Atlantic coasts, cruise ships, and even a converted dairy barn. We have played in every state in the union and most of the provinces of Canada, as well as England, Holland, Germany, Belgium, Greece, Puerto Rico, the Philippines, and Uruguay.

So there you have it! I love playing tour guide, so that's what I'll do for you here. I'll be your tour guide through my experience of being in The Association. I promise your tour will be anything but dull! There's some great music in store for you, as well as history, love, drugs (it was the *sixties*…), and well, maybe we should just go ahead and get started now that you know what's what…

Have fun, kids!

Disclaimer #2

IN 1966, BEECHWOOD MUSIC Corporation, a subsidiary of Capitol Records, Inc., together with Price/Stern/Sloan Publishers, Inc., published a book written by The Association, *Crank Your Spreaders*. (The word "spreaders" refers to the wing windows of your car that you had to push out or crank to open.) It featured poetry, prose, illustrations, musings, and God knows what from the heads of the six of us in the band, which at that time included me, Terry Kirkman, Jim Yester, Ted Bluechel, Brian Cole, and Jules Alexander. As we told the *Los Angeles Times* about our "literary" offering, "It's the first in a series of one."[2] Of course, in this same article journalist Peter Johnson quoted us as saying, "If you are looking for some kind of label for us, you can write that The Association is the answer to Edward Albee, the Taft-Hartley Act, and World War II." I'd like to take credit for that statement—it could have been me, but then again, it could just as easily have been Terry, who told Johnson he played "underwater Chinese kazoo," or Brian, who claimed, "I played flower pot and volleyball on our last album." You pretty much could never predict what was going to come out of our mouths. And that's the way we liked it.

There was a 1969 edition of *Crank Your Spreaders* that added the work of Larry Ramos (our six-man band became, for a time, a seven-man band before Jules left for India and Larry was on the road with us, getting ready to take his place; Jules would later rejoin the band, at which point we became a seven-man band again). In both

2   Johnson, Peter. "Hit Not a Miss—Association: Offbeat Rock'n'Roll." *Los Angeles Times*. April 3, 1967.

editions of the book, I wrote the following foreword, which still rings remarkably true, perhaps even more so, as I sit here fifty-four years later, marveling at my attempt to recollect memories of the times we spent and the music we made from the cobwebs of my mind.

***

Many times I have asked myself why we should want to write a book. In answer to my own question, I ask, "Why should we write a book?" The reply not only *seems* illogical, but it *is* illogical. But these answers must be questioned at another time.

Books (as everyone is aware of) are, for the most part, printed on pieces of paper and fastened together with glue or staples or string and stuff…which is why we have chosen this media.

We shall attempt to convey to the reader (reador, readers, or readee) something that's neat, I bet. If you don't agree with all the views and ideas, that's alright too; just don't come running to us when you're sorry later because we'll all probably be sorry later ourselves. But right now we can all be sorry for many things together (I could give you several examples, but I'm sure you have enough).

When writing a book there are several rules that should be observed; it's the least you can do if you're not going to follow them. The most important of these are the guides on illustrating:

1. Do not use cheap, distracting illustrations of no consequence.
2. Use only those that merit observing—such as gas stations, apartments, milk, some small fires, or a gorilla or two dismounting. Even these, as snazzy as they are, can be disconcerting, so it is usually better to blend them in by printing the text over them, thereby creating a unity and feeling of oneness heretofore unknown in the physical world.

Now you may begin the Author Purification. Thus: lock yourself in the bathroom for a duration of 72 to 345 hours (depending on the holiday) and eat the Author Purification Diet, which is one meal a day eaten at 9:42 a.m., made up of 37 unleavened chocolate chip cookies and a quart of akadama[3] with a graham cracker crust. This meal may be eaten at any chosen speed or taken through osmosis.

Strive to maintain a constant state of confusion. This level is easily attained by continually asking yourself the musical question, "What color is the sound of one hand laughing?" and walking around a dead Cornish game hen at high noon (a craven coward?) on the corner of Melrose and La Brea, chanting, "Don't act crazy!" This will help cleanse you, both spiritually and mentally.

***

CONSIDER YOURSELF WARNED. (AND sincere apologies if you're now craving chocolate chip cookies.)

Though there won't really be any illustrations this time around (just photos), I'm going to tell the story of The Association like I remember it (quite the feat, when you consider how much marijuana I've smoked in my lifetime). I can't predict what you'll think or say or do—my version may differ from any of the other guys if you talked to them, but I can promise you one thing: it's gonna be a helluva ride.

So please, fasten your seatbelts. I'll convey something neat, I bet.

PS: When you crank your spreaders, be sure to watch out for water balloons that may come hurtling at you through the window.

Russ Giguere
Los Angeles
August 2019

---

3   Akadama is both a soil (used for things like bonsai plants) and a Japanese sweet red wine. Here I am referring to the wine!

Ray Bradbury Was My Hero

I NEVER MET MY father.

I get it—your mind is probably jumping to the movie-plot-worthy notion that he was some sort of dirtbag, a two-timing jerk, a ne'er-do-well. But that couldn't be further from the truth.

My dad was a handsome fellow—a fine, upstanding Navy man who had been born in Flint, Michigan, and worked as a chief pharmacist's mate in the dispensary at the Portsmouth Navy Yard in New Hampshire. He married my petite, blonde, blue-eyed mother, Marguerite Bamberger, on a cold winter day on February 16, 1942. Not long after their honeymoon just south of the White Mountains at Tobey's Motor Court in Plymouth, he was shipped south on his second enlistment and returned home for short furloughs only. In August 1943, when Mom was seven months pregnant with me, Dad was killed by a torpedo from a German U-boat off the coast of Virginia. Such was the fate gamble a young pregnant bride wagered, marrying a serviceman at the height of World War II.

Russell Henry Giguere, Sr. (yes, that's right, I'm named after him) was on a gunboat called *Plymouth* (yes, it had the same name as the town in New Hampshire where they honeymooned), which was actually a gift of William K. Vanderbilt to the US Navy. Well, technically he sold it to the government for one dollar, so I'd say it was a gift! It was reputed to be the "finest yacht afloat," according to the Navy. That probably had something to do with the gold-plated fixtures and swimming pool it had when it was a yacht. (Not that the Navy enjoyed those; that swimming pool became the mess hall and kitchen!)

On August 8, 1943, my mom received a telegram from Western Union:

The Navy Department deeply regrets to inform you that your husband Russell Henry Giguere Chief Pharmacists Mate US Navy is missing in the performance of his duty and in the service of his country. The Department appreciates your great anxiety but details not now available and delay in receipt thereof must necessarily be expected. To prevent possible aid to our enemies, please do not divulge the name of his ship or station.

Three weeks later on August 30, New Hampshire Republican senator Styles Bridges wrote my mother a letter:

Dear Mrs. Giguere:

I was shocked to hear that your husband has been reported missing in action and want you to know that I am thinking of you in these trying hours. I hope sincerely that you may soon receive encouraging news and that he will return to you safely.

Very sincerely,

Styles Bridges

All 2,265 tons and 265 feet of that ship had sunk in less than two minutes and with it, my father. The incident was described as follows:

The *Plymouth* was a convoy escort ship—a patrol gunboat (PG)—that cruised the East Coast, protecting the supply convoys so vital to the war effort. Its usual run was between New York City and Key West. On the evening of August 5, 1943, just after 9:30 p.m., the *Plymouth* picked up evidence of a nearby German U-boat on its sonar. While the *Plymouth* was maneuvering to drop depth charges on the U-boat, the German submarine fired a torpedo which struck the 264-foot *Plymouth* abaft of the bridge. The incident occurred about 90 miles off the coast of North Carolina, almost directly in line with Kitty Hawk—famous for the Wright brothers' first manned aerial flight. This area was commonly known as "Torpedo Alley," as German U-boats hunted down Allied convoys there, sinking over 300 ships; a vastly underpublicized reality of World War II.[4]

Seventy-five men died and eighty-five survived, most of them those who were lucky enough to jump overboard in time and not drown in the mess of shipwreck, oil, smoke, fire, or sharks they had to battle ninety miles out at sea. Those who survived were rescued by *Calypso*, the Coast Guard cutter located just eight thousand yards away.

I was born two months after the *Plymouth* sank, on October 18, 1943. All of the bios on me out there will tell you that I was born in Portsmouth, New Hampshire—I lived there in my grandmother's house with my mom—but truthfully, I was born in a naval hospital just over the bridge in Kittery, Maine.

Why do I even bother mentioning all of this? You picked up this book because you want to read about the music—the hits, the touring, the fans, the sex, the drama, everything 1960s, everything rock and roll—but this story is how I best remember it and if there's one thing you should probably understand upfront, it's that I never knew my father. Why? Because I think that never knowing my father made me the kind of kid, and later, man, who works hard, tirelessly, at whatever his job is. I watched my mother keep it together (gracefully, I might add) for me and my half-sister, Judy, and later my other half-sister, Nancy, and half-brother, Tyson, so to the extent that observing my mother's behavior influenced my life, it is certain that "keeping it together," pressing on, was all I knew. Then again, perhaps my nonstop work ethic was my way of proving myself to the world, of making my mom proud for two people—her and my absent father. Though I wasn't conscious of it and had for all

---

4   Devlin, Philip R. "Memorial Day Tribute: The Amazing World War II Tale of Survival and Heroism of Roger H. Fuller." *Manchester Patch*. May 25, 2011.

intents and purposes a fairly idyllic childhood, before I ever became a musician, or a "rock and roll star" per se, I was likely—if not to me, to other family members and at times to the outside world—the boy without a father.

Life went on. Mom was still young and pretty. She had me and then was married again within eighteen months. Who could blame her? It's tough to raise a child alone and she wanted a husband for herself and a father for her son. Her second husband was a spineless guy. His mother lived with us and fed lies about me and anything and everything she could to her son and my mother. He was too weak to stand up to his own spiteful mother. Eventually my mom had had enough and delivered an ultimatum: "Either we live here, or your mother lives here, but not both." By this time, my mom was pregnant with my younger sister, Judy, but she had no problem walking out the door. My mother never asked him for a dime. The marriage was so quick and I was so young I don't even remember it—I'm simply recounting how it was all explained to me.

What I do remember is sitting with Judy at the kitchen table when I was about eleven or twelve, long after we had moved to San Diego.

"If my father was killed before I was born, but we were both born on the East Coast, and you're my little sister," I ventured, "then *WHERE DID YOU COME FROM?*"

Judy stared back at me, her eyes as big as saucers, as we both realized she didn't know the answer to the question, either.

We sat my mother down and demanded an explanation. "*What happened here?*"

And that's how we found out there had been another husband sandwiched in the lineup.

My memories of New England include snowball fights and sliding from atop a mountain of snow piled as high as the second-story window of the house, all the way down to the ground below. Our backyard on Salter Street in Portsmouth had a river and a small dock, and my Uncle

Bob, Aunt Jeannette, and cousins Paulie, Jan, and Bobbo lived next door. I can still see the fishermen repairing their nets and the lobster traps piled on the dock across the river. My grandmother would put me in a boat and row across that river to pick up my grandfather and uncle who worked at the navy yard. She also taught me how to do the Charleston when I was four. I learned to sing songs like "Rag Mop" and "Ragtime Cowboy Joe" by listening to them on the radio.

My mother's sister, my Aunt Millie, was married to a submariner named Jack Camp and lived in San Diego. During one fateful phone call to my mother in New Hampshire, Aunt Millie said, "Margie, there's no winter out here, and there's lots of men. Come out here." And with that, we packed up, moved west, and moved in with Aunt Millie and her two kids, my cousins, Jack Jr. and Gail. Jack Sr. was away at sea more than he was home.

Aunt Millie worked as an Arthur Murray dance instructor and taught me everything she knew. "Do I really have to learn this stuff?" I'd whine. "Russell," Aunt Millie would say patiently, "you'll always be grateful I taught this to you." Years later, when The Association guest-starred on Carol Channing's TV special, "Carol Channing and 101 Men," where we appeared with George Burns, Eddy Arnold, Walter Matthau, and The US Air Force Academy Chorale, we sang a shortened version of "Along Comes Mary" as "Along Comes Carol," and as they outfitted us in nineteenth-century costumes, the producers asked, "Which of you guys can dance?" Larry Ramos and I were the only ones who raised our hands, and so we got our dance groove on 1960s style with Carol in her miniskirt, white tights, and white boots. The YouTube video of our performance will show you I was having a grand time since I'm dancing like a fool with a big grin on my face. And so Aunt Millie was right. But I get ahead of myself.

San Diego was apparently good for me. I recently reread my mother's handwriting on the back of an 8" x 10" photo of me as a five-year-old not long after we'd moved there. She titled it "Peck's Bad Boy," after a fictional archetype characterized for his naughty, mischievous behavior. She wrote, "His arms show up his nice tan. Isn't his face dirty? The man two doors down said he never saw such a dirty face so he just had to take his picture. He needed a haircut also, as you can see. I'm crazy about this, as you can't always get one like this so good. Under all the dirt you can still see how swell he does look. He really has improved one hundred percent out here." I guess Mom thought the West Coast sun was good for my attitude!

"Peck's Bad Boy 1948"—Mom loved this shot of me taken by our neighbor Carr Tuthill, a curator at San Diego's Museum of Man.

Once we'd been in San Diego for about a year and a half, my mother met a tall, handsome redhead by the name of Bob Bilyue from Stillwater, Oklahoma. Bob had been a machine gunner in the Marines and served in the Philippines. He also watched as the flag was raised by Marines at Iwo Jima and knew the war journalist Ernie

Pyle. Bob came through San Diego and once he got a taste of the Southern California weather, there was no way Bob was going back to Stillwater. He met my mother at the Hacienda Club on University Avenue, on a night when Roy Hogsed and His Orchestra were playing. Roy was best known for his hit, "Cocaine Blues," which hit No. 15 on the country music charts in 1948. Mom married Bob and had two more children: my half-sister, Nancy, and my half-brother, Tyson. My new dad owned two top-of-the-line gas stations in San Diego and did pretty well for himself, so much so that he sold the gas stations and went into water softener and garbage disposal sales.

Things went south, however, when Bob started writing bad checks and had to do jail time in Chino. Chino was a minimum-security prison—when you went there, they'd tell you how to break out: "Throw your jacket over the fence so you don't get cut, hop over, and run like the dickens," because if they caught you, you sure as hell weren't going back to Chino, which was a country club compared to the maximum-security clink they'd send you to if you tried to escape. Bob wasn't the most terrible guy in the world, but he became a drinker and philanderer. We visited him once in Chino, but eventually, my mother divorced him while he was in the slammer. I'll never know what made him write bad checks. But he was my stepfather from the time I was six until I was about fourteen or fifteen, so he was the closest thing to a dad I ever knew.

As a kid, I built forts and rafts, dug caves, and played Cowboys and Indians. I preferred to play an Indian. We would see Arabs on television and then we would play Arabs, too, putting on robes and using broomsticks for horses. When I got to junior high, I took Mechanical Drawing, Metal Shop, Woodshop, Printshop, and Calligraphy. I even received the 1957 "Best Dancer" award (the title came with a six-inch-tall plastic trophy) for winning a competition at the end-of-the-year dance at Woodrow Wilson Junior High. I asked Barbara Dumler to dance because we'd danced together before and I knew she was good. "Oh, cool," she said. The contest came down to two couples, a very popular buttoned-down duo, and me and Barbara (I was always on the fringes of the social scene; I didn't care about popularity). At the end of the song, the applause meter registered the same rating (which was totally bogus—there was no way the performances were equal) for both couples, so they had us dance to yet another song. We really dialed it up. After that, there was no mistaking the pair that deserved to win. When the second dance finished, they ran the applause meter test again, and Barbara and I were the clear winners. (Thanks, Aunt Millie!)

In the seventh grade, I handed in a book report on a collection of Ray Bradbury short stories—it was either *The Golden Apples of the Sun* or *The Martian Chronicles*.

"We can't accept this," the teacher said.

"Why not?" I asked.

"Because this isn't *literature*," she said, peering down her nose at me, drawing out the last word like it left a bad taste in her mouth.

"What do you mean it's not literature?" I asked. "Have you read it?"

"No," she admitted. "It's not on the list."

As a young boy, I'd been an avid reader, devouring piles of books I carried home from the library. (I read less by the time I was in high school.) The lady who checked out the books would ask my mother, "Is he really going to read all of those?"

"Oh, yeah," she'd say, "some of them two or three times."

By the time I finished junior high, I'd read something like a thousand books—everything Jack London ever wrote, everything John Steinbeck ever wrote, you name it—but I hated stupid lists and rules. I didn't love the system. In fact, I did whatever I could to bust it, so I turned in the same three book reports three years in a row. I remember one of them was *Captain Courageous*—I never even read the actual book, only the classic comic. (There were no computers then, so it was easy to get away with handing in the same thing year after year.) It's safe to say that none of my teachers thought of me as a sterling academic, but then again, I'm not writing this book to share my illustrious history making straight A's, now am I?

Hoots at the Ice House
1962–1964
(with a lil' bit of 1960s history...)

"W HY WEREN'T YOU IN class?"

"I was busy."

"Do you have an excuse?"

"I said I was *busy.*"

The previous day, Mom had stood outside the front door to our house and watched me walk down the road from the bus stop. She had never done that before. When I reached her, she told me a policeman had stopped by the house to tell her I hadn't shown my face at school for some time. When The Man calls on your mom personally, you know it can't be good. There was no dodging the firing squad on this one. I'd been caught red-handed, and it was fight or flight.

The Hoover High guidance counselor barreled ahead, "'Busy' doesn't work, Mr. Giguere. You have to have a written excuse."

"Well, what happens if I don't?"

"You missed one hundred days of school this year. You're out of school more than you're in it. They'll have to expel you."

"*Please* don't *expel* me." I honestly couldn't give two shits.

"Russ, you can't just stop going to school."

"What's the alternative?"

"You have two alternatives. You can go to the California Youth Authority, or you can get a job."

The California Youth Authority, known today as the California Division of Juvenile Justice, was a division of the California

Department of Corrections and Rehabilitation. In other words, the education, training, and treatment services it provided was basically jail for those of us deemed "serious youth offenders."

"I guess I'll be getting a job."

They set up four interviews for me, and I accepted the job that put me to work full-time as a shipping clerk and involved attending school a mere four hours a week at E. R. Snyder Continuation High School in San Diego, about a five-block walk from work. The standing joke was that E. R. Snyder was the only person who ever graduated, so they named the school after him. I'd walk into the room, sit in the back, and read. I never said a word. I did this until the time I turned seventeen and a half.

I'd had some job or another since I was twelve years old, everything from cleaning gas stations to polishing and greasing carousel horses, manning the brass rings, and serving as the safetyman for the Balboa Park merry-go-round. Everything in Balboa Park was free up until the age of twelve, so I practically lived at the zoo until I started working. In my later teens, I sold popcorn and candy at the Starlight Opera, an outdoor amphitheater also in Balboa Park. I loved seeing all of the big musical productions—*Bells are Ringing, Carousel*—they would usually do four or five shows per week over a two-week run.

As a teenager, when I wasn't working, I was playing guitar and singing, but even my years in the 110-member all-male Glee Club in junior high hadn't helped raise my confidence to the performance level it needed to be at if I wanted to fulfill my dream of playing guitar and singing solo in front of an audience. So by the time I was fifteen and a half, I was spending many an evening at the Upper Cellar, a San Diego coffeehouse at 6557 El Cajon Boulevard that sat about fifty people and served no alcohol, just coffees and teas from around the world. There was a small wooden platform against a wall in the middle of the room that served as a makeshift stage, with the four lights hanging from the ceiling working together to serve as stage lights. When I started, I cleaned the floors and tables, and worked my way up to serving customers and even co-designing the menu cover with Morris Lafon, who would later move to New York City in the 1970s and make a bit of a name for himself acting in downtown experimental theater productions.

I also fell in love with one of the waitresses, Birdie McNichol, who was dating another guy when we first met. When she broke up with him, a few years later, I was nineteen and I made my move. Now, don't go thinking that I was moving in on another man's woman— let's be clear here, I'm not that kind of guy. I waited until the coast was good and clear. Birdie would later become my first wife. She was like Lauren Bacall in *Key Largo*, only sexier.

Birdie was a music major putting herself through school working at the Upper Cellar, serving as musical director for a Lutheran church choir, and cooking dinner five nights a week for several San Diego State University students. Bob Stane, the Upper Cellar's owner, was one of her clients. Incidentally, one of Birdie's roommates at that time was none other than Judy Henske, a stunning six-foot, model-tall singer/songwriter who would later marry Jim Yester's brother, Jerry, of the Lovin' Spoonful, The New Christy Minstrels, and the Modern Folk Quartet (MFQ). Judy would also be part of a short-lived band, the Whiskeyhill Singers, formed by Dave Guard after he left the Kingston Trio. The Whiskeyhill Singers lasted about six months and was comprised of Judy, Dave Guard, Cyrus Faryar, and David "Buck" Wheat. (Cyrus would later join the MFQ.) The Whiskeyhill Singers' main claim to fame would become the four songs they recorded for the *How the West Was Won* soundtrack— they actually recorded more than four, but only four made it onto the album. (What is it they say about six degrees of separation? I've found that in this life, and especially the music business, it's often far fewer.) Judy was later known as "Queen of the Beatniks" and performed with up-and-coming stand-up comedian Woody Allen (whom she also dated) in the Greenwich Village Clubs—it's rumored she's Woody's inspiration for the title character in *Annie Hall*—a fairly substantial claim, considering Annie was an aspiring singer from Chippewa Falls, Wisconsin, Judy's hometown.

Judy went from a folksinger to a real chanteuse. I saw her at a gig she did at The Troubadour in the mid-sixties with legendary jazz guitarist Herb Ellis. She did tunes like "Miss Otis Regrets," "'Til the Real Thing Comes Along," "High Flying Bird," and other standards, along with some blues songs she was known for belting out, like "Duncan & Brady" (in the song, Duncan shoots Brady with a shining star). She was one of the funniest people on stage that I ever saw, and a big favorite with local talk shows.

But back to Birdie. Birdie was smart, easy on the eyes, and she spoke the language of my other love, music. With her perfect pitch, she would be instrumental—no pun intended—in making all of the written notations of our vocal arrangements on *Insight Out* (1967), The Association's third album, while we were in the recording studio. Our arrangements took ideas from everybody. Birdie would write down everything as it was happening and changing in real time—she really made sure everything was dead-on. *Insight Out* had two No. 1 hits on it, "Never My Love" and "Windy," and the album climbed all the way to No. 8 in *Billboard* on September 2, 1967:

1. The Beatles—*Sgt. Pepper's Lonely Hearts Club Band*
2. Monkees—*Headquarters*
3. The Rolling Stones—*Flowers*
4. The Doors—*The Doors*
5. Jefferson Airplane—*Surrealistic Pillow*
6. Young Rascals—*Groovin'*
7. Engelbert Humperdink—*Release Me*
8. **The Association—*Insight Out***
9. Aretha Franklin—*I Never Loved a Man the Way I Loved You*
10. The Temptations—*With a Lot O' Soul*

Incidentally, I saw The Doors (No. 4 on the list) perform before they ever hit the charts. One summer night in 1966, a friend of mine and I went to the Whisky a Go Go on the Sunset Strip to hear some music. The opening band, unheard of at the time and calling themselves The Doors, came on. The lead singer, Jim Morrison, was so drunk he could barely stand up. We walked out. Less than a year later, The Doors had their first hit, "Light My Fire." Regarding "Windy," sometime in the 1980s, when The Association played with an orchestra in Detroit, the conductor, who had studied with Leonard Bernstein in New York, shared what Bernstein told his students when he played them our song: "*That* is a perfect record." Bernstein even sang "Along Comes Mary" to demonstrate the Dorian mode octave as part of his "Modes of Music" section in the series of Young People's Concerts[5] he gave in the sixties. But I'm getting ahead of myself once again.

I made friends with Bob Stane while working at the Upper Cellar. Bob had put himself through San Diego State College as a marketing major while running the joint. "I had been exposed to coffeehouses and I was looking for a new career," Stane said. "I was not happy working day hours. I am not a morning person. Getting up in the morning was painful to me. That limited my options. I had done a lot of jobs. I had surveyed for the railroad, I'd worked in mines...I got involved in coffeehouses when I went to the Unicorn on Sunset Boulevard in Hollywood, in 1957. Now, I don't know for sure, but I have this memory of Theo Bikel playing guitar and singing there. It was a turning point. I looked around and within ten seconds I thought, 'I can do this.'"[6] Many of the acts that appeared at the Upper Cellar, like Mason Williams (of "Classical Gas" fame), Paul Sykes, and Judy Henske, also then traveled north to perform at The Ice House, a comedy and music club in Pasadena. On one occasion, Bob took a performer from the Upper Cellar to audition at The Ice House and asked the owner, Willard Chilcott, if he liked the act. Willard didn't, but he said he'd be willing to give Bob anything if

---

5   "Calling Card." *The Times*. November 28, 1966.

6   Roland, Terry, "Bob Stane Remembers the Upper Cellar and the Coffeehouse Era." *San Diego Troubadour*. November 2016.

he would come up from San Diego to run The Ice House. Bob asked for half ownership, to which Willard agreed, and the rest is history… Bob ran the club for seventeen years. Bob sold the Upper Cellar to Dave Schoolcraft, a DJ who worked for the local radio station, KPRI. Dave changed the name of the coffeehouse to The Greenwich West.

Bob penned a successful pamphlet released in 1960, *How to Run a Coffee House* (which has the menu cover Morris Lafon and I designed on the front of it). That pamphlet was such a hit, Playboy called and asked him to work out of their Chicago headquarters and standardize all of their clubs around the country. The money was too good to turn down, so Bob left for the Windy City and whipped them into shape over the next six months while simultaneously continuing to run The Ice House via phone through Lori Spring, the manager he hired to take his place while he relocated. By the end of those six months, his mission was complete, and Bob could no longer hack the Windy City's weather or Playboy's dress code, so he moved back to Pasadena permanently. "I've got it set up here now so the secretary can run things," he explained as he fled the bone-chilling Chicago winter. No one had ever heard of anyone quitting a job with Playboy!

But back to the Upper Cellar—now The Greenwich West. As soon as I turned eighteen and was able to stay out past the citywide enforced youth curfew of 10:00 p.m. (a popular trend during the 1950s juvenile delinquency scare—"Keep violence down and protect your children by keeping them indoors at night!"), I began programming the coffeehouse's entertainment, selecting the movies for movie night, deciding which night would be poetry night, jazz night, and so on and so forth. I also designed some of their posters. One of our most memorable performers was a homeless man who would sign up for poetry night, reciting classics such as Hugh Antoine d'Arcy's "Face on the Barroom Floor," Ernest Thayer's "Casey at the Bat," and Robert Service's "The Shooting of Dan McGrew." He'd deliver an impressive, theatrical performance, pass his hat around to collect a fat wad of cash tips, and waltz right out the back door until the next poetry night, when he'd do it all over again. The artist Richard Allen Morris would read poetry and create tension in the audience by rocking back and forth on his heels slowly, looking like he was about to fall over.

Even though we were all in San Diego, there was a buzzing music scene that acted as a feeder and stepping stone to the Los Angeles music clubs. I met Mason Williams at the Upper Cellar, as well as Paul Sykes and Randy Sparks before Randy formed the Randy Sparks Three (which Paul would also join, and not to be confused with the Randy Sparks *Trio*, which was the next venture Randy formed with his wife, Jackie Miller, and Nick Woods, before founding the fourteen-member group, The New Christy Minstrels). Bob recalls of Randy, "He is one of the best single acts I have ever seen in my life. He sang, played guitar, and was a comedian full of funny patter. I mean, he tore the paint off the wall. This was a full five years before The New Christy Minstrels." Paul Sykes had one of the best voices I've ever heard; he eventually gave up music to return to his work as a florist. In fact, he even turned down an offer from Randy to join The New Christy Minstrels—rumor is he didn't want to be part of such a big group (by the time they recorded their debut album, they had gone down from the original fourteen members to just ten). Paul was a damn good singer (and a damn good florist).

Now settled back in Pasadena, Bob Stane invited me to spend New Year's Eve 1961 with his family. He took me to the Troubadour, the legendary music club at 9081 Santa Monica Boulevard in West Hollywood, where I first met owner/manager Doug Weston. Even living 120 miles away in San Diego, I had heard about the club: Doug had first opened it in 1957 as a coffeehouse on La Cienega Boulevard, before moving it to its current location in 1961. At six and a half feet tall, Doug was a towering figure, literally and figuratively—a complete force of nature, his presence couldn't be ignored. When he died in 1999, the *Los Angeles Times* pop music critic Robert Hilburn wrote, "Doug Weston was arguably the godfather of the Southern

California singer-songwriter movement in the late sixties and early seventies, someone whose unshakable belief in the inspirational power of music made his club both a showcase and meeting hall for much of the best young talent of a generation." True—all of that. Larry Murray of Hearts and Flowers remembers, "People had love-hate relationships with him. But he really held that thing together in a subtle manner, and really made things happen. For example, if you were an unsigned act and he could kind of spot if you were gonna do something, he'd hire you, and you'd have to sign this deal with him that you owed him two to three more engagements at the same price. So you worked for twenty-five dollars a night. Like, three years later, you were making $2,500, and Doug would go, 'Oh, by the way, on the Saturday of Easter, I would like to exercise my option.' Managers, mainly, hated him for it."[7]

The Troubadour accommodated up to three hundred people— for a live music venue, it was an intimate performance space. Weston said, "What we do offer an entertainer is a place where he can check up on his own validity. The Troubadour gives them a chance to get back to that atmosphere and make sure their music is still valid. It is so much more satisfying than the big concert halls where the closest person in the audience is fifty to a hundred feet away. The people who play our club are sensitive artists who have something to say about our times. They are modern-day troubadours. It is important for them to get away from the crowds and check their own validity once in a while. We provide them with the atmosphere in which they can do it."[8]

Linda Ronstadt wrote in her memoir, *Simple Dreams*, "The limited space of the Troubadour put the bathrooms in a back-hall area off the performance space. That meant everyone from the bar had to travel through the room where the stage was in order to visit

---

7   Unterberger, Richie. *Turn! Turn! Turn!: The '60s Folk-Rock Revolution.* Back-beat Books, 2002.

8   Hilburn, Robert. "Atmosphere, Talent Key to Club's Success." *Los Angeles Times.* August 2, 1970.

the plumbing. Even if you were an up-and-coming hopeful hanging out in the bar but too broke to pay the admission fee, you could get a rich sampling of what was happening on the stage every time nature insisted. If you had been hired in the past by owner Doug Weston to play at the Troubadour, you got free admission, so when somebody interesting was playing, we veterans would crowd the staircase and the upstairs balcony night after night to see our favorites." Linda Ronstadt, Tom Waits, Elton John, The Eagles, and many more owe the launch of their stardom to Doug.

To give you an idea of the influence Doug had, Elton John's first album, which was released in the United States on July 22, 1970, landed on the desk of Doug Weston as a booking request. Elton John was a complete unknown—no one had ever heard of him. After listening to the album, Doug immediately booked him for six shows August 25 to August 30. Robert Hilburn, the *Los Angeles Times* music critic who had interviewed Doug Weston earlier that month about the Troubadour, would write about Elton John's performance: "Tuesday night at the Troubadour was just the beginning. He's going to be one of rock's biggest and most important stars." *Rolling Stone* pointed out, "The stakes couldn't have been higher: His debut LP, which had come out that spring, wasn't selling."[9] After those concerts at the Troubadour, "Your Song" hit No. 8 on *Billboard* and was later voted No. 137 in *Rolling Stone*'s "The 500 Greatest Songs of All Time."[10] Thanks to Doug Weston, Elton John soon became a household name.

So you get it now—the story of Elton is just one of countless artists Doug introduced to the masses. When I first heard "Rocket Man," which Elton wrote with Bernie Taupin and wasn't released until 1972, I immediately thought of it as *my* song. They say it's inspired by the Ray Bradbury story, "The Illustrated Man," and

---

9   Weingarten, Christopher, Browne, David, Dolan Jon and others. "The 50 Greatest Concerts of the Last 50 Years." *Rolling Stone*. June 12, 2017.

10   "Special Collections Issue: 500 Greatest Songs of All Time." *Rolling Stone*. December 2004.

so maybe that explains my affinity for it. Elton doesn't even know me, I thought. How could he write this? That's how much its lyrics resonated with me.

Anyhow, back to my first visit to the Troubadour with Bob—we saw Oscar Brown Jr. perform live; to date it is still one of the best shows I've ever seen. Oscar was a prolific singer/songwriter perhaps best known for "Afro Blue," "Work Song," and "Jeannine." On that same trip, I joined Bob at work at The Ice House every night, where I met comedian Pat Paulsen while he was working there. This was several years before Pat hit it big with regular appearances (and a 1968 Emmy win) on *The Smothers Brothers Comedy Hour*.

Pat Paulsen would become a dear friend of mine. He first met the Smothers Brothers when he sold them his song "Chocolate," but Pat also had his own act at The Ice House. Once we formed The Association, Pat did "cranial painting," a PR stunt Bob Stane invented, wherein Pat would hang upside down from a tripod and paint with watercolors on butcher paper using his head and beard (grown specifically for the stunt) while we played our music in the background. Bob Stane muses, "I learned a lesson about promotion and publicity.... At first, I called the three local television stations and they all said this was a publicity stunt, not a news story, and they wouldn't cover it. Then, one of the stations called and said they had a three-minute slot they needed to fill during the news hour and wanted to come film the cranial painting process. After they made an appointment—and I found 'appointment' to be a key word to use—I called the other two and let them know about the appointment the other station had made for the cranial paintings, so they said that they would like an appointment, too. It opened up the door, just by using that word, 'appointment.'" His idea was wild and wacky, and by golly, it worked, and brought both of us publicity.

In his later years, Pat announced he would walk on water. He'd show up for the appearance in a white robe, and then ask for absolute silence and meditate for some time, before walking serenely off the

Santa Monica Pier! The newspapers reported, "If anything, Mr. Paulsen sank faster than the normal rate."[11]

Believe it or not, Bob Stane once had to talk Pat out of quitting show business, just before he hit it big. This was long before Pat went on to run for president...in 1968, 1972, 1976, 1980, 1988, 1992, and 1996. What can I say, he thought it was funny!—it was, and *he* was. Mason Williams remembers being at dinner with Tommy and Dick one night and saying, "It would be great to have a candidate on the show." Tom then said, "Why not Pat Paulsen?" And the idea took off. When the Smothers Brothers first asked Pat to run for president in 1968, he said, "Why not? I can't dance—besides, the job has a good pension plan, and I'll get a lot of money when I retire."[12] Mason says, "Hubert Humphrey told Pat, 'You know, Pat, you might have cost me the election,' because thousands, maybe millions, voted for Pat." Pat could have you laughing so hard you felt your sides would split, particularly with his political humor: "All the problems we face in the United States today can be traced to an unenlightened immigration policy on the part of the American Indian,"[13] or "I've upped my standards. Now, up yours,"[14] or even, "I am neither left wing nor right wing. I am middle-of-the-bird"—I could go on and on.

The humor Pat utilized in his *The Smothers Brothers Comedy Hour* appearances (where some of his writers included Mason Williams, Rob Reiner, and Steve Martin) and in his presidential campaigns paved the way for people like Jon Stewart and Stephen Colbert to exist today. In his book, *Dangerously Funny: The Uncensored Story of "The Smothers Brothers Comedy Hour,"* David Bianculli writes, "In terms of introducing and encouraging new

11   Grimes, William. "Pat Paulsen, 69, a Parodist of Presidential Doubletalk." *The New York Times.* April 26, 1997.

12   Glass, Jeremy. "The 9 Craziest People Who've Ever Run for President." Thrillist.com. May 7, 2015.

13   Mankiw, N. Gregory. "Give Me Your Tired, Your Poor and Your Economists, Too." *The New York Times,* February 9, 2013.

14   Smith, Chris. "Primary contests evoke Sonoma County memories of comedian Pat Paulsen." *The Press Democrat.* February 13, 2016.

talent, pushing the boundaries of network television, and reflecting the youth movement and embracing its antiwar stance and anti-administration politics, the show was, quite literally, their finest hour…. Mostly they were in the right place at the right time, reacting to the sixties as events unfurled around them." The show's soaring popularity and the brazen reaction to politics it generated sent people like President Nixon, who advocated for more governmental control of broadcast media, into a tizzy. Pat Paulsen, in one of the editorials written for him on the show, said, "The Bill of Rights says nothing about Freedom of Hearing…. This, of course, takes a lot of fun out of Freedom of Speech." Ultimately CBS yanked *The Smothers Brothers Comedy Hour* off the air in 1969, bogusly citing a violation of their contract by failing to turn in a copy of that week's show in time—Tom and Dick later sued CBS and won. Though the lawsuit victory came far too late to save their show, it did much to further the cause of freedom of speech and cement their pioneer status in history as television's founding fathers of political satire.

Why in the world am I going on and on about Pat Paulsen and Tom and Dick Smothers, you ask? Because what Tom and Dick Smothers did for audiences, who were gathering around the television to hear and feel the state of world affairs reflected back to them, had been happening in the lyrics and composition of folk-rock and the rock and roll music scene since the early 1960s. Indeed, television, which was still a relatively new medium at the start of the decade—nine percent of households (six million) owned one in 1950, compared to ninety percent (sixty million) of households in 1960—demonstrated its rising power in September 1960, when forty percent of Americans tuned in to watch then Vice President Nixon go head to head with John F. Kennedy in the first televised presidential debate, where a pale, underweight, five-o'clock-shadowed, nursing-an-injured-knee Nixon, in a hastily applied pancake job, faced off with the handsome, younger, well-rested JFK. JFK went on to win the election by 303 electoral votes to Nixon's 219, and a little more than only 112,00 popular votes. Many people attribute the trajectory of JFK's victory as beginning with that televised debate, when information was no longer about content only, but also about the visuals accompanying that information.

That presidential debate was widespread proof of how moving images reaching a mass audience had the power to influence opinion and culture. Perhaps nowhere was this more prevalent than when The Beatles first appeared on *The Ed Sullivan Show* on February 9, 1964, and Beatlemania, all music and mop tops, officially penetrated the USA.

All of this is to say that in early 1960, while I was on the cusp of experiences that would lead me to become part of The Association, American culture was entering an entertainment revolution: radios in every household slowly turned into television sets in every household—and so sensory-wise, you could no longer just hear; you could also *see* what you were hearing, making entertainment that much more accessible. Talk shows and variety shows tested the boundaries of this new format, and this experimentation was mirrored in the developing sounds of popular music, which had morphed from the big band and sweeping doo-wop love ballads of the 1940s and 1950s to the electric sounds of the 1960s that were expressing unrest, discontent, and (gasp) sometimes deep sadness, a far departure from the songs our moms and dads grew up with or the traditional folk songs that shared sadness in a more removed fashion via a story told in third person.

Arlo Guthrie said, "The corporations, businessmen, and women who were controlling the entertainment business did not understand the lyrics of the songs that they were selling. The guys on the radio didn't get it. The guys that owned the radio had no connection with the music, in terms of understanding it. For the first time, there was an explosion of all different kinds of music being played. And the lyrics were unintelligible. Not just the lyrics—the philosophy, the heart of it, was unreadable, unknowable, to the people who controlled the industry. So all of a sudden, all around the world, for a very short time…imagine a world where everybody's got a radio, and all of a sudden everybody's saying what they really think, in words you could understand, but your parents couldn't…A floodgate had opened, because we were using a language that couldn't be understood over whose system we were using to communicate it. And it was so wonderful."[15]

As I continue my story and you try to place who and what The Association was in this time period and look at the spectrum of the whole decade, remember—as *The Smothers Brothers Comedy Hour* would shed light and focus our laughter on the very things going on politically that were making us uncomfortable, for the other solo musical acts and groups that came up with us at the same time, it was no longer only about great music you could dance, sing, or groove to, it was about using the art as a means to express feelings of the counterculture that weren't always pretty or safe—rage, anger, fear, sorrow, and more.

Anyhow, back to that 1961 New Year's Eve trip to visit Bob Stane, where I also met Doug Weston and Pat Paulsen. Bob and I spent New Year's Day watching the Rose Parade on television while his family went to watch it in person. I then returned to San Diego, and it wasn't long before Bob stopped in at The Greenwich West on a brief trip into town.

"Russ," he said, "my light man is leaving The Ice House. Would you like to replace him?"

"When would that be?"

"In a month or two."

"Perfect."

I thought I'd found my dream job, or if not my dream job, at least one in which I'd be getting paid to work full-time in the field I wanted to live and breathe in: music. I was already used to working with talent and managing people on a small scale at the coffeehouse, and now I would get paid a regular salary to run the lights and sound

15   Unterberger, Ritchie. *Turn! Turn! Turn! The '60s Folk-Rock Revolution.* San Francisco, CA: Backbeat Books, 2002.

full-time for a nightclub in the big leagues, and it would leave me time to work on my music, all the while remaining in close proximity to the Los Angeles music scene. On September 23, 1960, when The Ice House first opened, Chuck Immordino wrote in "Chuck's Corner" in *The Pasadena Independent*, "The Ice House, a theater restaurant featuring folk music in concert, full-course dinners and imported beers and wines, will open this evening. The Ice House will feature top-name folk song interpreters from all over the world. The Ice House should not be confused with a beatnik coffeehouse. It will be a complete gourmet restaurant and will take its place among the other fine eating places in Pasadena. The food will be expertly prepared by Chef Pierre Boissy—former catering manager at the Americana Hotel in Miami and a man with thirty years cuisine experience." Immordino also quoted The Ice House's original owner and creator, Willard Chilcott: "Local night life activity is limited, and The Ice House was conceived to bring the foremost professional music artists in the country to Pasadena."

The Upper Cellar had another regular customer, Carl Heckman, whom Bob would ask to run the Glendale Ice House. Carl was about ten years older than me and was a civilian electrician employed on North Island Naval Base in Coronado. He'd come to the coffeehouse in the evenings after work. He looked sort of like a bulldog—a cigar-smoking, sweatshirted, flat-topped bulldog. He had a huge magazine collection, just stacks and stacks, including every copy of Paul Krassner's *The Realist*. He also had a great record collection, too—comedy, jazz, blues, folk, flamenco guitar, Ken Nordine (Word Jazz albums)—it went on and on. Carl was an artist/chef/poet at heart, so in a way, he was the perfect choice to run the Glendale Ice House.

Two months after Bob's offer to run lights, I bid goodbye to San Diego, declared my love for Birdie with the promise we'd carry on our long-distance relationship while she finished school, and moved to Los Angeles with a sleeping bag, suitcase, and the dark brown LG50 Gibson acoustic guitar with a sunburst on it that I'd bought for fifty dollars from Ed Harris, my high school friend who lived three blocks down from our family. In Pasadena, I lived in the Catalina Continental, a two-story rooming house designed by famed architect brothers Charles Sumner Greene and Henry Mather Greene. This Greene & Greene house had at least two rooms with secret panels leading to very small closets. The Greene brothers also designed The Gamble House, a Pasadena landmark that was the former home of David and Mary Gamble of Procter & Gamble and is now held up as a beacon of American Craftsman architecture. I lived in the attic of the Catalina Continental while I waited for the light man who was on his way out and showing me the ropes to vacate his room. Eventually, I'd graduate from a single room with a communal john down the hall to two rooms and my own private bathroom.

Mondays were my day off. On Sunday evenings, when I wasn't planning on doing a hoot at the Troubadour the next night (more on that shortly), I'd take a Greyhound bus to San Diego, where Birdie would pick me up, we'd go to her house, and she'd go to class—I would either sleep or go to class with her. Then we'd hang out on Monday night and on Tuesday morning, I'd take a bus back to Los Angeles to make it to Pasadena in time for work at The Ice House. I never missed a day of work.

The Ice House was an altogether different beast than The Greenwich West. It got its name because it had, at one time, been just that; one of those places they stored ice to keep it cool back before the invention of the modern refrigerator. (I still have the old Ice House club logo, a pair of ice tongs holding a musical note, hanging on my kitchen wall—some man bought it at auction years ago and went out of his way to insist I should have it.) Located on Mentor Avenue just off Colorado Boulevard, The Ice House was on two levels and sat about 120 people in canvas director's chairs and had a restaurant that served food, beer, and wine. (They wouldn't serve hard liquor until the 1970s.) The club entrance was in the alley, which gave it a speakeasy feel. While I was at The Ice House, they would gut and renovate the room on the north side of the building, which had a much higher ceiling, expanding the seating capacity to something like 200 or 225 people on three different levels, with a fancy dark blue curtain as the stage backdrop and nine or ten large lights in their lighting plot—red, white, or blue backlights for the curtain, as well as five or six small spots downstage and large lights to wash the stage in color—a system that was a step up from the lights at The Greenwich West.

During the renovation, Pat Paulsen and I made extra dough painting walls during the day (and sometimes stuffing envelopes in the office, too)—seemingly boring work, but there was never a dull moment with Pat. Construction always stopped before the evening's entertainment began, so we never had to halt performances as a result of cosmetic work on the building. The only time The Ice House ever shut down was on November 22, 1963, the day President John F. Kennedy was assassinated.

The official title on my business card was "Light and Sound Technician and Hootenanny Coordinator." "Hootenanny" was a funny and fancy word for "open mic." Bob Stane managed the club, a man named Rudy was the bar manager, and I ran all the technical stuff that made the shows happen. Each night I would open up the club, count out the money, start the water to make the coffee, and select the music to play over the loudspeakers in between sets—I always played jazz, including the Dave Brubeck Quartet, Ramsey Lewis, Pete Jolly, and The Ahmad Jamal Trio—and the music was a welcome change from the usual live music. I would make the announcements for each act from the booth in the back ("Ladies and gentlemen, for your pleasure…") and work sound and lights at the same time. We had comedy acts, folk singers—duos, trios, quartets, Mexican bands, flamenco guitarists and troupes, mimes—if it could be classified as live entertainment, chances are it could be seen at The Ice House. There were two twenty-five-minute acts followed by a thirty-five-minute headliner act.

Miraculously, no one ever discovered I was color-blind—I flipped on the brightest combination of lights possible—the bluest of the blues and the reddest of the reds. I never missed a light cue. The rudimentary system was made fancier by the light gels that allowed me to illuminate the stage with a wash of colors, which was often needed—some of those folk singers looked like zombies up there!

The sound system was solid—the Smothers Brothers actually recorded a live album there. I'll never forget when, on a break in the middle of the live recording, Tommy Smothers singled out an audience member seated in the front row with his feet up, parked on the stage.

"Excuse me, sir, are you in show business?"

"No," said the man.

"Well," said Tommy, "get your fucking feet off the stage."

In terms of folk music and comedy, everyone who was anyone and everyone who didn't yet know they were going to be someone came through The Ice House. Lorenzo Music, known then as Jerry Music, had a folk music and comedy duo, Jerry & Myrna Music, with his gorgeous wife Myrna—I did lights for them at The Ice House, too. Lorenzo later wrote for *The Smothers Brothers Comedy Hour* and *The Mary Tyler Moore Show*, and cocreated *The Bob Newhart Show* and *Rhoda*, where he was also the voice of the only heard, never seen, Carlton the Doorman. I did the sound and lights for Randy Boone's act—Randy's star was on the rise at that time for his role in the 1962–63 popular comedy-drama, *It's a Man's World*, and he later went on to have recurring roles in the Western television shows, *Wagon Train*, *The Virginian*, and *Cimarron Strip*. He was a great storyteller. I share all of this so you can understand just how small The Ice House world was in the early sixties. Everyone knew everyone else, if not by name, then by sight, and though we didn't necessarily know it just yet, we were all on the way up. Born out of the Beat Generation, we were ready to break on to the scene, challenge the establishment, and forge a new way of expressing ourselves in the world.

You have to remember, too, that at this point in time rock and roll was still in its infancy and once Kennedy was assassinated in November 1963, America barreled full speed ahead into a cultural revolution. "Looking back through the decades, it seems clear that Kennedy's death marked an important turning point in American life, after which time events began to move in strange, unexpected directions. This was the moment, if there was a particular moment, when the cultural consensus of the 1950s began to give way to the oppositional and experimental culture that we associate with the 1960s."[16] In fact, perhaps more than any other time period prior, at the heart of this book when The Association was just forming, politics and culture were indelibly intertwined.

When Martin Luther King Jr. was assassinated in 1968, the Academy Awards broadcast was postponed, movie attendance dropped sharply,[17] and the Beach Boys were forced to cancel four of their concerts due to curfews being imposed in the South. Consider that some of the most radical legislation in the history of the United States—from the Civil Rights Act (1964) to the Voting Rights Act (1965) to Medicare and Medicaid programs (1965)—was passed in this decade, while the Vietnam War raged overseas into its second decade. Racial tensions were high, as evidenced by the Watts riots that erupted in Los Angeles in August 1965, not even a week after the Voting Rights Act had passed. Some historians even argue that the riots made white voters panic and switch their allegiance from the Democratic Party to the Republican Party. Needless to say, there was plenty of ripe material from which one could be inspired to write music encompassing not only songs about love and heartbreak, but also the unrest brewing across a country wrestling with its discontent.

The first combat troops—3,500 marines—landed at China Beach on March 8, 1965, joining 23,000 military advisers already there training the South Vietnamese. The day before *that* was Bloody

16   Piereson, James. *Camelot and the Cultural Revolution: How the Assassination of John F. Kennedy Shattered American Liberalism.* New York: Encounter Books, 2013.

17   "Martin Luther King's Death Postpones Oscars." *Variety.* April 8, 1968.

Sunday (the United States Bloody Sunday, not to be confused with Northern Ireland's Bloody Sunday that occurred fewer than ten years later), where civil rights demonstrators, in a movement supported by 1964 Nobel Peace Prize winner Martin Luther King Jr., as they were trying to walk peacefully in protest from Selma to Montgomery, were physically blocked and had tear gas released on them, before being beaten by Alabama state troopers. People were downright hot and bothered, and their feelings were bubbling to the surface. The songs musicians wrote reflected life back to a population hungry for a new way to express their feelings and experiences.

Musically speaking, at the start of the 1960s, we were a few years into the popularity of Dick Clark's television show, *American Bandstand*—it had gone national on ABC in 1957. We were also only a few short years on the heels of what was known as rock and roll's first tragedy: the February 3, 1959, plane crash near Clear Lake, Iowa, referred to as "The Day the Music Died" in a Don McLean song of the same name. That plane crash resulted in the death of Ritchie Valens, Buddy Holly, and J. P. Richardson (the Big Bopper), who had been on the Winter Dance Party Tour of the Midwest with Dion and the Belmonts. And all of *this* was long before the drug-related deaths of Jim Morrison, Jimi Hendrix, Brian Jones of the Rolling Stones, and Janis Joplin by the early 1970s. I mention these musicians not only for what they have in common—their untimely early deaths at the age of twenty-seven—but because their music stands in stark contrast to the untimely demise of those on the Winter Dance Party Tour with Dion and the Belmonts just ten years prior. If there's one thing I hope you're getting, it's that there was a lot of dramatic cultural, social, and political change in a short period of time.

Bob Dylan said, "It's just like when talking about the sixties. If you were here around that time, you would know that the early sixties, up to maybe '64, '65, was really the fifties, the late fifties. They were still the fifties, still the same culture, in America anyway. And it was still going strong but fading away. By '66, the new sixties probably started coming in somewhere along that time and had taken over by the end of the decade. Then, by the time of Woodstock, there was no more fifties…I guess the fifties would have ended in about '65."[18]

Anyhow, back to what was going on at the time I began working at The Ice House and later, performing. In the fall of 1963, American newspapers were covering the Beatlemania that people were buzzing about across the pond, and CBS ran a special about The Beatles on their morning news program with Mike Wallace on November 22, 1963. They never re-aired it on the evening news with Walter Cronkite because it was trumped by President Kennedy's assassination. By the end of the year, however, enthusiastic listeners of that first CBS broadcast had convinced American disc jockeys to play music by The Beatles, which led to "I Want to Hold Your Hand" being their first hit single in the United States, along with a release of their album three weeks early in the states, and on February 9, 1964, after already selling one million albums (in the US), they appeared on *The Ed Sullivan Show*. I always thought they sounded like The Everly Brothers, but with one more vocal harmony part.

Henry Diltz, one of the original members of the Modern Folk Quartet, recalls watching the live broadcast of The Beatles' first US appearance. "We were on the road. And instead of driving all night, we made sure we had a motel room early enough to watch *Ed Sullivan*. And we were mesmerized. I mean, we had sort of heard of The Beatles, and maybe had heard one song on the radio. You'd think, 'Wow, that's really something.' But to see them standing there, these four guys, playing their instruments, making that music…it was the joyfulness that got everybody; really infectious and joyful music."[19] Beatlemania distracted our sad spirits, and lifted Americans out of the doldrums we'd plummeted to in the wake of Kennedy's assassination. Dr. Steve Williams, Associate Professor of Sociology at the University of Southern Indiana, explains with regard to The Beatles, "Instead of

18   Gilmore, Mikal. "Bob Dylan Unleashed." *Rolling Stone*. September 27, 2012.

19   Cody, John. "Looking Back at Los Angeles' legendary 1960s Sunset Strip." *BC Christian News*.

having songs written for them, and using studio musicians, now they were writing their own lyrics and music. They played all their own instruments and toured as a group, which meant they controlled what they're expressing. Combine that with folk music expanding lyrical content and suddenly...Things were being expressed in ways they weren't before. Now, not only was there suggested sexuality of rock 'n' roll, there's an actual free love movement."[20]

At the same time The Beatles took the US by storm and Dylan was breaking the folk music rules by ditching his acoustic guitar, The Rat Pack, a group of entertainers including Frank Sinatra, Dean Martin, Sammy Davis Jr., and their pals was also playing what would be their last concert for twenty-three years. James Wolcott wrote in "When They Were Kings" for *Vanity Fair*, "...the Rat Pack performed during the same period that the Beatniks rolled onto the scene—Jack Kerouac, Allen Ginsburg, William Burroughs...At first the two outfits couldn't seem more bizarre-o worlds apart, the Rat Packers showing the money in their sharkskin suits and slick grooming, the Beats bumming around in fleapit pads from Monterey to Morocco on the path to Buddha-hood. Yet both were a reaction to the suburban conformism of work-home-family in the Eisenhower era. The Rat Pack, like the Beats, disdained middle-class moderation in their pursuit of free-wheeling kicks."[21]

The Kinks, The Who, The Rolling Stones, The Hollies, and The Dave Clark Five were also part of the British Invasion infiltrating American pop music charts with their hits. "The Beatles loomed over their era possibly like no other artist has since. From January 1965 through January 1966, they enjoyed six No. 1 US singles in a row, a feat unbroken until the Bee Gees tied it in 1979 and Whitney Houston topped it with seven singles in 1988...The sunny "I Feel Fine" and "Eight Days a Week" matched the optimism of America rebounding from President Kennedy's assassination. The hopefulness continued

---

20   O'Nan, Angela. "Rock 'n' roll and 'moral panics' – Part One: 1950s and 1960s." University of Southern Indiana University Communications. February 20, 2017.

21   Wolcott, James. "When They Were Kings." *Vanity Fair*. May 1997.

through the first half of 1965, as blacks secured the right to vote in the South and President Johnson vowed to end poverty with such Great Society programs as Medicare and Medicaid…1965 was a year with one foot in the world of doo-wop…and the other in the future as British art school rockers transmogrified the blues with fuzz boxes and distortion."[22] Rock and roll's popularity was heavily influenced by demographics at the time; half of the US population was under the age of twenty-five, while forty-one percent were younger than the age of twenty.[23]

So you get it: the country and rock and roll were changing, and rapidly. Let us also not forget the abundance of sex and drugs (oh, please, let's not forget)! This was an era long before AIDS and Nancy Reagan's "Just Say No" antidrug campaign. With the Supreme Court's ruling on Griswold v. Connecticut in 1960, the pill was suddenly available in all fifty states. Sex not only for function, but also for pleasure, was becoming more…prevalent (thank goodness). At the same time, US Production Code allowed the Hollywood movie, Sidney Lumet's *The Pawnbroker*, to show breasts on screen for the first time. And forget marijuana! (Okay, I admit, personally I can never forget marijuana…) However, I'm actually talking about LSD at the moment—*One Flew Over the Cuckoo's Nest* author Ken Kesey took advantage of the legality of LSD (it wouldn't become illegal until late 1966), and hosted parties in the San Francisco Bay Area to encourage LSD experimentation. In 1967, Paul McCartney admitted he'd taken LSD. *Life Magazine* reprinted a quote from him that had appeared in *Queen*, a UK-based magazine. "After I took it [LSD], it opened my eyes. We only use one-tenth of our brain. Just think what we could accomplish if we could only tap that hidden part. It would mean a whole new world."[24]

---

22   Jackson, Andrew Grant. *The Most Revolutionary Year in Music 1965*. New York: Thomas Dunne Books, 2015.

23   Braunstein, Peter, Phillip E. Carpenter and Anthony O. Edmonds. *The Sixties Chronicle*. Lincolnwood, IL: Publications International, 2007.

24   Thompson, Thomas. "The New Far-Out Beatles: They're grown men now and creating extraordinary musical sounds." *Life Magazine*. June 16, 1967.

So I think you can safely say that in the "swinging sixties," for those interested in expanding musical experimentation into sexual or chemical experimentation, there were *options*. I stuck mostly with pot: the joke among my friends and me was "Just say how much." For an early twenty-something guy with his life in front of him, it was an exciting time and place to be alive.

As The Ice House grew, so did the depth and breadth of the acts. When I began working there, Gale Garnett had a huge hit with "We'll Sing in the Sunshine," a song that went all the way to No. 4 on the charts. I remember when The Dillards—Doug Dillard on banjo, Rodney Dillard on guitar and dobro, Dean Webb on mandolin, and Mitchell Franklin "Mitch" Jayne on double bass—hit town and played all the hoots. They were the best bluegrass group I'd ever seen or heard. The first time they came through town, they had just two microphones, and by the next time they came through they'd graduated to four microphones, and it was a whole different show.

You've heard The Dillards even if you don't realize you've heard them—Doug and Rodney performed most of the 1967 *Bonnie and Clyde* soundtrack, along with Glen Campbell. After Elektra released their first album, "Back Porch Bluegrass," The Dillards were invited to audition for *The Andy Griffith Show*, where they were offered to be the Darling family even before the audition was over. Their television appearances on a hit show did much to expose many Americans to bluegrass music for the first time. Many years later, Doug went on to play and tour with The Byrds. Folk-rock (what The Association was first known for; indeed, I can go so far as to say we *trailblazed* folk-rock into the fabric of American music, as I'll share later) borrows from many music styles, including bluegrass.

If there's one thing I don't like and The Association doesn't like, it's being pigeonholed. We had many influences, just one of which was bluegrass. Of course, The Dillards, like most other groups, including us, had humble beginnings. When they ran out of money on their first trip from Missouri to California, they got a gig playing the Buddhi Club in Oklahoma City and were able to earn enough money to complete the journey and reach their destination (and thank goodness for music history, they did!). Bob Stane said of The Dillards, "They were perfect in all ways. It was instrumentally perfect, the vocals were perfect, the humor was great."[25] A man by the name of Tom Campbell was responsible for booking the entertainment acts into every land at Disneyland. He booked all sorts of bluegrass, folk, and country players he first saw at The Ice House, including The Dillards, and later, The Association. The Association would work every land in Disneyland long before we had a hit record.

My job at The Ice House came with a few unlisted responsibilities and perks. We had so many acts coming into town for two weeks or a month at a time, and since the talent's time was free all day long until the evening shows, they wanted to take in the sights. I quickly became an expert Los Angeles tour guide. One time I drove down to Mexico with Canadian singer Karen James; her guitarist, Doug; and the Gold Coast Singers—a duo that had a big hit with "Plastic Jesus," which Billy Idol would later go on to rerecord: "I don't care if it rains or freezes / As long as I've got my Plastic Jesus / Ridin' on the dashboard of my car." We were harassed by plainclothes policemen with relentless, ridiculous questions such as, "How much do you make a year?" until they found out Karen was Canadian and changed their tune and were as nice as could be. In the 1960s, if you had long hair or looked anything like a hippie, the authorities took it as an invitation to badger you as they saw fit.

Speaking of hair, a few years later, one interviewer asked me backstage, before an Association concert at a college in the Midwest, why I had *short* hair.

"I'm gonna do you a favor," I told him, "and not answer that, because your question is irrelevant."

---

25   Roland, Terry, "Bob Stane Remembers the Upper Cellar and the Coffeehouse Era." *San Diego Troubadour.* November 2016.

I stood up and walked out to grab some fresh air and relax. I didn't want to start the concert irritated. An irate mom, who had just dropped off some kids for our concert, approached me as I stood outside.

"Why do you have *long* hair?" she asked.

This, on the heels of a question asking me the exact opposite! In truth, I had neither long nor short hair; it was something in between. I laughed at the absurdity of it all and went back inside to do the concert. I mean, what can you say to that? Hair and skin color are comparable in one thing, and one thing only: neither of them are the gauge of anything whatsoever.

There was a time when security at Disneyland gave our light man Pete Stefanos a hard time for his long hair. It must have been the combination of his stature (he was six feet tall) and his locks. He also had a black belt in karate, so they may have sensed he could have kicked their asses if he wanted to.

"How did you get in here?" they asked him.

"I work with The Association, I'm working at The Golden Horseshoe," he explained.

"Well, stay in your *land!*" the guy shot back. All because of the length of his hair!

In the summer of 1968, my daughter Jill was born. The doctor kept poking his head in while Birdie was in labor to ask, "How is everything going?" "Fine," we'd say. And then he looped back around to catch her when she came out! Shortly after her birth, I stopped in Portsmouth to visit my uncles George and Bob Bamberger and my cousins, whom I hadn't seen since Judy and I had left for San Diego with my mother in the late 1940s. In a story on my visit, the local paper wrote the following about me and my hair (or in this case, lack thereof): "The twenty-four-year-old rhythm guitar player is not the typical rock and roll star. At the present time he doesn't have long hair! When offstage, he doesn't dress in mod clothes or Nehru jackets, either. Giguere caused some commotion the other night when he appeared on a television show minus any hair, whatsoever, on his head. Why did he cut his hair? 'I didn't want to comb it,' he simply replied with a laugh. 'My hair was once a foot long, and it waved and curled and bounced when I walked. I loved it,' he said. 'The hair really keeps a lot of people away from me, but I don't care. Now the short hair kind of puts people off, too. I just enjoy getting people exasperated!'"[26]

It's true, I cannot lie; I don't care if you're exasperated by me or not, I'm always going to tell it like it is. The fact is, people judged men by the length of their hair in the 1960s. That may even still happen today, but trust me, it was worse then. There was a case that went all the way to the Massachusetts Supreme Court about a high school senior, George Leonard Jr., who played nightly in a successful band, in which he was known as Georgie Porgie. The principal kicked him out of school and told him not to come back until he got a haircut. His father filed a lawsuit saying Georgie needed to keep his hair long for his job (as a musician). Ultimately he lost, as the Supreme Court sided with the principal and said he had a right to tell Georgie to get his hair cut and then expel him when he didn't comply. Unbelievable! This was a court case about the length of a guy's hair! While we were in the middle of a war overseas! I mean, there were far more important issues with which we should have been consumed. Personally, I loved watching people get their panties in a twist when I made them uncomfortable because of some label they put on me based on what my hair did or didn't look like. My 1968 buzz cut came about when my daughter Jill was born with a few wisps of hair, and I shaved off all of my hair the day after her birth to see if our hair would grow out at the same rate. As it turned out, mine grew much faster!

But back to my early days working at The Ice House in Pasadena. I had to be familiar with all of the museums in town because musical guests were constantly coming and going for gigs (arriving from out of town) and asking questions—this is how I became well

---

26   Fuller, Bruce. "Member of 'Association' Home for Visit." *The Portsmouth Herald.* Portsmouth, NH. August 16, 1968.

acquainted with Descanso Gardens and The Huntington Library, Art Collections and Botanical Gardens—I've never seen anything in the world like The Huntington's succulent garden. Their art collection has an incredible set of twelve Paul Revere silver spoons, each with an apostle on them. Descanso Gardens became the backdrop for the cover of *The Association's Greatest Hits* album. I also became an expert on Forest Lawn Cemetery, or, as it was affectionately referred to, "Disneyland of the Dead," where you can find the graves of Humphrey Bogart, Nat King Cole, Errol Flynn, and more. (Los Angeles Tourist Sidebar: If you want to see the graves of as many stars as possible, I recommend you check out Forest Lawn Glendale over Forest Lawn Hollywood Hills. Forest Lawn had these great coloring books—one year I bought a bunch and gave them all out as Christmas gifts.) Clearly, I acquired a bevy of useless trivia in my unofficial role as ambassador to Los Angeles tourism.

When I wasn't working, playing guitar and singing, or offering up tourist tips, I could be found catching an afternoon movie screening at one of several local movie houses, which let all card-carrying Ice House employees in free of charge. I saw every single movie they screened. Later, when Birdie moved in, if we weren't going to a Monday hoot at the Troubadour, we would catch the shows and ride the rides at Disneyland, where we also enjoyed free admission, thanks again to Tom Campbell, who booked the acts there.

So I ran the lights, sound, and the Sunday night hoots at The Ice House in Pasadena. The Monday night hoots at the Troubadour were the bigger stakes gig of the two for any performer who signed up—you were, after all, that much closer to the Hollywood lights. Hootenannies were like an organized evening of cabaret—you'd sign up for a time slot—if you were a musician, you'd do four or five songs, and if you were a comedian, you'd do ten minutes of your best material. I'd put my own name on the list at The Ice House one Sunday a month, and at the Troubadour one Monday night a month. By this time, I'd decided I wanted to be a professional singer. There was just one problem: the cold terror I experienced performing in front of live audiences. I had no choice—I wanted to be a pro, so I had to get over it. I knew that if I wanted to conquer my stage fright, I was going to have to get used to playing in front of people. So in my two-year stint working at The Ice House, I did twenty-four sets at Ice House hoots and twenty-four sets at the Troubadour hoots. With this consistent commitment, my confidence grew, and my stage fright was cured.

I saw a lot of the big names at each of the clubs, while I was working there and after—some of them before they were ever household names: David Letterman, the Smothers Brothers (they were already a major concert act and pretty big in radio when I met them, but weren't yet on television—by the time they did get there, The Association was also making waves, and they had us on three times), Jay Leno, The Eagles (years after I worked at The Ice House, during the time I left The Association, I saw the guys who would go on to form The Eagles play as Linda Ronstadt's band in a Troubadour hoot—I even sang backup with them!), Steve Martin, Lily Tomlin, George Carlin, Modern Folk Quartet (the most handsome male quartet that ever was—their banjo and clarinet player, Henry Diltz, who already shared his experience of watching The Beatles perform live on *The Ed Sullivan Show*, would become a major rock and roll photographer, shooting over eighty album covers while Chip Douglas, their bass player, would later produce all the hits from The Monkees), Doug & Jennifer (a duo act of Jennifer Warnes and Doug Rowell), and many more. Doug would eventually carve my guitar and costar in a national tour of the hit Broadway musical *Hair*, and Jennifer catapulted to fame with "Right Time of the Night" in the early seventies, and later "Up Where We Belong" with Joe Cocker, before also collaborating with Leonard Cohen on some of his music, tours, and albums. I saw Fred Willard as part of the best comedy duo I've ever seen, Willard and Greco (with Vic Greco), and also as part of a comedy quintet, the Ace Trucking Company (where the members included Fred, George Memmoli, Michael Mislove, Bill Saluga, and Patti Deutsch), long before they appeared on *The Tonight Show with Johnny Carson* and over a decade before there was ever a *Saturday Night Live.*

In 1966 at a Troubadour hoot, I saw the first set Buffalo Springfield ever did (it was incredible). I saw my buddy Mason Williams from my days at The Upper Cellar, The Ice House, and of *The Smothers Brothers Comedy Hour* fame (he was their head writer) play silly and exquisite folk music on both his six- and twelve-string guitars. He could also play the banjo and wooden recorder. Mason introduced me to one of his dear friends, the American artist Ed Ruscha, whom he'd gone to school with, and we all had a lot of good times together. In working on this book, Mason told my coauthor Ashley, "Russ and I hung out a lot together…one of the things about Russ that I think is important is that he had excellent taste. If he recommended an album I should buy and listen to, I did, or if it was a movie he had seen that he thought was great, I would always go check that out. He had his thumb on the pulse of what was going on in LA and had a great sense of what was worth the time to check out."

Mason and I actually bought pot together for the very first time—we'd certainly smoked it before, but never purchased it. See, when I was thirteen, I was harassed by a cop in a park near my friend's house in San Diego. My Levi jeans were rolled into cuffs about a third of an inch wide, and he bent down to check within them to see if I was hiding anything.

"Son, you're going to have to roll those down all the way."

"What is it you're looking for, officer?" I asked.

"Marijuana," he said.

"I'm a thirteen-year-old boy!"[27]

I made a mental note in the back of my mind after that experience—if that cop is so against marijuana, and so focused on suppressing it, then it must be pretty good! Mason and I bought

---

27   I gave an interview in 1970 to *The Purdue Exponent* where I tell this same story, only in that version, I was twelve. I swear I told the story incorrectly to the paper. I was thirteen!

a pack of cigarettes, emptied them one by one, and filled them up again with marijuana. "Some dope fiends," we chuckled to ourselves. Mason's bass player, Tandyn Almer, would pen the music and lyrics to our first hit, "Along Comes Mary," at the age of twenty-three. (Tandyn also happened to be a piano player.) Why do I mention "Along Comes Mary"?

Because in discussing Tandyn's lyrics and the controversy that would abound over "Along Comes Mary"—"Was it about marijuana or was it about the Virgin Mary?"—I can only respond, *What do you think? We're just getting into my story, but you can probably guess the answer!* On NPR's "All Things Considered," former *Rolling Stone* editor Parke Puterbaugh remarked, "It ["Along Comes Mary"] is a breathless set of lyrics. There's a lot of harmonic complexity, so it was a pretty challenging piece of music, especially for the time. There is the just torrents of words and the internal rhyme and the enigmatic lyric, which are a cut above typical pop fare." Terry Kirkman says, "When musicologists look at 'Along Comes Mary,' it is an accepted identified benchmark in American popular music as a total departure from any form that had preceded it."

I remember Roger McGuinn (known then as "Jim" McGuinn), who would become the lead singer and guitarist of The Byrds, sitting in the lobby of The Ice House fingering a pop music/rock and roll ditty (a Beatles tune I can't recall at the moment) on the guitar. "This music," he said, "is finally the cross between art and money." I also remember the purity of the singing voice of David Troy ("Diamond" Dave Somerville), the original lead singer of The Diamonds. They had big hits with "Why Do Fools Fall in Love" and "Little Darlin'." Dave sang his ass off and gave great concerts all the way through to his death in 2016.

If you weren't alive during this time period I'm talking about, you might be reading and thinking like you were when you saw my name on the cover of this book: "Who are all these people and all these names and why should I give two shits?" Well, these names are truly some of the greatest there ever was, both in comedy and in music. In the case of many of them, they paved the way for the later successes of other major rock and roll stars and bands, simply because their talent and music existed. The scene was so tight and so small, it would be like turning on your television today to watch your favorite stars on your favorite shows, all of whom just happened to be your friends. Without the Smothers Brothers, Steve Martin, and Jay Leno, there would never have been a Stephen Colbert, Jerry Seinfeld, or Chris Rock. Without Buffalo Springfield, The Byrds, and—dare I say it?—The Association, there never would have been an Aerosmith, Maroon 5, or Backstreet Boys. The 1960s music culture in Los Angeles was full of pioneers who didn't even know they were pioneers—we were merely doing what we loved, making art and music in response to the world around us, fighting war with songs of love and peace, and cracking jokes to break the tension of the social unrest. In the words of Bob Stane, "We had winners on this stage every night. A lot of people who made it. We had award winners in every field. Oscars, Emmys, Grammys. You'd find Oscar winners in the kitchen talking with the cook. Leonard Nimoy would come in. It was just a brilliant place."

When I performed at the hoots, I sang some of my favorite blues tunes, which I learned from the records of Sonny Terry and Brownie McGhee, Josh White, and Big Bill Broonzy. At The Ice House in the mid-1960s, the country was at the height of what is now called contemporary folk music, or the folk revival. It began in the 1940s with a resurgence of square dancing and folk dancing, ebbed in the 1950s with McCarthyism and left-wingers like Pete Seeger being forced to testify in front of the House Committee on Un-American Activities (HUAC), and then rose again to popularity with the spread of folk music in coffeehouses and the chart-topping hits of The Kingston Trio. So at the time I was working at The Ice House, we had the British Invasion on one side, and folk revival on the other. Folk music was the primary attraction at the Ash Grove, a popular Los Angeles folk club that was open from 1958 until 1973. Chris Hillman of The Byrds explains, "Within a two-mile radius in Hollywood was the Ash Grove, and up the street was the Troubadour, and it was worlds apart in the folk music period, prior to the Beatles. So at the Troubadour, you would hear the Modern Folk Quartet or a Kingston Trio-type band, down at the Ash Grove you'd hear—and I did see—the Stanley Brothers, Bill Monroe, Flatt & Scruggs, Mance Lipscomb, and Lightnin' Hopkins."[28]

When Bob Dylan broke open the folk music genre and stood it on its head, his actions spurred internal debate amongst many a band ("Should we go electric?")—case in point being The Scottsville Squirrel Barkers, where they split; Chris Hillman went electric and formed The Byrds. (In the sixties, it was popular for many a band to name themselves after animals, fruits, vegetables, or just include a plain ol' direct reference to drugs.)

As I was growing more comfortable singing in front of a crowd, I began performing a Johnny Cash song, "Frankie's Man, Johnny," a story of a man who gets caught in the act just as he's about to do his woman wrong:

Then, in the front door walked a redhead, Johnny saw her right away.
She came down by the bandstand to watch him while he played.
He was Frankie's man, but she was far away.
Frankie smiled at the redhead; she smiled back at him.
Then he came and sat at her table where the lights were low and dim.
What Frankie didn't know wouldn't hurt her none.
Then the redhead jumped up and slapped him, she slapped him a time or two.
She said, "I'm Frankie's sister and I was checking up on you.
If you're her man, you better treat her right."

---

28   Cody, John. "Looking Back at Los Angeles' legendary 1960s Sunset Strip." *BC Christian News*. 2009.

I learned "I'm Just a Man" from The Grandison Singers, a black gospel trio from the Big Apple who played the club, and other great songs like "The Wagoner's Lad":

> *Hard luck is the fortune of all womankind.*
> *They're always controlled, they're always confined.*
> *Controlled by their parents until they are wives,*
> *Then slaves to their husbands for the rest of their lives.*

"The Wagoner's Lad" formed the crux of the lyrics at the heart of The Kingston Trio hit song "Pullin' Away."

Traditionally, folk music was played on guitar or other guitar-like instruments (banjo, ukulele, etc.) and handed down through oral tradition, with the original author unknown—you learned the stories and the songs from the people who taught them to you, not from a piece of paper. Doug Dillard, for instance, taught me "Polly Vaughn," a story about a woman who appears as a ghost at the murder trial of her lover to clear his name:

> *In the middle of the night Polly Vaughn did appear,*
> *Cried, "Jimmy, oh, Jimmy, you must have no fear;*
> *Just tell them you were hunting when your trial day has come*
> *And you won't be convicted for what you have done."*

You couldn't beat the stories those folk songs told. I sang them because I loved them, and I was honing my skills and developing my stage presence. I never did learn to read music formally—I think I made it through one or two guitar lessons as a teenager. I wasn't interested in learning any single-string stuff—all I wanted to know were the chords and the rhythm so I could play the songs I wanted to sing. And so I learned everything by ear. To this day I like to say that as a guitarist, I'm an excellent drummer—meaning I have good rhythm—and as a baritone, I can squeak out a little tenor when needed. I sang and played rhythm guitar with The Association, but there were three of us on guitar, and guitar wasn't my strength in comparison to some of the other guys, so eventually I stopped carrying mine and stuck to the tambourine, cowbell, and other percussion accompaniment as well as my part on the vocals, while also singing the lead on songs like "Cherish" with Terry and "Windy" with Larry Ramos.

Henry Diltz, who I mentioned was an original member of the Modern Folk Quartet before becoming a famous rock and roll photographer, remembers the first time the MFQ made their continental US debut at the Troubadour. The MFQ had started in Hawaii, where they'd enjoyed success as regulars at a Honolulu coffeehouse. But when they played the Troubadour, "No one had ever heard of us," Henry said. "We sang 'The Ox Driver's Song.' When we got to the chorus of the song, we broke into this strident four-part harmony and at that moment in the song, the whole audience rose as one, applauding. It was shocking. We were like, oh my God, what is happening? What's going on? We'd never had that happen. People were just blown away by this four-part harmony...we were like The Four Freshmen singing folk music. And so these bigger chords you could do more with musically became popular. And they put The Men together, I think, to take advantage of that, to be able to sing fatter chords. You can hit jazz chords and more musical chords that way." (The Association was born out of that folk-rock group, The Men, which I'm getting to, I swear...)

Henry's right—most folk groups were solo singers, duos, or trios—nothing larger. The MFQ opened the door wide for bigger bands like The Beach Boys and The Association to push to create bigger, more impressive sound. To be sure, groups like The New Christy Minstrels were certainly large and harmonizing beautifully, but they were sticking mostly to traditional folk music, and not experimenting much with style or sound. As we were rising to prominence, music producer Phil Spector, a key player in shattering the confines of aural expectations in rock and roll and perhaps even more notorious for his casual wielding of guns during marathon drug- and liquor-fueled recording sessions, was experimenting beyond standard percussion, bass, and guitar with his Wall of Sound, where he used new combinations of unusual instruments foreign to rock 'n' roll—calling it a Wagnerian approach to rock and roll. And of course Brian Wilson created *Pet Sounds*, which was incredibly original in that no one had ever heard music like that before, and furthermore, you couldn't easily label what it was you were hearing. Experimentation was met with unpredictable mixed results, for as a musician you had to contend with the expectations of the record label and your audience.

Brian Wilson's *Pet Sounds* odyssey took up more (than) ten months and cost a then-unheard-of $70,000, making it one of the most expensive albums ever recorded at that time. The Capitol executives were hoping for a hit-packed album to recoup their sizable investment. But when they heard the final mix that April, they were puzzled—and horrified—by the decidedly un-sunny sounds. Instead of a celebration of youth, Capitol got a melancholic musical missive straight from the heart of their young maestro. "It was played at a sales meeting, and the marketing guys were really disappointed and down about the record, because it wasn't the normal 'Surfin' USA,' 'Help Me, Rhonda,' 'Barbara Ann' kind of production," remembered A&R rep Karl Engermann. "Capitol didn't see the evolution," Bruce Johnston lamented. "*Pet Sounds* was so radical compared to the nice 'Barbara Anns' we had been making, which Capitol had been successfully selling and they just wanted more."

Unsure how to market Wilson's introspective artistic statement, Capitol hedged their bets by hastily preparing a greatest hits compilation and throwing their full promotional machine behind it. *Best of the Beach Boys* was rushed into shops less than two months after *Pet Sounds'* release. It promptly went gold, while *Pet Sounds*, effectively left to sell on its own merits, barely cracked the Top 10.

It was a major drop-off from the Number One million-sellers of prior years. Capitol felt vindicated, and Brian Wilson was crushed. "In my heart of hearts, I think that the reason [*Pet Sounds*] isn't a billion-selling album is simply that the label didn't believe in Brian," Johnston reflected on the album thirtieth anniversary. "They turned their back on him by releasing *Best of the Beach Boys*. Why wouldn't you allocate a massive budget to promote *Pet Sounds*? This album is timeless and forever, and the label turned it into an ignored stepchild."[29]

Considering that the whole reason a record exists in the first place is because of the talent, ingenuity, and creativity of the musicians behind it, you'd be surprised by how little influence bands actually have over what the record companies do with their music… but more on that later.

While I was working at The Ice House, I met Ted Bluechel, Brian Cole, Terry Kirkman, and Jules Gary Alexander, four of the six original band members of The Association. Ted Bluechel had been a champion pole-vaulter and first chair drummer in his high school band in Southern California. While attending El Camino Junior College and on track to become a zoology teacher, Ted started playing guitar in The Cherry Hill Singers, a quartet made up of three guitars and a banjo. I worked the lights and sound for their sets at The Ice House. A 1968 article in the *Illinois State Journal*, "…And Just Who Are The Association?" highlighted promotional information that was circulated about the group. Regarding Ted, the material boasted, he "is the sex symbol of the group; is called 'pig,' reason for given nickname is that he used to live on a pig ranch; other reasons infer that he likes to drink between performances and has a hairy chest, whatever that has to do with it. Ted also has five furry little (she) rats." I don't ever remember Ted being a drinker, but

---

29   Runtagh, Jordan. "Beach Boys' 'Pet Sounds': 15 Things You Didn't Know." *Rolling Stone*. May 16, 2016.

he's certainly one of the sweetest guys I've ever met, up to that point and to this day. He introduced me to lip balm (which I always have in my pocket) and blueberries, and in the band, he sang baritone and played the drums and occasionally guitar.

Everyone in the group would eventually have what we called a "free association" name. Mine was Quivers H. Orion. Quivers because the full form of my first name, Russell, could be considered to have a homonym, as in the *rustling* of leaves...which we then bastardized and decided rustling was quivering—hence "quivers." (Go with me for a moment here.) And the "H" is for my middle name, Henry, and then my last name, Giguere, means "hunter." And Orion, as in the constellation, was a hunter.

Ted's free association name was Punky Coldbubble. (Teddy Boys were part of the British subculture; the name referred to young men who wore clothes inspired by the style of the Edwardian period, therefore "Punky"; when you turn blue as in Ted's last name, Bluechel, you're cold, hence, "Cold"; and a shell, as in the second syllable of "Blue-chel," is a "Bubble.") What can I say? It was long before the days of personal digital devices, and we had a lot of time to occupy in the long hours we clocked on the road. Ted also turned me on to The Beach Boys. Until Ted opened my eyes, I thought The Beach Boys' music was only for rich, white kids. Boy, was I wrong. They have one of the most complex, innovative rock and roll sounds and their sophisticated harmonies still stand the test of time. See if you can listen to a Beach Boys tune without tapping your foot or singing along. Anyhow, Mike Whalen, whom you'll learn also figures into the early beginnings of The Men, worked with Ted in The Cherry Hill Singers.

Brian Cole was brilliant, perhaps too brilliant for his own good. As Jules puts it, "Brian was an extremely intelligent man, head up his ass, but he was fantastic." He could crack a joke anytime, anywhere, anyplace—often at the expense of the company the joke was told in (just ask any of the former wives or girlfriends of The Association band members). Brian would find out what your button was, and then push it, again and again. And then again. And then one more time still, for good measure. Brian preferred slippers—he had some kind of a problem with his feet, so slippers were more comfortable—he had an entire collection in all kinds of styles, many of which looked like actual shoes, yet the only time he wore actual shoes or boots was onstage. Brian was an expert at recognizing regional accents and placing from what part of the country people came. He knew I was from the New England area immediately when he heard me pronounce closet ("cluzzet") and helicopter ("heelacopter"). Over the years on the road, Brian and I both got so good at nailing accents that we could guess where someone was from within a hundred miles—north, south, east, west, and in the middle. He collected watches, gold, and other fine jewelry items—I accompanied Brian on several trips to pawn shops and he knew what he was doing. When we boarded the plane back home to the United States at the end of our European tour, Brian lined the bottom of his coat pockets with small diamonds he'd purchased to avoid paying any extra taxes on his gem purchases. He loved to take a hundred one-dollar bills to a print shop, ask them to stack them all together and put glue on one end of the bills to form a small tablet of one-dollar bills. Brian would then peel dollar bills from that notepad as he needed them to pay for purchases, while onlookers stood by, mouths agape. He was also the first to have one of those chains that attached to your belt and hooked to your wallet. The only people who did that were bus drivers, truck drivers, bikers…and Brian. Nowadays, kids wear them all the time, but back then, it was an unusual sight.

Brian was probably the most interesting guy among us in the whole band—an original to say the least; he drove some members of the group crazy, usually intentionally. Though he never let on, I think he got a kick out of other people's reactions to him—the more intense the response, the more it inspired him to increase the weirdness of his behavior.

Brian sang bass and played bass in the band, but to him, his musical abilities were secondary; he thought of himself more as an actor—in fact, in the beginning when we were all rehearsing together, he made extra money on the side by giving invited talks to acting school students. His "free association" name was Orate Mondo Bituminous—within that name is a reference to William Jennings Bryan (the orator, because Brian was a big talker); Mondo, meaning world (because Brian told me "Leslie," his middle name, means "world"); and Bituminous (coal, a homophone for his last name, Cole)—ultimately all harkening back to Brian's affinity for the theatrical. Brian could entertain an audience with his incredible memory and vast trivia knowledge. You could quote a line from any Shakespearean play no matter how obscure, and he would tell you the play, the character, and the act the line was in—and if he knew the publication, he could tell you the page number to find it on.

Terry and I always sang lead on Dino Valenti's "Get Together" in concert. We called it "Dino's Tune." You can hear us sing that song on our live 1970 album, though it was the Youngbloods and their 1967 recording that made it famous. What's funny about that particular song is that Dino Valenti got busted for grass while riding in a car with friends, but the police broke into his apartment and took him in for speed, and all of a sudden he was facing ten years in the slammer. "To finance his bail and subsequent court appearances, he sold a song, 'Get Together,' to Frank Werber's SFO Music Company. He relinquished all rights to the song, thereby effectively cutting himself off from the usual penny-per-record share of royalties. Having been recorded on albums by such artists as Jefferson Airplane, the Youngbloods, Fred Neil, and We Five, not to mention singles success by the Youngbloods, the song has sold nearly two million copies, becoming an anthem of sorts for the gathering 'hippie' tribe. So Valenti lost out on something like $20,000. 'A lot of people say I was stupid for selling all my rights to the song, but for ten years of my life, man, I can write another song."[30] When we performed "Dino's Tune" live, Brian would always recite an excerpt from James Thurber's 1939 antiwar story, "The Last Flower," before we sang it. I can still hear him saying that last line, "One man / And one woman / And one flower." We wrote to James Thurber's publisher asking for permission to use the excerpt Brian performed on our 1970 live recording, but the publisher declined. Early pressings of the live album include it (the publisher's decline of permission came after we'd already recorded it). If you're lucky enough to have a version that includes the poem, know that you are one of the few! Brian was instrumental in much of the onstage banter we developed in our repertoire in between songs to entertain the audience and cover string changes, any sound issues, really anything that might come up in live performance—in fact, much of the time, Brian and I would hold down the fort onstage together. We could talk to anyone about anything for any length of time.

Brian was bisexual, but it was the 1960s—you were whatever you were, you did what you wanted to do, and no one talked about it. The entire time I knew Brian, he always lived with a woman. He did have liaisons with men, however, including Michael Shere, the light man at the Troubadour, who was the best light man I ever met. Michael was gay and often flirted with me; I never took offense and never knew anyone else to, either. Our manager, Pat Colecchio, whom I'll tell you about soon, swore that one night he and Bones Howe were mixing tunes on our fourth album, *Birthday*, when they heard a door open and close and Brian popped up in the control room decked out in full drag—wig, dress, makeup, heels. I wasn't there to witness it, but regardless of any sexual preference, with his flair for the theatrical and the shocking, it seems exactly the type of stunt Brian would pull just to elicit a reaction.

Eventually, Brian would venture beyond the group's affinity for marijuana and acid into drugs involving needles, dangerous dalliances that would cost him his life when he died from

---

30   Fong-Torres, Ben. "Folk Focus: Dino Valente." *Rolling Stone*. February 1, 1969.

speedballing—shooting heroin, and then cocaine—in 1972. He once told me he wanted his tombstone to read "It Didn't Look Deadly to Me." I can still see the wistful look on Brian's face as he admired my healthy veins just one day before he died.

"Oh, come on, let me shoot you up," he said.

"Brian, you're not going to touch these veins. I don't even like it when they have to take blood! I'm going to let you shoot that crap into my body? I don't think so."

One time I was at a party and looking for a bathroom when I opened a door and saw a bunch of people doing lines on a glass-topped desk. Ever friendly, one of them asked, "Would you like a line?"

"Sure," I said, figuring it was coke. I'm not a heroin kind of guy. But I did those lines, and the next thing I knew, I woke up in the garden. I think what heroin provides people is oblivion. I do not require oblivion.

My friend Danny Hutton of Three Dog Night vividly remembers visiting Brian at his house in Benedict Canyon, discovering that he was doing speed, and then shoving Brian's needles down the garbage disposal, which Brian was not happy about.

"The one thing I tell people, and a lot of people don't get it or believe it—it was a very innocent time," Danny says. "It's always written about the drugs and sex and all that stuff. But everybody for a period of time thought the drugs are not habit-forming and free sex is okay and the peaceful love kind of thing. When I look back, it was just very innocent and sweet. I've got some lovely memories of that. Later on, the hard drugs came in and people with guns and it got very dark. People would go to rehab five times and you thought, oh, maybe this is addictive. And a lot of people started dying…I have a phone book—I look once in a while and I just see names (of people who've died) crossed out."

But in 1963 before the hard drugs, Brian was an actor/singer who played bass in a trio folk group called the Gnu Folk, and they also performed at the hoots. He was living with his wife, Molly, and two young sons, Jordan and Chandler, in Portland, Oregon, when Molly gave him one year to make it in Los Angeles. Brian met Terry and Jules at the Troubadour.

When I first met Terry Kirkman, I was struck by how much he looked like actor George C. Scott. I can't even count on my fingers and toes the number of instruments he can play. He always had several harmonicas in various keys in his pockets, or a recorder in his belt, ready to play at the drop of a hat. Like Mary Poppins keeps pulling treasures out of her bottomless bag, Terry was always fishing out some hidden instrument. In the band, Terry sang baritone and played the recorder and other brass and reed instruments, including the flugelhorn and saxophone, respectively. Terry shares:

I was born into a relatively musical family. My mother was a piano player, monster church organist, and was a music major. My father, though I never saw him play, played in dance bands. We moved to Pomona, CA, probably right at the beginning of WWII. We moved into an apartment house that was all people who worked in defense plants. We couldn't get a piano, so my mom somehow got a marimba—I saw her play it. I was probably three and I climbed up on a chair and taught myself to play "Jesus Loves Me." And that was it. It never occurred to me—no one ever pushed music on me at all. I would find an instrument and I would just start playing it. If I could get a song out of it, I would figure out how it works. It's really interesting to figure out when you get an instrument like a harmonica that doesn't have a system laid out in front of you. My brother played tuba and bass while he was going to college. The only instrument I ever learned to read music on was tuba. I played a different variety of brasses—saxophones, some keyboard, and recorder. I'd just teach myself to do it. I'd just pick it up. I couldn't play them really well, I would be pretty limited to three, four, five keys I could be comfortable in. It would be all in my head (writing music), and I don't know how that works. I hear the whole melody, I hear the bass line, as we start to lay it down and play it, you start to move things around and tweak them. I watched a snippet of Dylan in an interview from years ago where the news guy is saying, "So, I understand you wrote *Blowin' in the Wind* in ten minutes," and Dylan's famous answer is, "Yeah." He said "I can't tell you about it because it's just there," and that's pretty much how I wrote a lot of my songs. You receive them...I've had whole verses come to me like you were singing it. I go, "What is this?"

Terry had been in the National Guard, but at some point the army lost his paperwork and had to recreate his file from scratch, which meant they had to redo his medical examination. At that point, they discovered he had Osgood-Schlatter's disease (a painful swelling of the bump on the upper part of the shinbone, just below the knee), which had been previously diagnosed, but only after he entered the National Guard and his official paperwork had already been submitted. Terry was given an honorable discharge. While attending junior college in California, he and a few buddies paid eighty-five dollars each for a one-way ticket on a charter airline to Hawaii. The money ran out pretty quickly, and he needed a job. Terry walked five or six miles to a job interview and landed it, working as a sales rep for a paper company where Waikiki was his territory.

While in Hawaii, he ended up at a party at a doctor's house in the Honolulu foothills, where he met Jules on a rainy night. Terry had a broken guitar where he could play only one string at a time. But that night, he and Jules made music together. Not long thereafter, Terry paid seventy-five dollars to sail back to California on a 160-foot schooner in twenty-nine days—everything that could go wrong on that trip did go wrong, including running out of food, but he made it back to California alive. Once there, he went back to school and to work, managing and talent searching for acts to book at the Meeting Place, a club in the Inland Empire.

One of Terry's good friends and fellow music majors was Frank Zappa, and together they played folk-blues and jazz at suburban coffeehouses. Terry played in a Basque restaurant and a Latino band—basically whatever music work he could get, he took. Terry's free association name was Ripper Chapelman. (A tear, from the first syllable of Terry's name, is a rip, hence "Ripper"; and a "kirk," like the first syllable of his last name, is a Scottish word meaning church, hence "Chapel.") In terms of his songwriting, Terry is the mastermind behind what I call "thematic mothers"—he writes big music with giant themes. He also has what I refer to as Catholic-Jewish guilt—though he is neither Catholic nor Jewish. Terry, as the songwriter for "Cherish," has made the most money of all of us in the group, and has struggled with that guilt over the decades. I've told Terry my theory and he agrees. There are those in the group who wouldn't concur with me, but that's how I see it.

Jules Gary Alexander grew up as the child of divorced parents, surrounded by a large extended family in Chattanooga, Tennessee, before moving to California when he was in high school. He taught himself how to play guitar and formed a rock band called Terry and the Twisters. He left high school before graduating. A friend of his asked:

"Are you having a good time?"

"No, I hate school."

"Let's go join the Navy."

So they did. Jules was just seventeen. While in the Navy, Jules earned his high school equivalency diploma and became an optics guy, and met Terry at that party in Hawaii when he was stationed at Pearl Harbor. "We sort of looked at each other, and it was as if we had played together for twenty years." When Jules got out of the Navy, he moved to Pomona with his mom and grandparents. Not long thereafter he ran into Terry at a folk club and they started hanging out. Together, Jules and Terry began to work as musical troubleshooters for multiple groups, including The Cherry Hill Singers (which you'll recall had Ted in it) and Jackie and Gayle, two women who had formed their own group since leaving The New Christy Minstrels. Jules is very spiritual and scientific and can play any type of music with anyone—he's an incredible guitarist and he has what I call the "touch." He has always been held in high esteem by anyone who has worked with him. Terry and Jules would add dynamic chords to arrangements they were working on and change harmonies, shaping the music to have more of an impact. Jules sang tenor and played lead guitar in the band, and his free association name was Diamonds G. Crusader. ("Diamonds" are jewels, like his first name, Jules. G was for Gary, Jules's middle name. And "Crusader"? Well, Alexander the Great was a crusader, and "Alexander" was Jules's last name.) We affectionately called him the "Science Editor." Crisscrossing the United States in countless hours on the road, one of us from the band would see a geological formation and inevitably ask, "What's that?" A former optics guy in the Navy, Jules always knew the answer. He was and still is the Science Editor of the group.

So you begin to get the picture of how we all knew of each other and were floating in, out, and around the same places at the same time. When Terry first introduced me to Jules, I felt as though I'd met my long lost brother.

One night in 1964 at The Ice House, one of the opening acts was late.

"Russ, would you do a few songs?" Bob Stane asked.

Doug Weston had told me at a recent Troubadour hoot that he felt I was ready to go professional, and that meant a great deal to me—it did a lot for my confidence. I turned to Jules. "Jules, wanna do a few songs?" We had never played together before in our lives.

"Sure."

We went into the dressing room and keyed up the guitar and bass. There was always a stand-up bass at the ready in the dressing room for any musical act that needed it—all you had to do was tune it.

Not long after Jules and I played together on the stage for the first time, Doug Dillard was instrumental in helming the formation of The Men, the group I became a part of before we split and some of us went on to form The Association. Steve Martin said of Doug, "Doug Dillard was a banjo icon. He, along with his group, The Dillards, influenced so many players…He was fast, clean and a melodic player with his own style."[31] A few decades after our times together at The Ice House, I would ring Doug up.

"Do you have a tux?" I asked.

"Yes," he said.

"Do you want to play a gig with us?"

And that's how Doug ended up playing with The Association at the Executive Inn on the Ohio River in Owensboro, Kentucky (long before they imploded it in 2009), in the 1980s and later at the Kentucky Derby.

But on that night in 1964 at the Monday Night Troubadour Hootenanny, Terry remembers, "I…was standing in the balcony with Doug Dillard and my future Association partner, Jules Alexander, watching the beginning of that evening's lineup of open mic acts and listening to Doug state his disdain for the Troub's 'hoot' having become a slick, agency-fueled showcase rather than the come-one-come-all fun event for amateurs and pros alike we all enjoyed in the beginning of the folk craze…So that Monday night, after about half the honed and hyped lineup of acts had performed, Dillard turned to Jules and me and said something akin to, 'You know what, guys? [Screw] all this hype. Why don't we put some fun back in this damned thing and fill that stage with some honest-to-God folk music pickin' and singin'?'"[32] The hootenanny was a free for all—if you signed up, that time slot was yours, no matter if your talent was questionable or if it didn't appeal to the masses or if you were too stoned to recall

31   Lewis, Randy. "Doug Dillard dies at 75; banjo player, member of the Dillards band." *Los Angeles Times*. May 18, 2012.

32   Kirkman, Terry. "Part One: How I Found Myself in the First Folk-Rock Group." *Huffington Post*. September 29, 2012.

what it was you had planned on doing or singing. Such was the case
with people like Wild Man Fischer, the stage name for Larry Fischer,
who also frequented the hoots. Years later, in reviewing his debut
album for the *Los Angeles Times*, Pete Johnson wrote:

> A rather unusual album froze me between my loudspeakers
> late one night last week and, though I am not sure if it is
> entertainment and would be just as happy if I never heard it
> again, it left me with the feeling that I had just undergone a
> profound experience.

> Larry Fischer, age twenty-four, makes his recording debut
> with this two-LP set, called "An Evening with Wild Man
> Fischer"...a series of thirty-six performances which may
> disgust and dismay the unwary listener.

> "Wild Man Fischer is a real person who lives in Hollywood,"
> notes the album cover. "He used to be very shy. He didn't
> make any friends. One day he decided to become more
> aggressive. He would write his own songs and sing to
> people and tell them he wasn't shy anymore. When he did
> this, everyone thought he was crazy. His mother had him
> committed to a mental institution twice."

> His voice is ragged, pocked with seemingly uncontrolled
> screams, but strangely melodic. His singing style,
> developed during the past several years while he earned
> his living performing original songs for ten cents apiece
> along the Sunset Strip, is remarkable for it achieves a near
> impossibility: the creation of a rock 'n' roll song without the
> aid of instruments."[33]

Guess there's something to be said for sheer determination and
staying power! But back again to that night at the Troub in 1964.
Doug asked everyone who wanted to perform something to come
on up (he called this the Innertubes; I have no idea why), and so

---

33   Johnson, Pete. "An Evening with Wild Man Fischer." *Los Angeles Times*. May 5, 1969.

everyone got up on the stage: me, Terry, Jules, Brian, Ted. There were something like twenty-plus people crowded onto that stage, including David Crosby of Les Baxter's Balladeers (and later The Byrds and Crosby, Stills & Nash). "So many people wanted to be an Innertube that night it took about a third of our allotted time just to get everybody set up, tuned up (with each other), and settled on which song to sing first," Terry recalls.

Doug Weston decided this was a great idea to form a band and began taking names, but I hung back, skeptical. The group sang more than twenty minutes of folk song standards, though I couldn't tell you exactly what today—we had no idea just how important and historical that night would become. Singing together and improvising with a crowd of musicians for fun was one thing. Turning all of those people into one giant band was another. The whole thing was a good idea that had just grown too large—so I walked.

The Innertubes continued performing weekly at the Troubadour hoots, with members drifting in and out. Doug Weston then asked those of us who wanted to make the Innertubes an official group to show up in his office. Thirteen guys came: Jules, Ted, Brian, and Terry, and also Mike Whalen, Harvey Gerst, Nyles Brown, Steve Cohen, Tony Mafia, Steve Stapenhorst, Howard Wilcox, Sanny Delano, and Bob Page. Everyone sang, and everyone played an instrument— Ted was on drums, and there were electric guitars and a Fender bass player, plus ten more acoustic instruments. It was pretty wild, considering folk music wasn't known for utilizing these instruments, but they did what they wanted and went where the music moved them. (Which is what we later also did in The Association.) Doug decided to call this group The Men. Within The Men were the members of what would soon be known as The Association. Bob Stane said, "The Association (stood out). There was the question as to whether they were folk music or rock. It didn't matter…their first time onstage and they were perfect. They could come in and play just as they did on the audition at The Ice House and the people would be blown away…If you could hear them as they were in 1965, they would blow the room away. They were perfect."[34]

To be honest, I'm getting a little ahead of myself—at my age, I never know how much time I have left, so I want to make sure you get the whole story as it comes to me! The point is, you can't understand The Association without understanding how the group was born out of the origins of The Men and also how the music of the 1960s was so revolutionary, so I sometimes feel like I have to hop ahead in time to tell you what went on to happen so that you can better grasp the many pieces that together make the full picture. Plus, I do like to smoke a little weed, so it's best if I tell you now, since I might be occupied later and can't promise I'll remember *what* it is I wanted to tell you!

As I mentioned earlier, in July 1965, Bob Dylan played at the Newport Folk Festival. It was his third year playing there, but the first time he took his guitar and *plugged it in* to an amplifier in front of an audience. This offended legions of pure folk music lovers who shunned the electronic sound and caused a ripple of commotion over the boundaries delineating folk music and rock and roll. To my knowledge, the first electric guitar Bob Dylan ever played actually belonged to The Men. It was the early 1960s and he was playing at the Music Box, the legendary Los Angeles music venue now known as the Henry Fonda Theatre. After his performance, he came to the Troubadour to watch the Troub's evening's show and asked if he could play one of the electric guitars and jam with the house band.

Anyhow, in 1964, the thirteen members of The Men began performing at various clubs around Los Angeles and received favorable reviews including "Folk-Rock Introduced in Loud, Lively Event" in the *Los Angeles Times*:

---

34 Bob Stane actually says 1964 in his original interview (Roland, Terry, "Bob Stane Remembers the Upper Cellar and the Coffeehouse Era." *San Diego Troubadour*. November 2016). 1964 was the year The Men first formed, but by the time we broke up, became The Association, and had developed the beginnings of our unique sound, it was 1965.

Thirteen is going to be a lucky number for a group called The Men, who opened in a folk music revue at the Music Box Theater Monday night. The thirteen-member chorus and orchestra have come up with a brand-new formula called folk-rock and if the loud cheers of the audience can be taken as an indication, the aggregation is well along the road to success.

All is not folk-rock with The Men, however. They present a goodly portion of undiluted folk music, and their program also includes smatterings of bluegrass, blues and spirituals. These they achieve with agreeable effect, often achieving a striking harmonic blend in the process.[35]

The title of the article, not to mention its content, by the way, is further proof it is The Men who launched folk-rock into the music lexicon. There are historians who will try to tell you that folk-rock was first mentioned in a June 1965 *Billboard* article talking about The Byrds, Sonny and Cher, the Lovin' Spoonful, the Rising Sons, and Jackie DeShannon. But the press I just shared with you was six months before that. Let the record be known!

The members of The Men got a furnished house together in West Hollywood, actress Faye Emerson's old place. Soon, though, thirteen men dwindled to eleven as some band members decided they didn't want to make the commitment, and just as eleven were dwindling to ten, Terry and Jules cornered me.

"Russ, Mike (Whalen) is leaving us to replace Barry McGuire in the New Christy Minstrels," Jules said. "Will you take his place?"

Mike Whalen, who had been part of The Cherry Hill Singers with Ted, had become the lead singer of The Men. Barry McGuire had been part of a singer-songwriter team with Barry Kane called Barry & Barry, and together they had played at The Ice House and the Troubadour. Both Barrys were asked to join the New

---

35   Clar, Mimi. "Folk-Rock Introduced in Loud, Lively Event." *Los Angeles Times.* August 27, 1964.

Christy Minstrels in 1962. Hilario (Larry) Ramos, who would join The Association several years later, was also in the New Christy Minstrels. (They were a large group, as I mentioned earlier, in case you couldn't tell.) The New Christy Minstrels would go on to play a week-long gig at the Troubadour that was so popular it would turn into a three-month gig, and their debut album, *Presenting The New Christy Minstrels*, would win a Grammy and reach No. 19 on the charts, staying there for ninety-two weeks. They enjoyed quite a bit of popularity until the British Invasion's stronghold grew. That's around the time Barry McGuire left the New Christy Minstrels and Mike Whalen replaced him. The Mamas and the Papas would go on to sing backup on several of Barry's solo albums. I always say I came *this close* to being Barry McGuire. (Once again, when it comes to the 1960s Los Angeles music scene, regardless of who was already famous or who was about to become famous, everyone knew everyone else.)

"I don't know," I said to Terry and Jules. "Number one, you guys are big," I said, remarking on the sheer size of the group, "and number two, I haven't heard your music."

"Come on out," Terry said. "We'll do a set for you."

I loved them both, so I agreed.

Doug Weston found himself too busy managing the Troubadour to manage The Men, so The Men teamed up with former actor turned manager, Dean Fredericks. Dean was among the many actors who also frequented the Troubadour. A Purple Heart World War II vet, at six feet three inches tall with olive skin and in his mid-forties, Dean was strikingly handsome, and had already established a respectable Hollywood acting career. He had made a name for himself as the title character in the hit TV series *Steve Canyon*, based on a comic strip by the same name, and playing Kaseem, the Hindu manservant of the lead Johnny Weissmuller character in *Jungle Jim*, as well as having a recurring role on *The Adventures of Rin Tin Tin*. This is long before the days of equal opportunity and equality in Hollywood, and minorities were often portrayed by dark-skinned Caucasians. A few years prior to working with us, Dean had portrayed Captain Frank Chapman in what became a sci-fi movie classic, *The Phantom Planet*. He would later turn down an offer to be Mr. Clean in ads and personal appearances (simply because he didn't want to shave his head!)—apparently his high cheekbones made him look the part. Dean also had a business partner, Joe Koistra. I'm not really sure why these guys were keen on managing us, but they obviously perceived our enterprising talent to have moneymaking potential; they dug us and our music.

But back to that day Terry and Jules asked me to listen to The Men. Dean and I watched them do about five songs. They were excellent. The harmonies were unbelievable. I don't even remember what they sang, but I do remember they were really good. Afterward I did maybe four songs for them, and they asked me to join the group.

In 1964, I left my job as a light and sound technician and hootenanny coordinator for The Ice House and joined The Men, the first band ever to be branded as folk-rock. (You may have heard rumors of other bands holding this title, but as I just proved to you with that *Los Angeles Times* article, they're all wrong!) Not long after, our lives would change forever.

The Men Become The Association
1965–1966

WE WORKED ON OUR sound on the proscenium stage at a rehearsal hall and event space located on the second floor of the Larchmont Music Hall at 230 N. Larchmont Boulevard. It's now a yoga studio.

A few months later, in the middle of a rehearsal where we were working through some new arrangements for the group written by a composer by the name of Ruby Raksin (brother to composer David Raksin), someone called a meeting, and it was immediately clear there was a feeling of discontent in the air, often inventively labeled as "creative differences" and apt to happen in large groups where people wrestle for power and greater input. Quite frankly, the song we were working through was boring and not the kind of music that The Men did. After enjoying continued success performing at the Troubadour, we were looking for a record deal, but hadn't yet found it—some of the guys were selling their cars to pay for their existence. One of the guys, I can't remember who, pulled out his notebook and began firing questions at Terry Kirkman, raking him over the coals with accusations. "You said you were going to call this guy…" and "Why aren't we doing such and such…?"

I was silent, wondering what this guy's beef was—we had a good thing going and we were just getting started—there were no valid complaints to be made. Plus, I was the last to join, so I figured keeping my mouth shut to gauge the situation fairly was the best course of action.

Jules stood and cut him off. "I'm tired of this bullshit. I just want to make music. I'm outta here." And with that, Jules left.

The time for keeping my mouth zipped ended as soon as it had begun. "I don't even know what you guys are talking about. I'm going with Jules," I said, and walked out. My gut was calling the shots.

"Guys," Terry said, "I'm going to leave because I don't want to be held responsible for this at all." Ted, Brian, and Bob Page stood up in solidarity with Terry. "You know, you just lost your band," Terry said on his way out the door, with Ted, Brian, and Bob following. In fewer than two minutes, The Men had fallen apart, and those of us who'd walked away found ourselves standing together outside on the sidewalk.

Jules remembers telling those of us who had defected, "'Let's put together a band and do what we said we're going to do.' Dean had just arrived and asked, 'What's up?' And I told him, 'We have to do this,' and Dean said, 'Do you want a manager?' And I said, 'Yes'!"

Terry lived close by at 721 N. Alfred Street in West Hollywood, so the six of us—Terry Kirkman, Jules Alexander, Ted Bluechel, Brian Cole, Bob Page, and I—piled into our respective cars, picked up a bottle of red wine, and headed to his house to smoke dope and figure out our next steps. Conveniently, we'd left The Men in an ideal vocal combination; there were still two tenors (Bob and Jules), one bass (Brian), and three baritones (Ted, Terry, and I) among us.

"Why don't we just continue on?" Terry suggested. It seemed like a great idea—after all, we'd just trimmed the fat and what remained were the group members who wanted to focus on making music and not get caught up in any unnecessary drama.

There was the dilemma of what we should call ourselves. Someone suggested, "The Aristocrats," after that famous dirty joke involving the description of an obscene family talent act that ends with "The Aristocrats!" as the punch line.

"But what does 'aristocrat' really mean?" Brian asked.

Terry's girlfriend, Judy Hyatt Gelbord, a Troubadour waitress who would soon become his wife, pulled out the dictionary to look up the official definition of aristocrat according to Merriam-Webster, but it didn't ring true. Judy's eyes scanned the page and she came across "association."

"Here's an interesting one. 'A group of people united for a common goal,'" Judy read aloud. Heads nodded in agreement. The Association would be our name.

We began rehearsing the next day as a six-man band. The Men fizzled out after our exodus, so Dean Fredericks and his partner Joe Koistra transferred their full support to The Association. A huge advocate of what we were trying to do, Dean personally bankrolled the endeavor. He put up $25,000 to pay us a modest weekly salary (Jim remembers it was five dollars!) and rent a house on Ardmore Street (now demolished) just south of Melrose, where we lived and rehearsed. Ted, Jules, Bob, Bob's wife, and I lived together in the house while Terry lived with Judy on Alfred Street and Brian lived with his wife and kids in Hollywood (they had since moved down from Oregon). There were only three bedrooms, but Jules built a fourth bedroom in the breakfast nook. Later, even before we had our first record, we would each have our own apartment, which goes to show we were making good money as a band well before we were on the national radar.

A thick coloring book of animals sat on a table in the group house. Everyone who walked through the door sat down to color. (If you haven't yet guessed and the water balloons mentioned in my disclaimer at the beginning didn't paint the picture clearly enough, we had a sense of humor.) Everyone who smoked dope chipped in to buy a pound (far cheaper than buying it by the ounce) and when we split it four or more ways, it wasn't that expensive. But we never bought a kilo. A kilo was out of our budget. A pound, we could do. When we needed to clean the weed, we removed a screen from the living room window, washed it, and then used it as a strainer to clean out the marijuana seeds and stems—let's just say we were inventive and resourceful beyond just our music. All of the pot was good smoking quality, and not nearly as strong as the stuff that's available today. Just before we lived in the house on Ardmore with The Association, about five of us from The Men lived in a house on Wooster Street, where Jules had a room in the garage. Many times, Jules and I would look at each other, nod, and then head to his room in the garage to get high before coming back inside the house.

The neighborhood the Ardmore house was in also had a tortoise that loved to make social calls by yard-hopping from house to house on the street. The couch on Ardmore saw its fair share of houseguests for a night or two or a smoke or two, including Donovan, Ron Long from one of the funniest improv groups there ever was (and the only one to make Bob Stane fall over in his chair, laughing), The Shaggy Gorillas Minus One Buffalo Fish; as well as Stephen Stills of Buffalo Springfield; and later Crosby, Stills & Nash. (Though when Stephen crashed on our couch he was still six months to a year from debuting with Buffalo Springfield.) Jim Yester remembers that somebody must have slipped Donovan something when he came to the house because he sat down at the table and colored in that damn coloring book for hours on end. When my mother remarried and moved to Japan with her fourth husband who was also in the Navy, they stopped by the house with Nancy, Judy, and Tyson to spend the night before they left for the airport. Ted and I drove them to LAX the next day so they could catch their flight to Japan. Judy didn't go with them; she returned to San Diego via the Greyhound bus. My mom would later learn we'd achieved international fame when they watched us perform live on *The Ed Sullivan Show* from the comfort of their living room in Japan.

I remember one time while Jim, Jules, Ted, and I were living in the Ardmore house, someone had a party planned—at whose house I can't remember. At the time, Jim was seeing Jo Ellen Shattuck, whom he'd later marry. She played banjo and guitar in a quartet called The

Femme Folk Modern. One of her bandmates was going with either Joe or Eddie of Joe and Eddie—a duo known for singing mostly folk and gospel. They had a spectacular guitarist named Louie Shelton—he was tall and skinny with hair like Clint Eastwood and man, could he play. Louie played in multiple bands and later produced music. Anyhow, the big thing I remember about this particular party was that Jules—who had a deserved reputation as a major guitarist—was planning on playing with Louie for everyone at the party. We were all stoked and really looking forward to this event.

When Jules and Louie finally sat down to play, they started with Dave Brubeck's "Take Five." They played like they were from the same cradle. We were all thrilled, and so were they. Magnificent guitarists. Magnificent party. Magnificent night!

The Ardmore house had a pay phone in between the kitchen and dining room. The phone number was listed in the phone book as "The Association—Neo-Rock Renaissance Artists Performing in Concert." No joke! This was in the days before people worried about stalkers. Ted's drums, the bass, guitars, and amps were set up permanently in the living room.

We rehearsed five days a week for six months, without exception. If one of the guys in the band was playing on a demo during the day, we'd shift the daily rehearsal to the evening. We were driven and dedicated. Early on, it became apparent that Bob Page wasn't a good fit, so we asked him to move out and replaced him. At the time, Bob had an on-again, off-again live-in girlfriend. We thought they were married. They were often butting heads with parents who wanted nothing more than for him to get a "real job." Bob had actually come to The Innertubes/The Men/and now The Association because he had been part of The Gnu Folk with Brian. We decided to part ways. "A banjo player with an attitude" was the way one of the other band members described Bob. Bob would continue performing for a while before leaving the stage altogether to sell instruments for Eagle Music. In 1971, he opened The Guitar Store, a guitar outlet near San

Diego. The Guitar Store was later renamed Buffalo Brothers Guitars in honor of Bob's mom, who said "raising her boys was like raising a bunch of buffalo."[36]

Jim Yester had grown up in a musical family, singing in parochial school, playing piano, accordion, and guitar, and performing Kingston Trio cover songs with his younger brother, Jerry, who you'll recall was a member of the MFQ and also a founding member of the New Christy Minstrels. "First thing I learned was harmonica while walking to school, self taught!" Jim says.

Jim's music roots ran deep. His dad, Larry Yester, had his own big band when he was just thirteen, and later ran a music school in Alabama with his sister, led an orchestra on the local radio, and was dubbed "The Accordion Man." He became so well known that he put together a volume called "Accordion Pieces" for Amsco Music Publishing's "Everybody's Favorite" series of 1939 music instruction books.[37] He almost had his commercial pilot's license and, according to Jim, was just forty hours short of getting it when he moved the family to California. Larry found work there in several movies as both a musician and a bit player. In 1948, he played accordion in the John Ford Western *Fort Apache*, and was a piano player with a speaking part in the Warner Bros. musical comedy, *April Showers*. After country-western musician Hank Penny opened The Palomino[38] (club) in North Hollywood in 1949, he played there, too. He also had a regular band, Larry Yester and the Melloaires, and they played George Pierce's Cafe on Ventura Boulevard in the San Fernando Valley and had a regular Wednesday night radio show. Larry later opened the Stardust restaurant/bar in Joshua Tree, and after Jim got out of the Army, he played twelve-string guitar and piano there, and occasionally tended bar, washed

---

36   https://www.namm.org/library/oral-history/bob-page

37   Valerie Yaros located this through an online used bookstore in 2017, and we sent it to Jim!

38   The Association played the Palomino in the 1970s, and Larry Yester came to see the band.

dishes, and waited tables. In 1962–63, Jim's brother Jerry Yester and Jerry's wife Judy Henske played there, too.

The Yester men—Jerry, Jim, and their dad, Larry, "The Accordion Man."

Jim was a falconer, which I always thought was funny because he has a hawklike look about him. We gave him the nickname "Birdman." Jim graduated high school, went to work in a pharmaceutical lab, and then, knowing the draft was imminent, joined the Army and was shipped overseas, where he was first assigned to an artillery unit and then a radio unit in Germany where he began performing comedy and folk music with Dennis Turechek and Jim Kirby as The Yesteryears. Many of their tunes were parodies about life in the Army. When the Army discovered his musical talent, Jim was transferred to the Armed Forces Special Services Entertainment Division, which sent him to entertain the troops throughout Germany and France. The Yesteryears came in second in the All Army Entertainment Contest, where the prize was touring Germany and playing with other acts for thirty days.

When Jim was discharged in 1964, he went to live with Jerry in Greenwich Village, New York City. Jerry was singing with the MFQ at the time. Then their father was injured in an automobile accident, so Jim moved back home to Joshua Tree to spend five months helping his mother run the family restaurant while his dad recovered. When his dad was able to return to work, Jim headed to Los Angeles and auditioned at The Ice House and the Troubadour.

While Jim was waiting to audition at The Ice House, he saw an advertisement on the backstage bulletin board for a musician/singer to join a non-folk contemporary group (we had posted the advertisement, but didn't mention who we were by name). He copied down the number and then did four or five songs for his Ice House audition.

"Listen," Bob Stane told Jim following his audition, "I can't use you right now, but the good news is that friends of mine started a new group, and they want you to call them." Bob Stane knew from Terry and Jules that Bob Page wasn't working out and we were shopping for his replacement. Bob Stane slipped Jim a piece of paper with our phone number on it, which just happened to match the one he'd copied down from the bulletin board!

"How high do you sing compared to your brother?" I remember one of us asking Jim at his audition.

"Oh, I have several notes above my brother," said Jim.

"Cool." We could barely contain our excitement.

Jules took Jim aside. "Come back in three days and this guy will be gone and you can move in."

And just like that, Bob was out, and Jim was in. Three days later, Jim moved his stuff into the house and began arranging, writing, and rehearsing music and staging with us. He sang tenor and played rhythm guitar. In the words of Del Ramos, Larry's brother who would work stage crew, run sound, and later perform onstage with us, "There's no one in the whole world you can admire more than Jim Yester. The nicest guy you'd ever imagine." Jim's free association name would be Two Kings Nevermore. (His middle name was Louis and his first name, Jim, was short for James; since James and Louis were both the names of kings, we called him Two Kings. And yesterday, inspired by his last name, Yester, is gone; it is "Nevermore.")

Jim and I were responsible for getting a pet for the group house. We went hiking in the Hollywood Hills one day, just below the Hollywood sign. A rabbit ran across the road and Jim jumped over a bush to catch it. We named him Phydeaux and brought him back to the house, but he only lived a few days before dying under the stove. Poor thing, he wasn't ready for big city life. We buried him in the backyard.

Terry, Jules, Jim, and I smoked a lot of pot—eventually we won Ted over and he smoked, too. Brian was a germaphobe, so he wouldn't share a joint. Terry would give it up once he adopted a child because he didn't want to get in trouble with the authorities and have his kid taken away from him. Terry also never took acid.

My friend Henry from the MFQ probably puts it best: "I always said the reason there was so much great music and peace and love in the sixties was because everybody smoked God's herb. I say God's herb, but it was pot, grass, *marijuana*. It wasn't as strong as it is today, so it gave you a kind of euphoria. It heightened your senses. That's why musicians smoked it a lot. It made you want to play music and listen harder…It's the kind of thing that makes you want to stop and smell the roses. You stop thinking, your mind stops whirling around and thinking of a hundred things, and you concentrate on something artistic. That's what pot does. On the road, if you're spending eight hours driving to a gig, take a couple of tokes and the afternoon is lovely. You have a lovely conversation, you listen to music, it's great."

I don't want to give the illusion that we all sat around on our asses doing drugs, because we didn't. We put in the time and worked hard to form our sound. This was the 1960s and rock and roll was still new. Young people loved it, but not everyone was sure how they felt about it just yet. We'd already determined we wanted a look to distinguish us from the other groups that were wearing mostly hippie attire or street clothes, so that's how we settled on wearing those signature suits you see on our first album cover. Fortunately,

Jim wore the same size suit as Bob. A review of one of the many concerts we did with The Mamas and the Papas in our early years commented, "...the sextet is so versatile, each guy can do a little bit of everything...vocally and instrumentally. These cats dress in Ivy League attire, clearly avoiding the long hair cliché characteristic of today's pop combos."[39] In a later June 17, 1967, article in Michigan's *Battle Creek Enquirer*, "The Association: Harmonic Sounds of Professionals," Joyce Lapekas wrote, "Onstage The Association may seem strange to the world of pop with their gray suits, vests, ties, and relatively short hair. This is part of their appeal as they seem to attract an older, more sophisticated audience than do other groups. Their fans come not to scream, but to listen to the detailed harmonies and meaningful lyrics." (Oh, Joyce, I beg to differ. We certainly had our share of screaming female fans.) But to be sure, audiences took in the music not only with their ears, but also their eyes. It's no accident The Beatles wore suits on their first live US television appearance on *The Ed Sullivan Show* in 1964.

Over July 22–23, 1966, we did two shows at The Fillmore in San Francisco, where we were headlining a bill with Quicksilver Messenger Service, the Grass Roots, and Sopwith Camel. With the genius of Bill Graham, who I'll tell you all about in a little while, the Fillmore had begun hosting rock concerts the year prior. Maybe he got the idea when The Beatles played Shea Stadium on August 15, 1965, for the largest recorded crowd at the time—55,600—and grossed $304,000, which was also unheard of at the time. Anyhow, The Association was, of course, a concert act, but we did occasionally play dance gigs—and the Fillmore was one of them. At the Fillmore, "concerts featured far-out light shows, uninhibited dancing, and whatever turned young people on at the height of counterculture."[40] It was located at the corner of Fillmore Street and Geary Boulevard

---

39   Harada, Wayne. "Everyone Gets Into Mamas-Papas Act." *The Honolulu Advertiser*. November 7, 1966.

40   Bream, Jon. "San Francisco's Fillmore: Where rock history plays on." *Star Tribune*. June 3, 2014.

and with more than a thousand seats, it was cavernous, to say the least—when it opened in 1912, it was called the Majesty Hall and Academy of Dancing and used for masquerade balls and other big events. As we were setting up for the concert, a petite young girl approached me.

"Who do you think you're kidding with those suits?"

"Obviously not *you*, dear," I said.

For the life of me, I honestly don't know what people are expecting to hear when they say things like that. Anyhow, for our concert, they set up folding chairs ten rows deep in front of the big Fillmore stage and people danced behind them. Large screens hung from the ceiling all around the room; colored lights pulsated on one screen, and movies on another. It was truly a multisensory experience. The combinations were infinite and so was the Fillmore! I remember launching into the bridge of "Cherish" while watching King Kong grab a biplane out of the air on one of the screens. This was just one year before the Monterey Pop Festival and at the time, Haight-Ashbury was a beautiful neighborhood of "beatniks...out to make it rich," to borrow from Donovan's "Season of the Witch." It was full of galleries, beautiful shops, and great restaurants. Once *Time Magazine* and the news media jumped on it with both feet in hobnail boots, it became crowded with homeless, drug dealers, runaways, and the people who prey on them.

But back to the endlessly fascinating topic of our suits. Phyllis Burgess, Entertainment Editor for *Teen Magazine*, wrote in the *And Then...Along Comes the Association* album liner notes, "They are one of the few groups who have worked up a program of funny, professionally tight acts for full entertainment of all-age audiences... Are they weird musicians, or just musicians that are weird? They don't wear their hair long...they dress in smartly tailored suits, the only time they take off their shoes is to shower or go to bed. Different, perhaps, weird...no. They are terrifically talented in many different musical and entertainment facets, and the combination of these six very interesting and individual personalities, plus their talented showmanship, gives them that rare appeal."

See? I'm right about those suits. The look was part of the whole experience. If we'd been wearing bell-bottoms and vests, Phyllis probably would have written that we were, most definitely, weird. To be sure, the six-part harmonies and catchy tunes were our ticket, but the three-piece suits we wore to be taken seriously helped. I always say the fact that Jim wore the same size suit as Bob was a sign from God—not that I'm dogmatically religious. The rule was that you only wore the suit when you were performing. The moment you stepped offstage, you took off the suit. No autographs in suits. People always thought we had multiple suits, but for a long time, we had only one suit and seven shirts each. As success came, we expanded the color palette to include black, blue, brown, and tan suits. At one point there was a fire at our dry cleaners and we lost most of our suits to the flames, and from then on we relaxed the dress code to more casual attire. I gave my original gray suit away to Goodwill in the 1980s. There's probably some actor wearing it in a community theater production somewhere right now, without a clue of the history contained within its fabric.

"Russell," I remember one of the guys saying to me, even back when we were still part of The Men, "it's fine if you don't want to wear underwear when you're not performing. But onstage, you've got to wear underwear."

What can I say? I preferred the natural way. I didn't want to snatch up my crotch in some piece of hot fabric. But I heard my band members' beef. I had a large blond Epiphone guitar. When it came time to go onstage, I took the underwear out of the Epiphone hole and put it on underneath my clothes. After the gig, the underwear went right back into the guitar hole. (It was the perfect-sized single underwear compartment!)

Terry, Jules, Ted, Jim and Jerry Yester, along with Brian Wilson, Roger McGuinn, and Lorenzo Music already knew one another from practicing Subud. Subud is a spiritual movement or practice (as opposed to a religion) that began in Indonesia in the 1920s, and was founded by Bapak Muhammad Subud Sumohadiwidjojo. (Fun fact: Listen to The Association's "Songs in the Wind," which Ted wrote and sang on the *Renaissance* album, and you'll hear "Bapak" in some of the background harmonies.)

You know, I should probably clarify something. I'm not exactly the go-to guy to explain anything religious—while I consider myself to be a spiritual person, I would say most of that is a product of being a California man through and through. Subud was about connecting to the world through the great life force within you by using a spiritual exercise known as the *latihan kejiwaan*. Everyone I knew referred to it as simply *latihan*. I know when Terry first went to the Subud building downtown, Cyrus Faryar of the MFQ stood outside waiting for him and said, "I knew someone was coming down that I had to talk to."

Whether it was Subud or having been traumatized by a television program that detailed the treatment of animals and the chemicals the food industry injected into them and their feed (this last one was my experience), all of us, except for Terry, were vegetarians at the time. We never spoke about it, it just happened. It was the 1960s. Immersion in a religion or practice where you could find yourself was all part of the experience—it was still several years before The Beatles would go to India to practice transcendental meditation, but the groundwork for alternative experiences was being laid by musicians and artists everywhere.

Group meetings were held every Thursday at the Ardmore house, where we'd discuss what we were doing and how we were doing it. We never listened to potential material during these meetings or discussed money—we stuck strictly to creative concerns. In each meeting we strove to answer the question: Were we doing everything we could to make the best possible sound to have the greatest chance possible of meeting our goal of having a Top 40 record within two years?

People would ask, "What makes you think you'll make it?"

"Well, we stand as good a chance as anyone," I would say. "We're more talented than most people. We can sing *and* play."

In rehearsals, depending on the song, sometimes we'd learn each of our vocal and music parts individually so we could master them on our own before putting the sound together, while other times we'd jam vocally to arrive at the desired harmonies and sound—the final arrangement of "Along Comes Mary" came about in this manner. There was no lead singer, per se; different guys would take the lead on different songs, though I did lead vocals on many of them.

Our work had to be precise, or we didn't stand a chance of reaching our goal. At night we'd catch the other acts at the Troubadour and Ice House as we worked our way up to performing at the clubs. Anybody who was anybody or on the way to becoming anybody in the music business was at the Troubadour or The Ice House at night to catch all the acts, unless he/she/the band already had a gig elsewhere. When Weston started the club "back in 1957, there was no place for musicians and comedians and people of that sort, who were inclined to congregate, to demonstrate their craft and have a community—so he started the Troubadour."[41] When the house lights came up at the end of the night, you'd recognize all the faces of your fellow rock and roll colleagues.

A couple of months into rehearsals as the Association, Terry brought his buddy, Frank Zappa, over to the Larchmont rehearsal hall to listen to us. Frank was one of the nicest, sweetest guys I ever met in the music business—I guess that's contrary to how his public persona is often perceived, but I have nothing but good things to say. At the time Frank sat in on our rehearsal, he was starting his own band, The Mothers of Invention. Unbeknownst to me, when the rehearsal was over, Frank pulled Jules aside and asked, "Do you and Russ want to join my band?" Jules had the foresight to tell him he thought we, The Association, were onto something too good to

41   Mulchin, Chad Zachary. "WeHo's Biggest Little Club: Troubadour Through the Years." *WeHoVille*. May 15, 2013.

let go of just yet. So there you go—we missed our chance to be in The Mothers of Invention.

TROUBADOURS WE HAVE PRESENTED

Smothers Brothers	Olatunji	Brasil 65
Miriam Makeba	Rooftop Singers	Judy Henske
New Christy Minstrels	Josh White	Nina Simone
Hoyt Axton	Jim Kweskin &	The Association
Sonny & Brownie	the Jug Band	Bro. Dave Gardner
Les McCann Ltd.	Goodtime Singers	Chad Mitchell
Travelers 3	Sabicas	Godfrey Cambridge
Randy Boone	Judy Collins	Muddy Waters
Lenny Bruce	Roger Miller	The Mitchell Trio
Clancy Brothers &	Journeymen	Mort Sahl
Tommy Makem	Glenn Yarbrough	Bo Diddley
Joe & Eddie	Modern Folk Quartet	The Committee
Oscar Brand	Bud & Travis	Ian Whitcomb
Chico Hamilton	Odetta	Flatt & Scruggs
Bob Gibson	The Byrds	Geula Gill Trio
Oscar Brown, Jr.	Rod McKuen	Peter Tork &
The Dillards	Buffy Ste.-Marie	Mike Nesmith of
Jimmie Rodgers	Bill Cosby	The Monkees
Richard Pryor	Nitty Gritty Dirt Band	Pat Paulsen
Tim Buckley		

The Troubadour put out this mailer in the 1960s, which demonstrates the diversity of folk, jazz, blues, rock and roll, and comedy talent it attracted. The Men began here before morphing into The Association.

Terry remembers one of the first places we ever performed at was a florist shop on La Brea Avenue. There was a huge bleacher-like shelf display of big clay flowerpots—the kind that are so large they rest on a floor, as opposed to a regular-sized shelf or windowsill. Dean Fredericks decided we could make a stage out of those shelves. "Get up there in your costumes and pretend it's a nightclub," he said. We did. (You've got to start somewhere. That sound in front of an audience doesn't magically happen without practice in front of lots of strangers, and Dean saw to it that we took advantage of every possible opportunity to have an audience.) We also performed at The Gay 90's Saloon, a sort of French Art Nouveau place that used to be at 157 North La Cienega Boulevard on Restaurant Row in LA. The place was a whistle-stop on the Tanner Grey Line Bus Tour. We'd play a fifteen-minute set for a group of tourists and then they'd leave, we'd take a quick break, and then do the whole thing all over again. That was the first place we ever sang "Cherish" in front of a live audience.

After six months of working on our sound, we started making the circuit in Southern California and slowly but surely built up a successful concert act following. We were the hardest working band there was. We did a hoot at the Troubadour and for the first six months alternated between headlining at the Pasadena and Glendale Ice Houses—one week in Pasadena, one week in Glendale, back and forth. We did an early concert at the Glendale Ice House with a Mexican band made up of the Arambula brothers. They called themselves Los Piccolinos, and the Spanish language paper, *La Opinión*, covered us in a July 8, 1965, photo and caption that mentioned, "The Association, a tremendous melodic ensemble with their wit and musicianship..." Dean Fredericks' wife translated that review for us because she spoke Spanish. We were in our infancy and already foreign-language publications were talking about us!

Terry remembers playing our first Troubadour hoot as The Association: "The audience was starting to come unglued over our sound. You could hear it. There would be a hundred people on the street smoking and people started piling in. We finished the set, adrenaline squirting out of our ears, we're all scared and then we're blown away, you went down the stairs from the stage, about eight feet, then the stairs up to the second-floor dressing room— you don't hang out in the backstage—at the top of the stairs are the MFQ watching us and...Jerry Yester says with tears in his eyes, 'You fucking did it, man.'"

After finishing school in San Diego, Birdie had worked for the Los Angeles public school system as a teacher for six months before leaving California and me to work for the Army Special Services in Germany, where she organized entertainment and special concerts at army bases around Europe. (She had actually met Jim Yester in Europe, and was surprised, when she returned to Los Angeles and

The Association had already formed and was just beginning to get on our feet on the stage in front of an audience, that Jim was part of our group! Talk about that small world thing again.) While she was away I was a free agent, but I didn't date anyone else seriously—I was busy with music. By the time Birdie returned from her year working in Germany, The Association was on its way to making music history. Birdie had secretly come to hear us play at The Ice House in Glendale and was impressed. We got back together, she moved in with me in the group house, and we soon married.

Although America wasn't yet involved in Vietnam, when a man turned eighteen, he had to register with Selective Service (which I'd done, in San Diego), and after he turned nineteen (which would have been 1962 for me), he was eligible to be drafted and had to have a physical at the draft board. My physical was in Downtown LA, as I was already living in Pasadena by that time. A bunch of people, including Bob Stane and my pal Carl Heckman, who managed the Glendale Ice House, advised me what to do at the draft board to increase my chances of *not* passing the physical. I was told by someone who knew (I can't remember who the guy was) that you filled out the forms in *pencil* and he told me to first answer "no" to the question "Have you ever had a homosexual experience?" erase it and check the "yes" box instead, then erase *that* and check "no" again. I did that, but I don't think they cared one way or another (they'd probably seen it before). I don't think they even noticed I was wearing contact lenses that corrected my nearsightedness. But one of the examiners did discover I had a perforated eardrum (I know it was from diving in the ocean and the San Diego Bay). The perforated eardrum meant I would not be classified 1-A—"Available for military service"—but instead 1-Y—"Registrant qualified for military service only in times of war or national emergency." The officer who gave me this news was quite sincere and sorry to disappoint me by not classifying me 1-A. I walked calmly outside and when I reached the sidewalk, I jumped in the air.

Flash-forward from that physical to 1965, and men were getting drafted into military service left and right. I was a peace creep. I was, however, still four years shy of hitting age twenty-six, when I would automatically become ineligible for the draft. An executive order stated that men who married *after* August 26, 1965, would be treated on the same level as single men in the draft, but men who had married *on or before* that date would remain one step lower than single men in draft eligibility. So one step lower on the draft eligibility scale as a 1-Y registrant improved my odds of remaining a peace creep that much more.

Birdie and I would be married by a minister at his home in between sets at The Ice House on August 26, 1965. I guess you could say we got in under the wire! Mason Williams was our witness. He held a light over the minister's shoulder so he could read the vows we had to repeat aloud.

Bob Stane loved to say, "Marry in haste, repent in leisure." Mason Williams and The Irish Rovers were the two acts on the bill at The Ice House the night of our impromptu ceremony. The Irish Rovers were an all-male Canadian folk group made up of Irish men. They had a big hit with "The Unicorn," a Shel Silverstein song that explains unicorns are not a myth, they're just creatures who didn't make the boat in time to be saved from Noah's flood. The Irish Rovers wouldn't release that song until 1968, but at that time they were already performing it live. In fact, they're still together, performing it live today, so their musical marriage, per se, lasted far longer than mine to Birdie. But more about her and the other loves in my life, including our wonderful daughter, Jill, later.

In an early review of our performances, the December 6, 1965, *Los Angeles Times* "Association Warmly Received at Ice House," said, "They are excellent musicians with good voices and the kind of verve and youthful warmth that make their wholehearted patter qualify as first-rate showmanship. They have a wholesomeness, a coolness and intensity about them that suggests the possibility the group may be able to span both the youth and adult audiences, getting a different kind of acceptance from each…it's all whoppingly entertaining… Their strongest capacity is top-flight musicality, the kind that is likely to make them an enduring presence." One of my favorite quotes about The Association is from a later April 2, 1970, article in *The Daily Utah Chronicle*: "Their music is without a label or class of love as a way of life, not merely a replacement of war." YES! Someone who got that we couldn't be placed into a labeled box.

To give you an idea of what else was happening when we received that early review, it was just days earlier, on December 3, 1965, that The Beatles released "Norwegian Wood," which was the first pop song to use the sitar. Six months prior to that, they'd released "Yesterday." Then, 1965 stretching into 1966 saw The Beatles have six No. 1 hits in a row, something that wouldn't be duplicated, as I mentioned earlier, until the Bee Gees came along over a decade later. "The desolate 'Yesterday' resonated with millions who felt a stable past was crumbling in the face of social upheaval. Parents began to see rockers as Pied Pipers leading their children to long hair and drug-soaked promiscuity…The pensive 'We Can Work It Out' bemoaned the fussing and fighting that dominated the rest of the decade."[42] In 1965 alone, the charts were topped with hits not only from The Beatles, but also the Rolling Stones, Herman's Hermits, The Supremes, and The Beach Boys. "Between 1965 and 1969, 85 percent of the Top 40 *Billboard* hits were written in a major key"[43] and the average song length was under three minutes.[44]

In the beginning, we packed all of our equipment into Ted's 1959 Chevy Impala (black, with red interior), and Terry's Ford Falcon. We then graduated to one boat-sized white Chrysler station wagon (that

42   Jackson, Andrew Grant. *The Most Revolutionary Year in Music 1965*. New York: Thomas Dunne Books, 2015.

43   Lametti, Daniel. "Pop Music is Getting Sadder—And More Ambiguous." *Slate*. June 13, 2012.

44   Knemeyer, George. "45's Taking Their Time (Longer): Poll." *Billboard*. August 1, 1970.

had the best car radio you've ever heard) and blue Dodge van with all of our equipment, amps, and guitars, and wardrobe of six suits with seven sets of shirts. We actually got the Chrysler before we cut our first record, which also goes to show we were already making a living with our music before we hit the big time.

While we gave concerts during the day and hit the club circuit at night, we learned pretty quickly that you couldn't trust the sound system at an unknown venue—the speakers and microphones were often of lesser quality, malfunctioning or altogether broken. So we invested in our own equipment—I think Shure cut us a great deal, and eventually, Shure featured us in their advertisements. In the summer of 1966, the Beach Boys ended up borrowing our sound equipment at a Las Vegas concert when we played with them on a joint ticket with the Sir Douglas Quintet. The sound system was a piece of crap. The Beach Boys were already an established act with hit songs, but the gentlemanly thing to do was to be generous and share our equipment.

In 1965, as the crowds increased and we headlined nearly every night at either the Glendale or Pasadena Ice House, we were also doing other gigs, like playing Tina Sinatra's graduation party with Canned Heat of "On the Road Again" fame, and playing clubs as far north as Santa Barbara and as far south as Orange County. (And no, we didn't get to meet Frank. He was probably on the road, working.) We traveled with our manager, Dean, and our sound and light guys, Steve Nelson and Pete Stefanos. Steve was tall, blond, and handsome. He was nearly an Olympic swimmer before his love of music and life on the road with us took over. Pete, on the other hand, was the heir to a large candy manufacturer, and we always threw him a couple of bucks to help us unload our equipment. He stuck around, helping out and touring with us for several years as our light man and later road manager before then becoming road manager for Three Dog Night until the lure of his family business took him away. So we were a six-man band with one road manager and a two-man crew.

An August 20, 1966, article in *The Ottawa Journal*, "The Association: Electric Switch Paid Off," read, "Six folk singers got together in February 1965, worked and waited for a year, change to electric instruments and then—'Along Comes Mary'...The Association started as folk singers but, like so many other folk groups recently, 'we saw that folk was dying so we tried it with electricity, although we aren't necessarily a rock and roll group.'" As soon as we turned on the electric amps and the red lights came on, a murmur would pass through the crowd. The audience was afraid our sound would be too loud.

"Why don't we just duct tape those lights?" I suggested. We did, and the nervous crowd buzz never happened again.

We'd go on to be the first electric group to break through the anti-rock music biases in major venues across the country, including Hollywood's Greek Theatre, the Cocoanut Grove, the Copacabana, Tanglewood Music Festival, Blossom Music Festival, the Latin Casino, Saratoga Performing Arts Center, and Ravinia Park in Chicago, to name a few. In Chicago alone, we broke attendance records on August 2, 1967, when 17,432 people jammed into Ravinia Park to hear us—destroying an attendance record (by 3,000 people) previously held by the Kingston Trio in 1958, and in August 1968 we did four back-to-back SRO concerts at the Chicago Opera House.[45] These kind of numbers were highly unusual in the era of pre-stadium concert rock and roll. This might not mean much now, but believe me, it was huge then. All of these venues had *never* had a rock and roll band perform in them. A 1987 article read, "In its early days, the Association frequently encountered resistance as the first electric act to play such established venues as Hollywood's Greek Theatre, the Cocoanut Grove and the Copacabana."[46]

Sometimes we'd smoke weed before we went onstage (though more often when we were home or not performing), but we never smoked at the club—we always went someplace else to do it: an alley,

45   "'The Association' At Mac April 27." *The Jacksonville Daily Journal*. April 18, 1972.

46   Kansas City Star. "Association music triggers cherished memories." *The Pantagraph*. June 22, 1987.

a car, somewhere out of the mainstream line of vision. Again, we didn't all do it all the time. But I'd be lying if I said I didn't! Everyone in the group experimented with peyote and psilocybin (mushrooms) and everyone, except Terry, as I said earlier, also experimented with LSD. (Terry would develop a drinking problem and an affinity for cocaine before giving it all up thirty years ago and becoming a substance abuse counselor.) I actually stopped taking LSD because some of the things I saw on it were so clear and so real, I thought to myself—what good is it to go through this experience if I can't manifest these things in my real life? I wanted to manifest what I'd seen on acid in my life, without the help of drugs. But weed, well, I've always been faithful in my devotion to weed. I never talked about it, though. Early on, when I could sense a journalist was about to pop the pot question, I'd leave the room quietly. We were well-dressed and our image was clean-cut, but that didn't mean we didn't know how to have a good time.

Danny Hutton has a great story he loves to share. When a band or musician is doing well, on a national or international level of fame, the business manager of that band or musician will often make investments with the income that is coming in to grow the money for the band. As Danny Hutton tells it, "People would say… The Association seems so clean-cut. I said, 'Are you nuts? Those guys party harder than anybody I know. They have a *pharmacy* somewhere in Vegas.' That was legendary with people I knew. I don't know how true that was." We definitely did not invest in a pharmacy in Vegas, or anywhere for that matter, but that rumor cracks me up to this day. And we did know how to party—that part is true.

When I read the interviews we did at that time, I can't help but laugh. *KRLA Beat* wrote in their December 15, 1965, issue in an article "Meet The Association Agents of G.R.O.O.V.E.," "If you were able to pin these master performers—all of them licensed to entertain and delight—down for more than five minutes at a time, you might be able to tack a label of sorts upon them. But beware—

they harbor a distinct aversion to tags deep within their souls and about the closest you will come to a definition of their activities is the following statement from Agent 00Terry: 'We have a jazz, folk-rock, Dixieland, several other sound-combination, making-a-unilateral-hexagrallagram type of music singing groovy songs.'" And then the journalist comments, "Nope—I don't understand it either, but it sounded very impressive!"

My friend Guy Pohlman, whose father Ray Pohlman did some arrangements for us, produced our live album, and was part of the Wrecking Crew, the legendary group of musicians who played the instruments on many famous recordings from that decade, perhaps explains it best: "When Kennedy was assassinated and the Vietnam War started, everything started to change. This is a very generational stage. It grows into them finding their own identity. All of the Baby Boomer kids at the time—a lot of the kids could see through the Kennedy assassination and when The Beatles came, there was a sigh of relief that something was out there for them...The Association is the grand apex of this story in that kids could differentiate between the music they wanted and the music their parents had wanted. Those who had hip parents could understand the music and those who didn't have hip parents took longer to get into the rock thing. Six-part singing is not easy. Any vocal group is not easy to put together and the sheer will of these guys to stay together and do it and to practice and not even have a record out and not fall apart... most groups fall apart fighting. There are a multitude of issues that come into a band that can make it fall apart." I met Guy at a dinner at his house in the 1960s when he was just eight years old—he was a child prodigy on the piano, so music ran in the family, that's for sure. Guy is still just as incredible on the piano. These days I see him several times a week, and we talk about everything from politics and women to music and food.

It would seem we sometimes had difficulty winning over those less hip adults. When we played Humboldt State in 1967, the reviewer wrote:

For the Association plays only to the young. No one over twenty-five could have stood the excitement—or the din.

The six, who average twenty-three years of age, shouted poignant lyrics at a half-inch range from the microphone and used nine amplifiers to back up their "show rock" sound. Even their quieter numbers called for a liberal use of drums, a constant jangling of tambourines and an enthusiastic stomping of suede boots...

After a first half which was mainly a warmup and bad jokes ("I tune by smell and I've got a cold," said one), The Association came back wilder than expected with "Poison Ivy," "Changes," and their hit song, "Cherish."...

If the dearth of adults in the audience proved their distaste for what he and his buddies call music, Kirkman was equally upset about the older generation.

"Adults seem to put you in strange categories," he panted, still trying to catch his breath after the exhausting performance. "They don't understand. They seem to think we're some kind of beatnik communists."[47]

It sounds like that journalist was having a tough time adjusting to our "liberal use of drums...constant jangling of tambourines and... enthusiastic stomping of suede boots." Linda Eastman, a rock and roll photographer who would later marry Paul McCartney, wrote about The Association in her book, *Linda McCartney's Sixties*: "Unlike most other California bands, The Association were very straight, very clean. They weren't exactly like The Beach Boys, but they had the same pure harmonies..." As I shared with the Elmira, New York, *Star-Gazette*, "It seems like we were just a tribe of nomads traveling around, but we have one common bond—our love of music."[48]

---

47   Connelly, Mary Jo. "Music for the Very Young: Lots of Noise at HSC Gymnasium." *Eureka Humboldt Standard.* January 18, 1967.

48   Ryan, Pat. "The Association's Bond—Love." *Star-Gazette.* July 20, 1967.

Ted remembers that when our first single, "Along Comes Mary," was released and was such a big hit, people would say, "Who are you guys? What do you guys call your music?" People feel more comfortable if they have a label they can put on you to describe you, but that can be a curse because then they only want you to produce that one type of thing over and over again. Vernon Scott of *The Raleigh Register* wrote about us in his October 12, 1966, "Hollywood Column": "Their hair is clipped already shorter than The Beatles. They are prone to wear jazzy clothes. But en masse, at least, they are less bumptious than their peers…Their sound is not folk-rock, but a combination of pop music, jazz, classics, some rock 'n' roll. But they can't be categorized. Actually, it's a very pleasant sound with entertaining shenanigans." I appreciate that the journalist felt we couldn't be categorized. I would just tell people, "We're The Association. File us under The Association."

Pete Johnson of the *Los Angeles Times* wrote in his January 28, 1966, article, "The Association Spreads Its Talents Into Folk-Rock Field," "Their act is composed of musical numbers ranging from jazz to classically oriented ballads, with a middle spectrum of hard rock and the much abused school of folk-rock songs." Dale Olson of *Variety* said, "Association has limitless potential in a strong format that has been so deftly designed, so carefully written, and so handsomely organized it seems a sure hit. To describe them one must consider the elements of folk, rock, jazz, and straight musicianship in a complementary design to put a new edge on modern musical presentation."

In a January 28, 1967, profile of me ("Russ & His Scene") in *KRLA Beat*, Rochelle Reed wrote, "He listens to very little pop music." Reed then prints my actual words to her, "The majority of pop music is worthless, and you can quote me on that, rather, say I find no merit in most of it. There's an awful lot of good to make up for the larger percentage of bad, however." That's me, never shy about piping up with my opinion. I still feel this way today. I subscribe to the sixties expression, "Fuck art, let's dance."

When you're thrust into the spotlight in your early twenties, you learn there's an art to doing these interviews, which we sometimes mastered better than others. Reed concluded, "It takes a racehorse constitution to keep up with Russ. It is especially difficult to take several sentences from the many he pours out and call it an interview. For Russ pours out words as fast as Jim sings 'Along Comes Mary,' which, if you've listened to the song, is very fast indeed."

In the early days of The Association, there was a new, popular cartoon on television called *Jonny Quest*. It was about a boy who accompanies his father on exciting adventures—just the sort of thing I would have loved to have done as a child myself, had I ever had an opportunity to get to know my father. At any rate, Hanna-Barbera saw one of our shows at The Ice House and asked if I would meet with them—they had cut a few records at the time, and two of them were hits from Danny Hutton, "Funny How Love Can Be" and "Roses and Rainbows," before he formed Three Dog Night—so I assumed Hanna-Barbera was interested in cutting a record deal with The Association, which was an exciting prospect, being that we were still a young group. I took a meeting in the Hanna-Barbera offices with Dean and Jules, where they asked me to make records as Jonny Quest and to play him in live public appearances for something like $600-plus a week—seems they thought I was perfect for the part with my blond hair.

"Can I still be in the band and do this?" I asked.

"No," they told me. "It will take up too much time."

"Well, I can't do it then," I said. "I've put too much time and effort into this."

So there you go! Jonny Quest wanted to break up The Association! The money was good for that time, but the offer didn't even compare to what I believed we were capable of doing with The Association.

Dean Fredericks helped set up a singles recording deal with Jubilee Records, where we released a cover of Joan Baez's "Babe, I'm Gonna Leave You" on which I did the lead vocals. Our version was more blues-like than Joan's original. It didn't go anywhere. The B-side,

"Baby, Can't You Hear Me Call Your Name," with vocal arrangements by Terry and Jules, also didn't go anywhere. Then one day, Barry DeVorzon, singer, songwriter, producer, composer, and founder of Valiant Records (and later the creator of MasterWriter, software for composing music), held open auditions at the Troubadour, where the prize was a record contract. According to Barry, by the end of the day at around 4:30 p.m., he was depressed by the lack of talent and ready to pack up and go home—that is, until we showed up in our suits and with our harmonies. We sang Bob Dylan's "One Too Many Mornings" and two other songs. Then they stopped us and Barry said, "I don't know what you guys got, but you sound so good." Barry would produce our cover of "One Too Many Mornings." The B-side had an original tune by Jules called "Forty Times."

Back then, you had the record companies and then there were the radio stations, and that was the order in which things were done. AM radio had started to go Top 40, but the stations that were still playing jazz and a mixed bag of standards from the 1950s couldn't go Top 40 because they were eclectic, so they started mixing things up by doing playlists of four or five song sets. The Association music didn't fit really fit in. "Much to the chagrin of a business that issued 11,000 records a year—7,700 singles and the balance LPs that Top 40 stations would not touch—AM played only from a list of thirty hit singles each week, with a few 'specials' thrown in."[49] It wasn't until 1967, when San Francisco DJ Tom Donohue wrote "AM Radio is Dead and Its Rotting Corpse is Stinking up the Airwaves" for *Rolling Stone*, that he ushered in the era of playing noncommercial music by album-oriented bands.

Valiant Records had had some success with hits like the Cascades' "Rhythm of the Rain," Shelby Flint's "Cast Your Fate to the Wind," and Barry's own group, Barry and the Tamerlanes, with "I Wonder What She's Doing Tonight." Though we were thrilled to make a recording with them, "One Too Many Mornings" was released on Valiant's

---

49   Sanjek, Russell. *American Popular Music and Its Business: The First Four Hundred Years: Volume III From 1900 to 1984*. Oxford University Press, 1988.

label to little fanfare—we sold about 10,000 records, but that wasn't exactly impressive. At the time, music historian Russell Sanjek wrote, "A single 45 had to sell 11,200 copies to break even, and if it did not, the manufacturer took a loss. This happened…to 74 percent of all 45s put on sale in 1968–69 and 61 percent of all popular LPs, which had to sell a minimum of 7,800 copies to recoup their initial cost." He's referencing 1968 and on, but this statistic was applicable to us—we weren't yet laughing, as they say, all the way to the bank. We also logged our first television appearance that December of 1965 on *Hollywood A Go-Go*, where we sang both numbers in a lineup that included Lesley Gore, Simon & Garfunkel, Bobby Freeman, Donna Loren, and The Sunrays, but it wasn't even a blip on the radar. Ten thousand copies weren't enough to make newspaper headlines, but it was enough to prove there was more music and money to be made under the right circumstances. It also helped convince our fan, record producer Curt Boettcher, to work with us to cut our first album. It probably helped that Ted had put in quality time with Curt dropping acid and going for leisurely hikes around Hollywood high as a kite—Ted gently pushed Curt toward the group, but Curt had a mind of his own and wouldn't have worked with us if he didn't want to. Curt had his own band, The Goldebriars, a quartet comprised of two women and two men. Curt was a weed and white wine kind of guy who also practiced Subud, and together, he and Steve Clark, more of a whiskey and whites guy, produced our first album. One of my songs, "I'll Be Your Man," made it onto the first album.

> *Where were you when I needed you so*
> *Where were you when I called your name*
> *Where are you now when I need you again*
> *I guess that things just stay the same*
>
> *Where's the feelin' you told me you had*
> *The feelin' you said would never change*
> *I was a game just like all the rest*
> *I guess that things just stay the same*

But if we ever meet again
And if-a you need a true lovin' friend
Just look my way and give me a smile
And you can stay with me awhile

If I could start all over again
You know I'd start again with you
So says my heart but my mind can see
That what we had is through

But if we ever meet again (meet again)
And if you need a true lovin' friend (true lovin' friend)
Just look my way and give me a smile (give me a smile)
And you can stay with me awhile

As long as you can
long as you can
long as you can
long as you can

I'll be your man

It's been so long, I don't even remember what inspired me to write that song, but I remember writing it while living at the group house.

We knew we wanted to do Tandyn Almer's "Along Comes Mary," after Jules played bass on the original demo, which Curt actually sang on. In the demo, Curt sped up the tempo of Tandyn's song. There was debate about a cowriting credit—Curt felt his contribution to the demo that led to us recording the song warranted a credit for him—but ultimately this was dismissed and all of the credit went to Tandyn. Anyhow, Jules played bass on that demo and then brought it back to the band house to play it for us on an acetate. An acetate record was good for maybe twelve plays before it would wear out.

As soon as we heard it, we knew we wanted to do the song. Our group had a democratic process where everyone got to vote on whether or not we wanted to work on a song. If there was a tie, we didn't do the song, but with "Along Comes Mary," an official vote wasn't even necessary, we were all so clearly excited by it. In a 1967 article in Santa Rosa's *The Press Democrat*, "Swinging Set: American Sound," journalist Sylvie Reice wrote, "They want the audience—the fans—to get to know each member of the group," and she then quotes Terry Kirkman, "Instead of submerging each separate personality, our group brings out and points up each personality. The individual and his rights are very important to our group." Terry was right. Everyone had an equal vote in the group. We didn't even have the sheet music to "Along Comes Mary"—we just started working on it immediately, making up the lyrics we didn't know, figuring out the chords and adding vocal harmonies.

Speaking of making up lyrics, Jim sang the lead vocals on the song. There was a time when, a day before we were to leave for a tour a couple of years later, Jim had a motorcycle accident and couldn't make the tour—mild panic ensued when we decided Jules would take over Jim's lead vocals on "Along Comes Mary"—and he realized he didn't know the words. He wasn't alone. As it turns out, none of us knew them! It's a fast-paced song with snappy lyrics and we'd all concentrated on our individual parts and left the lead vocal lifting to Jim. Jules called Jim at the hospital to get all the lyrics down and learned them in time for the tour.

By this time we were also growing our fan base in a major way. Our loyal fans followed us from live appearance to live appearance and called themselves The Association Admiration Aggregation (AAA). Eventually, they were twenty thousand strong—long before we got a record deal or had even "made it." The AAA sent out long, detailed newsletters (you might say they were thinly veiled love letters or odes) that began with grandiose statements such as, "The complete story of The Association, individually and as a group, could make *Gone with the Wind* look like a featurette between the cartoons" and "A fan, while interviewing Russ Giguere after a show, asked him how the group was formed. His reply, 'Through osmosis,' is incorrect. We all know they answered a newspaper ad that said:

'Wanted: Six young men, all good looking, who all wear grey suits with burlap vests, and who all play guitars.'" Any material circulated about us was inevitably wacky, but it certainly wasn't limited to the fan club literature. One of my most favorite excerpts is this multiple-choice selection about Brian that was part of a publicity packet:

BRIAN COLE IS: (Check one of the following)
1. A swell kid with a wonderful personality
2. A plethora of unreality
3. A reincarnation of William Jennings Brian (sic), Elmer Gantry, Mickey Mouse (or all three)
4. Irrelevant, immaterial, and has no bearing on the case in question
5. Does not apply
6. An intellectual poltergeist

We loved engaging our fans. In an August 1967 letter I responded to fan mail from a woman by the name of Sandra:

Dear Sandra,

Thank you, I'm glad you enjoy our music.

I was born in Portsmouth, NH[50]—raised in San Diego, Calif. And I have lived in the LA area for five years. I am twenty-three, a Libra.

Be Aware,[51]
Russ Giguere

I also kept in touch with fans via the rags:

Dear BEAT, up, down, back and dead:

Well, we are now in an airplane unable to land because of fog, so we can't play Davenport with the Spoonful tonight.

---

50   Not true. I was born, as I mentioned, across the state line in a tiny hospital in Kittery, Maine, but I was raised in Portsmouth, New Hampshire, before I moved to San Diego.

51   This sign-off from my twenty-four-year old self cracks me up. I'm thinking about adopting it in my letters again. We should all be aware, shouldn't we?

Instead we will have to fly to Minneapolis and land there. Oh well, we need an extra night of rest anyway!

The tour is going really well, the people we run into are almost always warm and friendly and the crowds have been good. This tour is going a little smoother than the others but is still exhausting.

We worked with the New Vaudeville Band in Madison, Wisconsin. They were really good. They are really neat to watch, a really fine group of really fine reallies. I hope we have the opportunity to work with them again.

Chicago was really neat too. They have a lot of groovy shops and clubs and their auditorium (McCormick Place) is a beautiful place to perform, fine acoustics, professional lighting and just generally groovy.

I still miss Los Angeles and the rest of California and, of course, love to everyone.

Soon,

Love,

Russ[52]

We knew the fans were who kept us in business. Chrystal Starr Russell (now Klabunde) made a coloring book for us and even had her work featured as an album cover on *The Best of the Lovin' Spoonful*. Though she never officially joined the AAA, she and her girlfriends made friends with the band. "We would do stuff like go to a concert and show up early and tailgate a dinner for them," Chrystal recalls. "We made BLTs and had them in the back of the station wagon. And because Jules was a vegetarian, we made him a veggie burger. We were vegetarians, too. There was a time they were playing in Palm Springs and we surprised one of our best friends by taking the whole group out there to see the concert on her birthday. Russ

---

52   "The Association Report From Their US Tour." *KRLA Beat*. Undated article from author's collection.

asked me to have dinner with him...I don't know whether he was hoping for something romantic, but it was nice...I think I was quite into Brian. My sister was in love with Jules, and our friend Pattie was in love with Terry and I forget who else in our group...We had a fourth girl who was hanging with that particular group...I think she was into Jim or maybe Ted. My sister and friend had already claimed [the] other ones...You can't have a crush on the same one!"

Marilyn Doerfler, who was at one point in time our publicist once Larry was part of our group, said, "They are their own public relations department, filling empty wave lengths with endless memories of happy moments. The intelligence that they display is sugarcoated with humorous finesse. Fun and frolic are their passwords."[53] Take this response I had for a little questionnaire that was later published in a piece about the band called "By The Nutty ASSOCIATION":[54]

RUSS GIGUERE

1. Q: Biggest Break in Career.
   A: 3 feet.
2. Q: Biggest Disappointment to date.
   A: A dinosaur.
3. Q: If you were stranded on a desert island and could have one book, one magazine subscription and one natural resource, what would they be?
   A: Dear.
4. Q: After the Association, I will become...
   A: Therefore I am.

What a gem! And here's Brian's:

BRIAN COLE

5. Q: Favorite Clothes?
   A: Mine.

---

53 Knapp, Jan. "Seven talented musicians." *Battle Creek Enquirer*. July 19, 1969.

54 "From the Nutty Association." Source unknown. From the author's personal collection.

6.   Q: Most Thrilling Experience.

A: Discovery of females at age 42.

7.   Q: If a fictional character of your choice was to move in next door to you, who would it be?

A: The great comic character John Lennon, who disguised as a mild-mannered hippie can jump into a closet and turn into himself.

1.   Q: What is a hippie?

A: They don't know…yet.

In those days, whether you were a jazz band, novelty band, country band, or classical artist, the break even for a record company was north of twenty thousand records. "Records were becoming an increasingly expensive gamble, with major-label promotion costs averaging about $25,000 per song."[55] We had those twenty thousand numbers in fans, but not record sales; we hadn't yet broken out on the national stage in the way we needed to. A record deal was the key to helping us get to the next level.

The music for "Along Comes Mary" was recorded at the home studio of Gary S. Paxton, a songwriter and recording artist who was also a record producer, label owner, and audio engineer. Enigmatic, strange, and brilliant, Gary was a workaholic who couldn't sit still. He was known for recording and producing the Bobby "Boris" Pickett hit "Monster Mash" as well as the Hollywood Argyles' "Alley Oop" and would later earn a Grammy nomination for his engineering work on "Along Comes Mary." In 1963, a couple of years before we were introduced to Gary, a local radio station had dismissed one of his records, Renfro and Jackson's "Elephant Game Part I," as "too black." In response, Gary organized a protest parade on Hollywood Boulevard with fifteen cheerleaders and an elephant pulling a VW convertible. He was arrested when the elephant got scared and defecated in the street. Gary would move to Nashville, convert to

---

55   A Voice. "History of the Record Industry, 1920–1950, Part Two: Independent Labels, Radio and the Battle of the Speeds." *Medium*. June 8, 2014.

Christianity, and eventually focus his work on gospel and country music, as well as be romantically linked for a brief period of time to Tammy Faye Bakker, the wife of televangelist Jim Bakker.

Anyhow, we recorded the music for "Along Comes Mary" on two four-track machines (that worked together to form the first eight-track) in a garage at Gary's home while he was in a bus parked outside that served as the makeshift engineer booth. No one had really done this before, and we were trying to capture all the sounds we needed to capture—the harmonies and the instruments. The tapes, believe it or not, would be synced together by ear. Later, Gary would move the booth to his upstairs bedroom and the recording area to the downstairs living room. This was a time when the rhythm track was recorded live, and then vocals and sometimes additional instruments were added.

We didn't play the instruments on the recordings in the first album—we used a house band. The house band was unofficially called "The Troops"—basically a group of fantastic studio musicians who would lay down hundreds of tracks for all the popular groups of the day (not unlike the Wrecking Crew). Vocal tracks are always recorded separately from the music tracks, and in those days, it was common to hire other California studio musicians to lay down the music tracks, and then we would just do the vocals. We got some flak for this, but all the groups did it. The Mamas and the Papas, The Carpenters, The Beach Boys, John Denver—the list is far too long to print. One of the original things the "Along Comes Mary" single does is the lead lick, that distinctive repeated pattern of notes you hear at the beginning of the song—those are actually a guitar, harpsichord, saxophone, and bass compressed together to sound like one instrument. Vocally, the album makes use of echo to give the sound a live concert hall feel, as well as overdubbing, wherein for each song we would sing along to a previously recorded version we had sung and then the two are played together at the same time, so the sound of the harmonies is fatter. Overdubbing was innovated by Les Paul in the 1930s and made popular by Les Paul and Mary Ford.

Terry played the recorder solo on "Along Comes Mary" and Jules was on guitar for several tunes on the album. We did all the vocals, hand claps, and cowbells, and everyone else was part of the Troops. Mike Deasy played lead guitar on most of the tunes, and he would later write "Wantin' Ain't Gettin'" on *Insight Out*, our third album, and be part of The Wrecking Crew. Jerry Scheff played bass, and he would later become Elvis Presley's bass player. Mike Henderson and Butch Parker, who had both gone to school with Ted, played saxophone (just Mike) and keyboards (Mike and Butch). Jim Troxel played drums, and Ben Benay played rhythm guitar. Ben would also go on to be part of the band Delaney & Bonnie as well as play harmonica on my solo album years later. (Spoiler! Yes, I did a solo album. I'll get to that later.)

Sound for a recording versus sound in a live performance was a different animal, and these guys knew how to do it. Besides, we could back up the sound with a live performance that delivered; nothing at all like the studio-enhanced sound of so many artists today. We laid down only a few of the vocal tracks at Columbia Records—I think we had enough money for maybe one four-hour session where we cut the vocals to "Along Comes Mary," "Cherish," "Enter the Young," and one other, so the bulk of the record was cut at Gary's house. We were green, so we spent a lot of time working out vocal stuff in the studio that ate up time and money; stuff we probably should have figured out before we were recording in front of the microphones, but we didn't compromise on sound, and we got it done.

And Then...Along Comes The Association was released in July 1966 and peaked at No. 5 in *Billboard* on November 19, 1966. The LPs ahead of us were *The Monkees* (No. 1), the *Dr. Zhivago* soundtrack (No. 2), *The Supremes a Go Go* (No. 3), and *The Mamas and the Papas* (No. 4). The Beatles were two steps behind at No. 7

with *Revolver*, and *The Sound of Music* soundtrack was No. 10 that week. So we were in good company.

Soon after we'd finished that first album, but before it was released, we had another gig at The Ice House. We had been working our butts off and decided that after we finished performing, we'd take some rare time off to celebrate. We got in our cars and drove to meet Curt Boettcher and Rodney Dillard's girlfriend at her house in Santa Monica to drive to Lake Cachuma near Santa Barbara. It was nearing dawn and whaddya know—KRLA Radio started playing "Along Comes Mary." We'd never heard it on the air before. We went wild, whooping, hollering, and jumping up and down on the street in this little residential section of Santa Monica. We had just heard our music played on a major radio station! We had made the playlist.

On July 16, 1966, *The Cincinnati Enquirer* published Lynn Magnan's letter to the editor:

TO THE EDITOR:

I'm sure many people are having the same problem as I— trying to understand the words to the song "Along Comes Mary," by the Associations.[56] I have the record and have listened to it thousands of times but no matter how hard I try, I can't seem to catch all of the words. I would really appreciate it if you would print the words sometime in "Teen-Ager."

Well, Lynn Magnan, the name's The Association (singular!), and I'm happy to share the lyrics with you now.

Every time I think that I'm the only one who's lonely
Someone calls on me
And every now and then I spend my time in rhyme and verse
And curse those faults in me

And then along comes Mary

---

56   If I also had a dime for every time someone called our band by the wrong name, I could have bought Niagara Falls and named it after us. It's singular—The Association!

And does she want to give me kicks, and be my steady chick
And give me pick of memories
Or maybe rather gather tales of all the fails and tribulations
No one ever sees

When we met I was sure out to lunch
Now my empty cup tastes as sweet as the punch

When vague desire is the fire in the eyes of chicks
Whose sickness is the games they play
And when the masquerade is played and neighbor folks make jokes
As who is most to blame today

And then along comes Mary
And does she want to set them free, and let them see reality
From where she got her name
And will they struggle much when told that such a tender
touch as hers
Will make them not the same

When we met I was sure out to lunch
Now my empty cup tastes as sweet as the punch

And when the morning of the warning's passed, the gassed
And flaccid kids are flung across the stars
The psychodramas and the traumas gone
The songs are left unsung and hung upon the scars

And then along comes Mary
And does she want to see the stains, the dead remains of all
the pains
She left the night before
Or will their waking eyes reflect the lies, and make them
Realize their urgent cry for sight no more

When we met I was sure out to lunch
Now my empty cup tastes as sweet as the punch

"Along Comes Mary" would be one of the songs on our first album, *And Then...Along Comes The Association.* Funny enough, "Along Comes Mary" was actually the B-side of our single, "Your Own Love," released March 8, 1966. God bless that DJ who first decided to flip it over and play the B-side instead.

There's one big thing I'd like to clear up before we get too deep into the story here. Early on, journalists would call what The Association played "folk-rock" music—but truth be known, our influences really did come from far and wide—folk, blues, jazz, gospel, pop, and rock. The Men, as I said, invented folk-rock. Not The Byrds. The Byrds were a great band, but they didn't invent the genre. The December 18, 1965 issue of *Cash Box* printed the following in the "Record Ramblings" column:

It was almost a year ago that we first came across the "Folk-Rock" phrase emblazoned alongside the door to Doug Weston's Troubadour on Santa Monica Blvd. It referred to the sounds of a group, which Weston called The Men. As it turned out they were never separated from the boys and within a few months they were disjoined from each other. Three[57] [sic] of its former members went on to become the nucleus for a vocal-instrumental sextet called The Association. They wore short hair, ivy league hopsack suits with six button vests. And together, they wove some musical magic at a Salvation Army [sic] building in Glendale, which includes a folk club called The Ice House.

For almost six months they labored away before auditioning for Valiant Records. Accepted into the Four Star fold, their first single, a Bob Dylan composition titled "One Too Many Mornings" was released without fanfare about three weeks ago. Habitues [sic] of The Ice House stormed the record shops and several hundred records were sold in the

---

57   As I mentioned earlier, six of us (not three) defected from The Men—me Ted, Terry, Brian, Jules, and Bob Page (who would be replaced by Jim Yester).

Glendale-Pasadena area. And just this weekend a Pasadena radio station, KRLA, started to play the side. The Valiant effort, it appears, is on the verge of an LA bustout. Too early to write finis to the Association's success story, it's rather late to suggest you race out to hear the sextet at the Ice House. They have just moved to the Forum Club in Montclair. If musical merit is any indication, they should prosper wherever they are. And just for the record their names are Gary Alexander, Ted Bluechel, Brian Cole, Russ Giguere, Terry Kirkman and Jim Yester. The group, incidentally, can perform jazz, folk, rock and roll and folk-rock with equal dexterity. Which brings us back to Doug Weston who started the phrase a year ago. If nothing else he deserves the credit—or is it the blame?—for that meaty metaphor...

So there you go. I said I would convey something neat, didn't I?

Along Comes Mary
1966

As I mentioned, we'd allowed ourselves two years to get a Top 40 hit. Hearing our song on the radio for the first time took us one giant step closer to our goal. Our fans from the AAA were leaving flowers onstage every night we performed. The burgeoning numbers of female fans (don't get me wrong, we had just as many male fans, but for the purposes of this story, I'm only going to mention the women) were just the beginning of what we would later call, in all our time on the road, the antidote to DSB (Deadly Semen Buildup).

Do everything you can to prevent DSB!

Whether you were single or not, the rule of the band was whatever you did with other women was your business—we would all look the other way and didn't want to know about it. The less we knew, the better. (Though I do recall a stunning female little person knocking on my hotel door late one night, looking for Brian—she was gorgeous. I discreetly directed her down the hall.) In the words of Jim Yester, "Relationships are difficult when you're on the road so much. It was a circus life, that's for sure. We were the major clowns." Ted Bluechel adds, "We had a thing about us—we press on, we don't stop, the machine is all-important. Make the gigs, get on the road, do the recordings and what was left over you give to the families, but that didn't nourish the family relationships very well." Me? I was faithful to my wife Birdie and later to my second wife, Penny, during the time I was dating or married to them. When I happened to be divorced, separated, or single, which I was at various times over the decades, I went out with anybody I wanted, and I managed to avoid toxic DSB while still having lots of fun.

For a group of virile men in their early twenties, the AAA was perfect training ground for years of practicing preventive DSB. Our manager Pat (I'm getting to him) had a framed black-and-white photograph of two beautiful women and a baby in a natural outdoor setting—the photo was haunting, almost mysterious. The women in the photograph are young and beautiful—they look like wood sprites with long hair, flowing dresses, and a literal babe (as in an actual baby) in the woods. The photo was framed with a note addressed to Brian and Terry, thanking them for a beautiful night. It hung on the wall of Pat's office for years. The note clearly or cryptically (depending on your interpretation) alludes to the child featured in the photo as being the end product, so to speak, of one of the band member's DSB practice—but no further details were ever provided.

As our music grew in popularity, the rave reviews trickled in. Brian and I developed a routine, an improvised repartee with the audience, to keep them revved up as we flowed from one song to the next. We also had an opener we used often that we referred to as "The Machine," wherein Brian would introduce us all in his dramatic bass voice, and we'd "come to life," robot-like, and start to play our instruments until we all dove collectively into the driving beat of the song with which we were opening a concert. "As the machine is completed, the clockwork ticking of the drum and the electronic blips of the guitar suddenly melt together and the group is into its first number..." We became especially deft at covering string changes for guitars when necessary, cracking jokes as needed. "Their act is a tightly organized mixture of patter, free-for-all humorous skits and musical numbers that somehow flow smoothly from skit to skit without pause."[58] A later May 3, 1967, article, "Students to Host 'The Association,'" in *The OshKosh Northwestern* said, "As any entertainer knows most performance 'sets' must include ad lib or short skits to

---

58   Johnson, Pete. "The Association Spreads Its Talents Into Folk-Rock Field." *Los Angeles Times*. January 28, 1966.

provide the transition from one number to the next. The Association follows the rule of thumb in its in-between act pantomimes. Their onstage charm and poise, rare for so young a group, has captured and enlightened numerous audiences across the country." *The Daily Tar Heel* of Chapel Hill, North Carolina, agreed. In the April 22, 1967, article, "Music is a Way of Life For The Association Men," Penny Raynor wrote, "Their performance pauses are filled with skillfully paced pantomimes, dramatic readings, and slapstick comedy guaranteed to capture the attention and appreciation of any stonefaced, unappreciative pessimist." *The Flint Journal* wrote, "Their sound sometimes approaches a thing of real beauty, and it's a sound, too, with a sense of humor. The group presents sketches that are rehearsed and presented in a way suitable as a self-sufficient act. One is a takeoff on television newscasts during which Brian Cole, the bass player, announces that 'Lynda Bird Johnson and Senator Everett Dirksen have just signed to do a remake of *Lolita*."[59] (Truly, Brian was an original.)

There were dissenters, however. To know praise when you hear it is also to know your critics. *The Lubbock Avalanche Journal* of Lubbock, Texas, shared in the December 7, 1967, article, "'Association's Decibels Up: Auditorium Acoustics Get Workout From Vocal Group," claiming, "Their own humor interludes were mild and aimed at the youthful level and quite rudimentary in their composition. A good writer might be of a beneficial nature in this department, too."

There was often an internal debate in the group about these bits—some members were adamantly against them and participated begrudgingly. In general, this shtick was not considered cool by the tragically hip of the time, but they never had any fun anyway!

We played high schools, colleges, junior colleges, churches—anyone willing to pay. You name a venue or a large space, and we played it. As I mentioned earlier, we played every single "land" there

59   Kiefer, Michael. "Association Proves it Has Class." *The Flint Journal*. March 8, 1968.

was to play in Disneyland, doing multiple gigs there, including a "Grad Nite" in 1966. During Grad Nite, the park was shut down at 10:00 p.m. and left open until 4:00 a.m. just for the schools celebrating Grad Nite. After the success of "Along Comes Mary," we played in Frontierland, along with Deep Six, Young Men from New Orleans, and Hearts and Flowers, while the Royal Tahitians played Adventureland and Port Royal Steel Drums and the Clara Ward Singers played Fantasyland. We had two preferred spots in which to smoke dope in Disneyland: Monsanto's "Adventure Thru Inner Space in Tomorrowland" (you couldn't pick a more perfect spot to smoke up at than a pitch-black attraction meant to make its audience feel as though they were shrinking to a size smaller than an atom), or more frequently, you'd find us stealing a toke in the gondolas above Fantasyland.

We had one-toke pipes made from cutting opium pipes shorter—one-toke pipes were far cooler than standard rolled joints. Jules even briefly dated a tall drink of water and lovely girl, Shannon, whom he met at Tomorrowland, where she worked. She was over six feet tall, and in the heels she wore as part of her "Tomorrowland" silver bodysuit costume, she was truly Amazonian. Jules is maybe five foot six. To see them walk down the street together and head into the Troubadour was a sight you couldn't help but grin at. It was sweet.

During one of those Disneyland gigs, security called Dean to the office just as we were changing clothes in the dressing room.

"We heard the boys have a song on the charts right now, and the song is about marijuana," said one of the security officers.

"Well, I don't know about that." Dean feigned innocence. He pulled a newspaper from his briefcase, waving an article under their noses about how a local Catholic school had named "Along Comes Mary" song of the year. They didn't know what to make of it and had no choice but to let us go on. People were obsessed with marijuana. *Newsweek* even ran a story in 1964 about how the 1959 song, Peter, Paul and Mary's "Puff the Magic Dragon," was about marijuana.

The *Ottawa Journal* is one example of newspapers that picked up the story. "At the time 'Mary' hit the charts, there immediately was a question raised about the chance of this song being another 'drug' tune, possibly about marijuana, often called 'Mary Jane.' I asked Brian Cole about this. His answer was, 'It depends on how you take it. In LA there is a Catholic parochial school that used the song for something and interpreted it as a tribute to the Virgin Mary. It isn't written as a drug song, but you could interpret it as one if you wanted to.'"[60]

With every live performance, we polished our sound. The New Christy Minstrels had long been performing "Cherish," which was written by Terry Kirkman and brought to them by Mike Whalen after he left The Men to join them, but Terry wouldn't give them permission to record and release it. We were also performing it for audiences. When Terry first brought it to the group, we were on the fence about singing it, but Jules and Clark Burroughs of the Hi-Los added a more complex chord structure to the vocals and instruments. David Jackson, who played with us in the 1990s, said, "Clark was very instrumental in the blend of The Association." And then Jim, during sound check for a gig at the Glendale Ice House, suggested we add the now very familiar "bum, bum" backups that start the vocal arrangement. He got the idea just as he pulled into The Ice House parking lot. In particular, Jules's input was transformative—he road-mapped the arrangement, sitting down one-on-one with each guy to teach him his part, so the sound became what you hear today.

Everyone in the band wrote and contributed arrangement ideas, but Jules was the guy who could make a piece of music soar and take it to a whole other level. You could feel that even though we were new and still gelling together more and more each week, the air in the audience would shift during "Cherish." After each performance of the song, there was a stunned mass silence, followed by thunderous applause. People sometimes bash "Cherish" for being schmaltzy or

---

60   "The Association: Electric Switch Paid off." *The Ottawa Journal.* August 20, 1966.

sentimental, but I think the key to its success, complicated harmonies and beautiful melodies aside, is that it is about a love you have deep in your heart, but never express.

> *Cherish is the word I use to describe*
> *All the feeling that I have*
> *Hiding here for you inside*
> *You don't know how many times*
> *I've wished that I had told you*
> *You don't know how many times*
> *I've wished that I could hold you*
> *You don't know how many times*
> *I've wished that I could*
> *Mold you into someone who could*
> *Cherish me as much as I cherish you*

Everyone on the planet has experienced this feeling at some point in their life. It's the containment of that secret that makes it thrilling. The closest thing I can liken it to is the feeling I experienced with my sixth-grade teacher, Mrs. Wragg. (Don't laugh, hear me out!) I would invent questions and problems just to have her beauty near me and to drink in her heavenly scent—typical adolescent boy fantasy stuff. And even though she was well out of my age range, my preteen self took personal offense to her getting pregnant by her husband. Mrs. Wragg, if you're still around, I hope you know I meant no offense. "Cherish" is all about that person you loved deeply, but never told.

The success of "Cherish" is probably best summed up with these words from an article when the record went gold: "Although most people outside the record industry are notoriously unaware of the fact, a gold record is extremely difficult to come by and is rarely won. For instance, of all of the singles currently in the top one hundred in the nation, only one has sold one million. And that one is 'Cherish.'"[61]

---

61   "Cosby, Association Win Gold Records." (Publication and date unknown; from author's personal archives.)

Incidentally, on our *Greatest Hits* album, the liner notes for "Cherish" mistakenly print the lyric as:

> All the feeling that I have
> Hiding here for your inside

Your inside?! Why, that's a different song entirely. You would think someone would have proofread those liner notes and caught that mistake!

With the success of "Along Comes Mary," we went back into the studio with Curt Boettcher, Steve Clark, and Gary Paxton to produce a full album. When the album was finished, Barry DeVorzon took a copy home to pick the cut we would release as the next single. He called his business partner the next morning and told him he thought we had a problem. Because Valiant had spent a long five months, one city at a time, selling us as a hard-rocking semi-psychedelic act with "Along Comes Mary," they thought the second release should also be up-tempo and in the same genre to match the brand, sound, and fan expectations. But Barry was drawn to "Cherish," which was pretty much the polar opposite of "Along Comes Mary." Barry grit his teeth, determined to release "Cherish" and hope for the best.

When it was originally recorded, "Cherish" was three minutes and fifteen seconds long. Terry remembers it was closer to three minutes and forty. This was the 1960s, and we were very aware that any song over three minutes in length wouldn't get airtime on the radio. So for that reason, hit songs really had to be three minutes or fewer, and most hit songs were in fact about two minutes and fifteen seconds in length. The disc jockey programmed their shows counting on this. Furthermore, 45 records (what singles were issued on, for the most part) were cheap to manufacture; it was far less expensive for Americans to buy one 45 record than to purchase a full album. And 45s could hold about three minutes of music without compromising sound. There was a way to put longer songs on a 45, which involved compressing the grooves, but it wasn't typically done.

In "Cherish," we cut the repeat of the last line, "…and I do…cherish you," and sped up the entire song. In an article for *The Huffington Post*, Terry wrote, "What I heard in my head when writing the song was more like The Righteous Brothers' super hit, 'You've Lost That Lovin' Feelin', (and with good reason—the song is BMI's #1 most airplayed tune!). Slow, heavy, sad, poignant, and heartbroken, with that heavy fat back pulsing beat—*ka bam chunga, bam chunga*—full of heart-wrenching soul. So very not like the German Youth March tempo we ended up employing to shorten the length."

I have to disagree with Terry's final assessment and the record sales would beg to differ as well, but the songwriter is entitled to his own opinion. It was still long by a few seconds, but not so long it wouldn't fit on the 45, so we put 2:59 on the record and released it—by the time anyone realized what we'd done (programmers everywhere were probably scratching their heads, wondering why their playlists were running overtime), it was already a Number One hit. *The Daily Tar Heel* later wrote in a November 14, 1968, article, "The Association's first song, 'Along Comes Mary,' gave a break to the feeling of discontent stirred up by the Beatles. When 'Cherish' hit the nation as a gold record, the Association explained their origin by saying that they evolved from nowhere and yet from everywhere." YES. A journalist who really got us, hallelujah already!

A lot of bands would try to repeat the success of "Cherish" over the next several years. One of the most obvious rip-offs would be the 1972 hit by Climax, "Precious and Few." Walter D. Nims, the writer of "Precious and Few," was approached by our publisher, Herb Hendler, who said, "Write me another 'Cherish.'" It's like Mason Williams explains—when something's popular in Hollywood, or in this case when a record hits it big, record executive thinking follows this three-point trajectory (Mason uses his own name in this example):

First:

"Who's Mason Williams? Give me Mason Williams."

Then:

"Give me someone like Mason Williams."

And inevitably:

"Who's Mason Williams?"

That's the arc of fame! Mason also loves to say, "A career has an agenda. A creative life has a veranda."

With Herb Hendler's directive, Nims produced "Precious and Few." One time on tour after we'd gotten back together in the 1980s, we were in front of a live audience at a large Riverfest of over ten thousand people where Climax opened for us. After we performed "Cherish," and after the usual silence fell on the heels of the song's conclusion, I took the microphone and said, "Precious and few *that!*"

I never said subtlety was my strong point.

Barry and his team at Valiant had poured blood, sweat, and tears into circulating "Along Comes Mary" to radio stations in major US cities, but "Cherish" took on a momentum of its own, and its success was like the spark of a flame in a forest. Barry had to beg the pressing plants for additional credit to make more records to keep up with the demand. It paid off. An April 22, 1967, *Billboard* article, "Warner Bros. Buys Valiant," mentions our four singles ("Along Comes Mary," "Cherish," "Windy," and "Never My Love") hitting more than $2 million in sales and our two LPs reaching $750,000 in sales, which allowed Valiant to report 1966 grosses of more than $1 million, or nearly $8 million by today's standards, with inflation. Indeed, Valiant was able to make such a profitable sale to Warner Bros. largely on the success of The Association.

The process for selecting the music we would record and how we all got paid in the group was, as I mentioned, very democratic. Considering we were a six-man band, the fact that there could even be a democracy in a group that large was remarkable. In mid-March 1965, *Billboard* announced Herb Hendler had joined Capitol Records as acting director of artists' contracts and acting manager of the Beechwood Music Corp. Beechwood was our music publisher. Ted remembers that Herb encouraged us to write our own material.

"That's what we're trying to do," Ted says, "but the problem is that when we do that, the rest of the guys don't get their songs worked on—we don't have time for it, therefore we don't make any money off that."

Herb asked Terry what he thought about giving up some of his songwriting credit, but he made it clear he wasn't up for that. Herb suggested if we couldn't get any of the writer's penny, we could take the publisher's penny and split it in half—the publisher would get one half, and the remaining 50 percent would be divided among the six guys. That deal is extremely unusual for the music business, but Herb negotiated it, and it made things easier for us, knowing that if things continued to go well and we weren't touring, our efforts weren't wasted or stagnant—we would still be earning royalties. If you were the songwriter, you got your songwriter check, a check from the record company, and a check from the publishing company. If you didn't write the song, you would get a check from the record company and a check from the publishing company. This deal helped us avoid some, but not all, of the money squabbles to which other bands fall victim. Danny Hutton puts it succinctly:

> …My favorite thing is if the band is all there and they're all together and they struggle and they do their first album and it ends up being a hit album, and then they have to start the second album and one or two of the guys arrive in Ferraris. And another guy says, "Well, how did you do that?" And the other guys say, "Oh, I got my songwriting royalties from the album." And everyone looks at each other and says, "Okay, this album is going to be different. We're all going to write three songs apiece!" And if it gets too democratic…you can't be fair when you're doing music. You've got to serve the music. You have to serve the song. You have to do the best song. It's not about everyone getting a fair two or three

songs. Because the public doesn't care about that—they don't know about that. On the other hand, how the hell do you do it? How do you say, "Look, I'm the better writer." The other guys say, "Screw you." That's one big thing.

And then there's the stupid thing where somebody has sex with somebody else's wife or girlfriend in the band. All those romantic Fleetwood Mac kind of things going on. And then you get the pressure on the road. You make a joke or something or say, "Pass the butter," and the guy punches you—says, "For three months, every morning in the same tone you've asked for butter." You just get all this crazy tension, the adrenaline when you get off the stage, and somebody blows it. It all adds up and in this funny way it's like the seven-year itch...Everybody changes and the innocence is lost.

David Jackson, who I mentioned played with The Association in the 1990s, believes, "The need to be the big dog is, in my view, the biggest stumbling block for bands." My buddy Bernie Leadon, guitarist, songwriter and one of the original founding members of The Eagles who dealt with his own internal band problems/creative differences, ultimately leaving the band in 1975, shares, "Most bands never get record royalties, which means most *members* of the band never get record royalties and they don't participate in the publishing. So whoever wrote the hits suddenly is getting all this money. And now you have this disparity of power and finances inside the band. Interestingly, one band that dealt with this brilliantly is the band U2, who formed a band corporation, but they decided that everybody would share in everything. Songwriter, publishing, everything. U2 shares everything even Steven—and guess what? They're still together." U2 splits all of the music credit equally, but the lyrics credit only belongs to front man Bono.

Well, The Association is still together, likely in part due to the publisher's penny deal we worked out among all of us long ago, but that's not to say we haven't had our fair share of disagreements, discontent, and comings and goings of band members. In the beginning, we sang songs written by songwriters outside the group (as with "Along Comes Mary"), and when it came time to make an album, we'd consider something like thirty to forty songs for recording. We called a listening session like this a lynching. Most songs didn't make it past the first ten seconds. Someone would put it on and someone else would say, "NEXT!" We knew when it wasn't for us.

I'm not going to lie. We passed on a lot of songs that went on to be huge hits over the years (when we first heard "MacArthur Park" it was twenty-two minutes long—Bones Howe told us it couldn't be cut, but a month later it was released at seven minutes and twenty-one seconds. So much for that judgment, and more on that later), but I don't have any regrets. Once we'd finished arranging a new song and rehearsed our complex vocal harmonies, it likely didn't sound much like what it did when it first came to us in demo form. Plus, what was right for us wasn't necessarily right for another band, and vice versa. We passed on "Joy to the World"[62] and "One is the Loneliest Number" (both Three Dog Night), "I Write the Songs" (Barry Manilow), and "Aquarius (Let the Sunshine In)" (The 5th Dimension), to name just a few in a long list.

To beef up an album we included original material from group members. Just because you were in the group didn't mean your song was a shoo-in. Your song had to be voted in, and it was only voted in if was worthy.

Curt Boettcher had arranged for Brian Wilson to listen to a tape of our first album before it was released to the public and he said it was "the best first album" he'd ever heard. This was the same year The Beach Boys released *Pet Sounds* with "Wouldn't It Be Nice," "God Only Knows," and "Sloop John B." I remember Dean Fredericks felt that letting Brian listen to our record was like showing the enemy

---

62   David Jackson, who later played with The Association, sued Three Dog Night over his credit for writing part of the lyrics of "Joy to the World."

our secret weapon. But Brian's endorsement only further bolstered what we already knew: our music had the potential for greatness.

And Then...Along Comes the Association cost $17,000 to record (which would be about $135,000 today). The *Los Angeles Times* mused on our lyrics:

Here is a way the world has changed, Mr. Block:

Parents used to be near enough to pass the butter while celebrities were remote as age and press and limousines could make them.

Today, parents are somewhere else—because they aren't home for dinner or because they tune to different frequencies. And the celebrities, especially the pop music celebrities, are companions and advisers and even makers of moral standards.

The heroes of the young are almost as young as themselves. Unlike idols of another time, they are also available—to talk and answer their mail, vulnerable to the audience that sits at their feet.

This may trouble you, Mr. Block. But it's true. Somewhere over that manic guitar, your child has been receiving real messages—while you were digging the nineteenth hole.

You may have waggled your finger; it probably proved you weren't listening. Or couldn't understand. Because out of the broken ear drums of pop, human affections are being glued...

...The Mr. Blocks are forever worrying words, such as profound questions as whether a song such as "Along Comes Mary" has to do with marijuana or a belle of the junior high.

Association bassist Brian Cole was claiming that a real adult should be "somebody with an open mouth—AND an open brain."

And Terry Kirkman was saying he had offended a disc jockey by really examining the various possible meanings of "Along Comes Mary"—more mental traffic than a rock station could bear. "That's part of the trouble," claimed Kirkman, "if you're going to talk to teenagers at all, then you better be prepared to get into it."

So, Mr. Block, if you'd like to have a voice, get into it. Into mysticism, drugs, religion, war and love. Otherwise you will have lost by default, to all those choruses you don't understand.[63]

That gives you a pretty good idea of how not only the celebrity culture but also the youth culture and influence was changing dramatically in that decade—our voices were being heard, much to the chagrin of some of the adults, and rock and roll was a great platform.

Now that you know a little more about our story and can refer to the lyrics—do you think "Along Comes Mary" was about the Blessed Virgin Mary or blessed marijuana? You have a fifty-fifty chance of getting this answer right, but if you get it wrong, I'll know you weren't paying attention!

These photos and this letter from Penny and Julie (last names unknown) were mailed to Brian and Terry. The child they are posing with is one of Brian's sons. Pat Colecchio loved these photos and this letter so much, he hung them on the wall of his office at 9124 Sunset for many years. The letter reads: "Dear Brian and Terry, We thought we'd write you and tell you that a year ago last October you planted a spiritual seed that has grown and led us into wonderful things."

---

63   Seidenbaum, Art. "Who Talks to Your Child—And on What Terms?" *Los Angeles Times.* May 3, 1968.

Wake Up and Smell the Jet Fuel
1966–1968

"ALONG COMES MARY" WAS climbing the US charts—ultimately it would reach No. 7 on *Billboard*. Half of the radio stations in the country wouldn't play it (because they thought it was about marijuana), but it was still a hit. We loved our manager Dean Fredericks—he had been the first to put his neck on the line, fronting the cash to rent the band's house and paying us to rehearse all those months—yet Dean was having difficulty parlaying our success on the airwaves into more opportunities nationwide and, specifically, more money. We knew there was money to be made, but no one knew how to go about it; we still had yet to perform outside the state of California. And so we made the decision to go with a new manager, Pat Colecchio.

Pat Colecchio was a dashing, handsome Italian man originally from Jersey City, New Jersey—a real lady-killer. He looked like actor Victor Jory. Pat had the natural charisma to back up his God-given looks. In 2006, when Pat was in his eighties, he went to Texas to live with Jules for a while. In the 2011 book *Where Have All the Pop Stars Gone? Volume 1*, Jules talks about the experience. "When Pat got here, he practically took over the town. By the time he left, everyone knew him. He was the godfather of this club we liked to go to. Pat was eighty-two or eighty-three...and he was dating thirty-year-old women. He wasn't a man, he was a force of nature. I would see things happen that were kind of spooky—like women would walk around him, then walk toward him. It was if he was a magnet or something." There was a time he took all of the women associated with the band—the wives, the girlfriends—to see Sinatra perform at the Cocoanut Grove. Pat was in his element, escorting a large group of beautiful women to see Sinatra!

But in 1966, Pat was working in a Beverly Hills shoe store, of all places, when Terry met him through his sister-in-law. Pat had served in the Navy and watched through his binoculars on the deck of the *New Mexico* in Tokyo Bay as General Douglas MacArthur and Japanese Foreign Minister Mamoru Shigemitsu stood on the deck of the *Missouri* a hundred yards away, preparing to sign the document that ended World War II. Pat had witnessed many of the deadliest naval battles in WWII, including Okinawa, where more than two hundred thousand people, including fifty-four of his shipmates and one-third of the civilian population, died. Having survived all those horrors, it's no wonder that he was attracted to the lure of the sun and stars in Hollywood when the war was over. Pat became a bookie, a boxing reporter, and eventually manager of that women's shoe store, where Lana Turner was his very first customer—a far cry from his battles at sea.

What made Terry think *here's the guy to manage us*, I'm not sure, but I'm glad he did. "It was bizarre, antithetical…We were simply introduced to him and he had promoted several things before and the shoe store was just how he was making money," Terry explains. "It was a really weird, unadvisable, emotional kind of panicky move" post-Dean Fredericks not being able to capitalize on the success of "Along Comes Mary." Pat would see us on the way to and through our most successful period of hit-making and touring. Jules remembers that the first gig Pat got paid us $1,000 for the night, more than we had ever made up to that moment for a live performance. Pat was a father figure to me. Promotional material on the group had this to say about Pat:

Pat relies mostly on his "best bet" instincts, combined with
an impulsive business manner and never-say-die attitude.
He can be found worrying out The Association's demanding

schedule anywhere and at anytime. Not to mention his duties as a friend, father confessor, and water balloon captain. All this he does with nary a wrinkle to his debonair self.

Dean Fredericks filed a Los Angeles Superior Court suit charging us with breach of contract, insisting he had tied us to a seven-year contract and that we had severed the pact six years early. Our publicist, Stan Zipperman, also filed suit against us, claiming fraud and breach of contract, boasting he had a hundred witnesses willing to testify, and asking for $100,000 in punitive damages. We made the cover of the November 5, 1966, *KRLA Beat* issue with the headline "The Association Play the Court Game," and the article "Association Sued by Former Publicist" ran with a publicity photo of the group and the caption "The Association are saying it isn't so," saying:

The lengthy complaint alleges, among other things, the following:

—Zipperman's contract for public relations and publicity services for the Association was improperly terminated.

—The Association induced Zipperman to execute the contract through fraud.

—It is well known in the industry that Zipperman was substantially responsible for the success of the Association.

What's the card game you play until the first player successfully plays all the cards in his hand and then someone shouts "Bullshit!" and the winner has to show his card to prove it's what he said it was? Oh, wait, the card game is called Bullshit. I call BULLSHIT! Yes, we had fans; we were getting air time and actually climbing charts with our third single after the first two fizzled out; we were getting standing ovations at the clubs and we were well known regionally, but the fact of the matter was that we weren't moving faster or further along with Dean or with Stan, and they didn't know how to get us to the next level. Ultimately, we didn't have anything binding in writing with Stan, so that lawsuit died rather quickly. Dean's contribution to the beginnings of The Association was invaluable—we were fortunate to have someone believe in us and not be afraid to put his money where his mouth was on an unproven group in its infancy. We ended up settling with Dean for $71,000, which would be about $578,000+ in today's money.

As I mentioned after the release of "Along Comes Mary," there was debate as to which song to release next from our first album— it's always an argument, as record executives and producers rush to weigh in on what song they think will fare best. Thankfully "Along Comes Mary" was our first release because "Cherish" was so drastically different and a true love ballad that if the order of the two singles had been reversed, fans probably wouldn't have accepted another song that *wasn't* a love ballad.

No matter who you are or what you do, people want to put you in a box or on a shelf with a name so they understand how to classify you and look at you. This makes me crazy. Once you make a hit like "Cherish," producers and higher-ups in the business want you to recreate another success just like that—when I say "just like that," I am referring to the sound, tone, and style. We would get asked about this sort of thing all the time. In a group interview for *The Purdue Exponent* on Wednesday, April 22, 1970,[64] the reporter asked, "I was wondering if you were thinking about any change in the traditional Association style?" Jim answered, "There's no plan of change. If change occurs it's just a natural evolution, of where each cat's music is at as expressed through the group. Now if a change occurs over a period of time, then it occurs. But we don't sit down and say, okay we've done this, now we're going to do this. No, that doesn't occur in our group of musicians." I chimed in with, "We don't feel there's any actual Association sound except for us six singing. Whatever we choose to make it is just a variation on the theme of us singing and playing."

Ultimately, no one can predict what will happen with the release of a single and it's all a crapshoot—the argument and debate process attempts to make the whole thing a little more educated or thought

---

64 The newspaper says Wednesday, April 21, but April 21 was a Tuesday that year, so it's an error. I'll reference this again later on, so just know that the date they gave is wrong.

out, but it's an illusion. There's a lot of instinct and luck involved. Pat stepped in just as we were in the thick of promoting our first album. He used his Italian charm and graces to convince the program directors at WLS Radio in Chicago to play the album cut of "Cherish," and because of the success of the extended airplay, "Cherish" was then released as a single.

You might be wondering how in the hell what song played or didn't play on a radio station in Chicago could possibly determine your fate. To put it into perspective, WABC-AM in New York's "share of the New York radio audience often topped 20 percent compared to an average of about 6 percent for today's highest-rated stations."[65] Television had only recently replaced home entertainment options, and radio was still popular and had influence. Marty Nicosia, whom we met in 1967 and would go on to become our road manager in the 1980s, explains, "...you could have a hit in NY or LA, but if you didn't have it in Chicago...they covered something like forty states—you could pick it up at the far end of Texas, bottom of Florida, in Canada—when they covered it, it was a nationwide hit."

Pat would tell you that when he started with all of us, we lived in small rented apartments and drove beat-up cars, and a year later we were driving Porsches. We weren't necessarily all driving Porsches, though we were driving better cars. I owned a Porsche for a hot minute, until I discovered I couldn't get my luggage to the airport without leaving the top down. And putting the top back up was a project in of itself; it wasn't automated. Birdie kept the Porsche I bought her, but I quickly sold mine and went back to my 1959 black VW convertible with a white top that I bought for $900 from comedian George McKelvey. Birdie and I moved to a larger apartment and soon, at the recommendation of our accountant, we went house searching. I rode with a realtor looking at potential houses. She took me to see a Frank Lloyd Wright house up a hilly street in Los Feliz, not far from the Greek Theater and Griffith Observatory—the now famous

---

65   Battaglio, Stephen. "Television/Radio; When AM Ruled Music, and WABC Was King." *The New York Times*. March 10, 2002.

"Ennis House" at 2655 Glendower, built in 1924; a spectacular house with a spectacular view. The street wrapped around everything but the very back, so I got a good look at the exterior. She told me the price was around $67,000.

"Why so cheap?' I asked.

"It would take that much just to fix the plumbing," she said.

To gain access to the pipes required disassembling the outside walls, made of decomposed granite and cement (the operative word being "decomposed"). I passed. Eventually, I bought a house in Beachwood Canyon.

Ted also graduated to a house, in Laurel Canyon—though again, it's not like all of a sudden we were getting mortgages on ten-bedroom houses in Bel-Air. "Cherish" would reach No. 1 on the *Billboard* charts in September 1966 and stay there for three weeks, ultimately ranking as the No. 2 song of the entire year and hitting No. 1 in Canada. To give you an idea of the other music that charted on *Billboard* as top songs for all of 1966, Sgt. Barry Sadler's "The Ballad of The Green Berets" was No. 1, The Righteous Brothers' "(You're My) Soul and Inspiration" was No. 3, and The Mamas and the Papas' "California Dreamin'" came in at No. 10. In 1967, we would receive three Grammy nominations (though we didn't win any): "Best Performance by a Vocal Group," "Best Contemporary Rock & Roll Recording," and "Best Contemporary Rock & Roll Group Performance," all for "Cherish." The album, *And Then...Along Comes the Association*, became one of the top-selling LPs in America.

Early in our cross-country travels, probably on our second tour because this was before we began carrying no fewer than three giant Rand McNally atlases with us on the road, we landed somewhere in the Midwest in the summer during a high corn alert. We picked up our rental cars, filled up on gas, and asked the attendant for directions to the school at which we were scheduled to play. He looked us up and down and then intentionally (as we would discover an hour later) misdirected us. That was how it worked then—somebody gave you a once-over and if he didn't like the way you dressed, looked, or smelled, he gave you wrong information. And so we found ourselves on a suburban street where a group of young kids were on a porch, listening to a record on a portable record player—and lo and behold, the record was our first album! It blew all of our minds, and I think the kids' eyes fell out of their heads when I told them we were The Association! We signed the album, got the correct directions from one of their parents, and kept going.

Money was beginning to flow and success was happening. People were interested in our music, and they wanted to know what we were thinking, not only about music, but about what was going on in America and in the youth culture. See, it was an escalation of America's celebrity culture craze, which has only ballooned further with YouTube, Instagram, and twenty-four-hour news and social media. (I'll stick with my no cell phone, no email policy, thank you very much—it's gotten me this far in life, and I'm afraid if I have a cell phone, someone will call me.)

Long ago, people worshipped gods and goddesses in Greek myths or historical figures like Alexander the Great. Once silent movies and then talkies happened in the US, we had the rise of the movie star, and in 1962, Andy Warhol started his famous Factory. In a February 12, 2012, article for *The Guardian,* "Andy Warhol's Legacy Lives On In the Factory of Fame," Alex Needham wrote, "In a critique of the Hollywood star system, Warhol turned the likes of the Santa Barbara heiress Edie Sedgwick into celebrities, instinctively grasping…that people need not be famous for acting, singing or doing anything other than being themselves." Now, I never hung out with or met Andy Warhol or his crowd—I'm merely pointing this out to give you some context and let you know Andy Warhol's Factory was all going on at the same time as the Vietnam War, the British Invasion, and the rise of The Association and other rock bands. And the Factory is emblematic of the huge reversal of what was going on in the 1950s, where women stayed home and there was a general post-World War II cultural conformity. With the 1960s, there was so much newness—so much anti-establishment challenging of the way things were by the youth culture in their twenties and thirties. We were the ones dressing differently, experimenting with drugs, protesting against the war, wearing long hair; we were the people asking questions, abandoning self-examination fears, putting what we thought and felt out there, saying, "This is who we are, fuck it, what are you going to do about it?"

At one point in 1966 going into 1967, three of us in the band, including me, started packing pistols. I carried a .32 automatic, Jules had a snub nose .38, and Brian had a .45 automatic. It wasn't to be macho, and we didn't talk about it—some of the other guys didn't even know. We had the guns so that if shit started happening, we were prepared and we would come out on top. It was self-protection only. It was a crazy time in America. I remember a party at a hotel in the South, after Larry, who was Filipino-Hawaiian, had joined the band. A man walked up to me and nodded disparagingly toward Larry, who stood a few feet away from me.

"That China boy with you?" he asked.

I looked that racist right in the eye and shot back, "He's my *partner. Why?*"

The man walked away. We were the good guys and if anything went down, we were going to win. Fortunately, nothing ever happened that required armament and we only packed for a few months. We never flashed those guns and no one even knew we had them. As more and more airports began using X-ray machines, we got rid of the guns. Terry remembers Brian getting kicked off of a plane for having a gun, but I have no memory of that.

Also on tour in the South circa 1967–68, there was a time when we pulled up to our motel in a bus. Lee Liebman, our road manager at the time, went inside—as he usually did—to register at the front desk. The woman at reception refused to allow Lee to sign us in, insisting everyone had to come in and sign the registration cards individually. This was highly unusual, but we had no choice but to comply. Some of the guys had to be awakened and worse, a very important game of Hearts was rudely interrupted. As we each signed our registration cards, the woman drawled smugly, "I just wanted to see if y'all could write."

"Lady, we don't want to *vote* here," I retorted. "We just want a place to flop."

People wanted to know what we thought and felt, as I mentioned. The Association was interviewed in the 1968 J. Marks book (with photographs by Linda Eastman, the future Mrs. Paul McCartney) *Rock (Music) and Other Four Letter Words: Music of the Electric Generation:*

> Terry Kirkman: I think the word "underground" is a very nice label for a bunch of people who are unaware of the world around them until all of a sudden they see something that had been there all the time—maybe for two or three years—and then they say "Oh, it's been underground!"
>
> Brian Cole: I think if they go out and look they'll find a lot more than if they just sit there waiting to die.
>
> Ted Bluechel: But you know, you have the same kind of scene with the young people, you know, the so-called hip people. It's not really a generation gap, 'cause there are just as many un-hip kids as there are old ones. Yeah, I know a lot of hip fifty-year-olds.
>
> Terry: The problem is that labels like that generation gap thing are such gross generalizations. You can't say that a cat who's fifty years old is square: he might be hip in other ways.
>
> Brian: So just being aware of what's happening in the underground movement today doesn't necessarily put you in the hip set.
>
> Larry Ramos: Yeah, but man, we're not discussing any part of the underground. What we're talking about is the idea of

a few journalists who make a buck off that sort of labeling. That's nowhere!

Terry: ...because you see, hipness is just something you realize. Humans have a higher value all of a sudden for some reason, because you've realized something in yourself, man; not in the underground. You can call it Christianity I guess; you can call it whatever you want, you know, but at that time, to me, like...the term hipness was once defined by someone as the sweet fragrance of serenity, ya know what I mean? And I think, not as drug-taking or being hip, or dressing hip, or dressing mod or whatever else's happening like that.

Russ Giguere: Wait a minute, guys, like, listen, you're not talking about hipness; you're talking about fads and stuff like that. Ya know, all the cats in Harlem were hip and hip means one thing: a cat that was aware. And that's all it was!

Terry: It means that they—ah—they get along well with their fellow human beings; they don't step on toes, they're relatively happy...or maybe even sad.

Brian: It had nothing to do with the way you dressed...

Russ: Wait a minute, let me finish. See, a hip person was an aware person and that's...the cats in Harlem labeled it that way. You can wear a Brooks Brothers suit, man, and you can still be hip. You dig?

Terry: I have a personal belief that if you are aware, I have a feeling that you don't classify everything.

Jim Yester: It's a matter of individual understanding and, you know, like, a certain degree of hipness for one person is a hell of a lot more for another, you know...

Ted: Also, if you're hip in Peoria, that's pretty damn hip...

Terry: Yeah, exactly. So it doesn't make a difference what you wear or how you dress, or how you do it up socially. It's a matter of how aware you are of what's happening around you. You don't accept all of it; but at least you know what's happening.

What came out of our mouths ran the gamut of both serious and insane. One time, I kid you not, a reporter asked me, "What do you think about the Pope's edict on birth control?" I was stumped that a stranger would even ask this question of a musician—one has absolutely nothing to do with the other. But without missing a beat, I fired back, "Well, I think if he doesn't want to take birth control pills, he shouldn't have to." (I mean, really. What was I supposed to say? People put way too much value in what "celebrities" think. Live your own life, chart your own course, and don't worry about what anyone else thinks.) Stick to asking celebrities about the things they're good at—in our example, our craft, our art, the *music*. If he were still alive today, Andy Warhol probably would have loved the rise of reality television and its subsequent birthing of so many random people, often of questionable skills, morals, and talent, achieving such wide-reaching fame and cultural interest.

In 1966, our publisher, Beechwood Music Corporation, capitalized on our success by publishing a book, *Crank Your Spreaders*, which featured original poetry, music, writings, biographies, illustrations, and more from each band member. Looking back at it now, you might wonder what drugs we were doing as we each came up with our contributions. Here is one of Jim Yester's:

CONTEMPLATION by Jim Yester

Here I sit on planet Earth: a sphere.
Revolving around the sun: a sphere.
Holding a California orange: a sphere.
Could it be that this orange has some cosmic relationship to
the Earth and sun?
Could this orange, this simple sphere, unlock some mystery
of life?
Could this ball of citric acid unleash some great mystical secret?

Could it be that I'm hung up contemplating my navel?

And here's this one from Ted, who dedicated his poem to our fans in the AAA:

> A poem by Ted Bluechel Jr.
> for members of the
> Association
> Admiration
> Aggregation (AAA)
> to use when
> a commoner parks
> his car, partially blocking off
> their driveway.
> You are
> an inconsiderate dumper
> who, over my drive-way,
> left too much bumper;
> so it seems so very neat
> that next time I'll call
> the Heat
> and you'll quit sending
> me on a bummer.

Or this excerpt from Brian's "Five Scenarios" (which he called a shooting script):

SHOT FOUR

(Interior: a flower store when neighborhoods were in flower—also in Vogue, which the CLERK is reading. We approach with caution and careless rapture.)

> ME
> (with tongue in cheek)
> Could I have some plastic flowers for some plastic people?

CLERK
(a tongueless cheek)
What kind, sir?

ME
(with finger in eye)
How about...Rhoda Hum-drum? Um.

And this from our manager Pat:

He was very young, perhaps less than teen,
he sold papers, shined shoes, worked a printing press,
looked at girls and played football—
    Life was fun
When he was young, yes in his teens,
he worked in mills, factories, sold apples on a stick,
and watermelons, drove a truck,
liked girls and played football—
    Life was fun
He was a young man—war was there—so was he,
he thought of girls and football—
    Life was hardly fun
He was a live young man, joined a carnival,
wrote sport stories, acted some, worked on construction,
on the docks, drew some pictures, boxed a little,
he loved girls and played football—
    Life sure was fun
He was a man, tended bar, sold everything,
promoted all that could be, owned a hotel,
restaurant, nite club, managed boxers, a singer,
a comic, acted some, directed some, produced some.
Adored women—watched football—
    Life sure was wonderful
A bit older...manage a "band," promote a "band,"
like & love a "band,"

idolize women, observe football—
    Life is better than ever

With Pat on our team, we got on the road and began promoting our album across the country. Pat went out on the first tour with us, but as our success grew, he stayed back in the office to manage us and hired a road manager, Lee Liebman, to join our sound guy and light guy on the road. Lee, may he rest in peace, was a damn good road manager. No matter what time you talked to him, whether the go time was midnight or 5:00 a.m., Lee was always dressed and ready to go. We occasionally busted his balls. One time he said, "I don't really think you guys should smoke pot while you're driving." Our reaction was simply to light up another joint!

Lee wasn't a stick in the mud, though. One time when we were in New York and staying at The Warwick Hotel, Lee knocked on my door to ask if I wanted to go to the American Toy Fair being held not far from the hotel. Are you *kidding* me?—of *course* I wanted to go! A toy fair? But the fair was only for toy industry professionals, so how could we get in? No problem—Lee registered us as the fictitious "Joel's Toys, Laguna, CA" and we breezed right inside. The toy fair was huge and wonderful.

Fall 1966 marked the beginning of how we would come to be known as the hardest working band in show business, which wasn't really a compliment. Rick Colecchio, Pat's son, would join us several years later as a crew member, and he estimates we were on the road some 285 days a year. A March 6, 1968, article by Kathy Beck, "'Association' Marked by Versatility, Talent" in Bloomington, Illinois's *The Pantagraph* said, "If the fellows and their comedy seem a little tired, it's probably because they do 250 concerts a year, including five this week." It was a roller coaster. To be in your early twenties, seeing the country through your work as a rock and roll musician, playing to sold-out audiences wowed by our sound, what could be better? The best art presents itself as effortless, which is why people who are looking to criticize might say that the art (the music in this case) you are creating is deceptively easy, as in, "I could do that." But they couldn't.

Danny Hutton describes our music: "Their sound was beautiful. It was intelligent, sophisticated, romantic, complicated music. It was not music a garage band would say, 'Okay, let's do an Association song,' not necessarily because they didn't like it—it's because they couldn't. They didn't physically or mentally have the chops to do it. I like their music because when you heard it, you couldn't just hear it and pick up on it and do it. You had to really sit [with it]—they would combine things sometimes. I knew technically they were combining things, but that would create a third sound and I couldn't figure it out. You had to be there or they had to tell you how they did it, which is a very unique talent. They definitely had their own thing, their own sound." A 1972 article wrote, "Another point to bring out is that despite the number of hits The Association has turned out, very few songs are picked up and recorded by other groups. The sound produced by The Association is so diversified among these individuals that it is almost impossible for this unique blend of harmony in instrument and voice to be duplicated."[66]

Bernie Leadon of The Eagles shares,

"So The Association, with *six* voices…a standard three-note chord only has three notes—then what do you do with the other singers if you are going to have multiple people sing? Well, one thing is—and also, this is an important thing about The Association—their vocal style really had jazz in it, too, because they sang what you call 'altered chords,' which is you stick a fourth note into the chord…the basic notes are tonic, dominant, like one/three/five, like the tonic note on third and the fifth, that's a standard pitch chord. Then you go up to the one again on the top, so there's only the three notes. If you're going to have four different notes at the same

---

66 Bergstrand, Tom. "Association Big Hit With Quad-City Audience." *The Dispatch.* August 23, 1972.

time, one of them has to be an altered tone, which would be like a seventh or a sixth or something like that."

To break Bernie's musical explanation down, our harmonies couldn't be replicated easily—they were created with great thought, care, and consideration.

So in those beginning days where we were crisscrossing the country, there were two station wagons packed with all of our equipment, me, Terry, Jim, Brian, Jules, Ted, Pat Colecchio, Steve Nelson (our sound guy), and Pete Stefanos (our light guy). You'd get to the gig in the afternoon, unpack the equipment, rehearse, and do a sound check, eat a sandwich or something, perform, and then do it all over again the next day, sometimes in the same location if it were a few days' stint, or we'd drive to the next place at the crack of dawn and repeat the drill. To amuse ourselves during the long hours of driving, we'd have water balloon fights between the two cars. Jim Yester recalls, "One time we were doing that and one car went way up ahead and turned around and came back the other way, Terry leaned out of the car, threw a balloon, it hit the windshield right in front of my face and the windshield exploded...My whole face was covered with glass. That ended the water balloon fights from the car." I was sitting next to Jim in the front seat. I got some chunks of glass on me, but it was inconsequential and nothing like Jim—his whole face was covered with a light dusting of glass. Thank goodness he had had the sense to close his eyes.

Ray Staar, who worked with us as our light guy from 1967–69, remembers another instance with Jim. "We were traveling through the mountains or the hills around Pennsylvania, very leafy, very green—we were coming back from some remote location, we were late, and I was driving one of the station wagons—Jim was riding with me. I was in a hurry, I hit a patch of water and spun out. We landed in the ditch next to the road. Fortunately, we weren't hurt. We drove away. Jim never said a word the whole time. He just sat there. I think he said, 'Are you okay?' and we exchanged assurances, but he never mentioned it to anyone, never said anything, Mr. Unflappable!" That's the kind of guy Jim is.

Anyhow, soon after our second album, *Renaissance*, was released in November 1966, Jules left the band. "The band wasn't going the way I thought it should go and I didn't think I could change it, so I said, '*Adios*.' That's really what it was," Jules said in *Where Have All the Pop Stars Gone? Volume 1.* "I was a terrible, terrible, terrible celebrity, mainly because I didn't like it," he added. "I really enjoy my anonymity: It's fun to be high profile, everybody goes, 'ooh-ooh' and that kind of stuff, but I'm just not good at it." Jules went to India when he left the band, and we replaced him with Larry Ramos. For a while, before Jules left and while he was teaching Larry his parts, we were a seven-man band.

Terry was the one who suggested Larry Ramos. At first he asked Mike Brewer, who would go on to write "One Toke Over the Line" with Tom Shipley, but Mike declined, and so he invited Larry, who had enjoyed success singing with the New Christy Minstrels. Larry said he was only interested in joining one of two bands—either The Beatles or The Association. Lucky for us we were one of his two only choices. Larry had started performing at a young age, becoming Hawaii's ukulele champion at age seven, and he'd also performed for a few years with the national tour of the Broadway hit *The King and I*. Larry traveled with a trap case, normally meant to store drums or other musical accessories, but he stored the raw materials to build models in it—and he would build them on the road. He didn't smoke marijuana, but Ted was influential in changing that. Larry had a penchant for the blues and was always trying to get us to record blues songs, but that wasn't really our bag. As we said in the group, "No whining," and the blues had too much whining. We didn't do music that whined.

Anyhow, one night on tour while Larry was traveling with us and learning our music before Jules left the band for India, we were all in the cars when Brian, riding shotgun, threw a firecracker out the window of his moving car. Only it didn't leave his hand and

instead blew it to a raw, meaty pulp. I don't know if he was on drugs
at the time, but he should have been. That night, Jules played bass to
replace Brian, and Larry made his (earlier than anticipated) debut
with The Association. Years later, when we got back together for the
first time, we took a break from a rehearsal and Terry went across
the street for a burger, where he got a trivia question with his meal:
"What 1960s band was the first band of mixed race to have a number
one record?" Terry asked all of us, but we didn't know the answer.
Imagine our surprise when he scratched off the answer to find "The
Association" staring back at him! (The number one record the trivia
question was referring to was "Windy," which we would record for
our second album and Larry and I sang the lead together on.) This
was particularly funny to some members of the band who felt like
Larry never identified with what he was, Filipino. Terry once asked
Larry, "How can you vote for a man (George Wallace) who, if he had
his way, would see to it that you were out of the country?" Larry said,
"I resent that remark," and everyone stared and said nothing. Politics
wasn't a safe topic then and still isn't now.

Ray Staar, who traveled with us and worked on our crew, recalls,
"It was very democratic with The Association. We always went in
the same class—the band members and the support group—we were
always on the plane together...All of the equipment fit into the back
of two Ford station wagons—everybody's amp, Ted's drums, it all
got into the back of those two vehicles. One time we were traveling
and sitting on a tarmac, somewhere up in North Dakota or South
Dakota, way up there, and we weren't going anyplace—there's no
planes, we're in this teeny airport. We start looking around and
outside we saw this stack of equipment sitting off on the side and
we're getting ready to take off. Peter got up and stopped the plane.
He knocked on the door to the pilot's cabin. He was a big Greek guy
you didn't want to mess with. He said, 'If you don't stop the plane,
you'll be looking at the biggest lawsuit you've ever seen.' That was
The Association's equipment. Pete and Steve got off the plane and

repacked the entire belly of the plane to make it fit. The ground crew couldn't do it, but we could."

The travel was rigorous, to say the least—not for the faint of heart. We would go on to play concerts in forty-nine states—we wouldn't play in our fiftieth state, Alaska, until The Association got back together (spoiler alert!) and did a concert with Wolfman Jack and Paul Revere and the Raiders in 1980. Some people thrived on the road; others deteriorated. Terry remembers, "Four days after you get home (from touring), your body lets go of everything that is stored up, and you're really sick. That was happening to all of us on a regular basis. It took us a really long time to understand that if you were going out for six or eight weeks, a week and a half before you came home, you started taking a bunch of vitamins and you quit doing stuff.[67] We were getting home, getting our clothes to the cleaners, and then going into the studio. There was no creative time at all. Unless you were locking yourself up in your hotel room, smoking pot, and eating franchise food all the time—that would be your creative time." Pat Colecchio remembers one of the band members physically assaulting another—not to the point where he had to go to the hospital, but still, it was "hardly a plus for the creative process,"[68] as Pat put it.

That was Terry's experience. We were healthy, just exhausted— if we weren't performing on the road, we were home sleeping at night and working in the recording studio during the day (to be honest, sometimes those day/night activities were reversed) or guest-

---

67 "Stuff" meaning the alcohol and drugs. Let's face it: mostly drugs. Well, mostly drugs for me and the others. With Terry it was mostly alcohol.

68 Unfortunately, Pat is no longer around for me to pick his brain about his experiences, and managers weren't really interviewed (like the band members were). Pat's son Rick is still around, and we are in touch. I am, however, in receipt of a scathing letter Pat once penned (not to me) to "that asshole ingrate whose camouflage of his own subversive dealings had the fucking nerve to demean me," so these words of his that you're reading really did come from his mouth, or that letter, I should say. (He had Italian blood, so when he was mad, he didn't mince words.) I'm not one to throw anybody under the bus, so we'll just have to leave it at that. You'll hear more from Pat later. (It was a long, double-sided letter.)

starring as the musical act on TV shows: *The Tonight Show Starring Johnny Carson, The Dick Cavett Show, The Ed Sullivan Show, The Hollywood Palace, The Smothers Brothers, The Joey Bishop Show, The Red Skeleton Show, The Steve Allen Show*, and more. When we did *The Andy Williams Show*, Andy asked to sing his favorite Association song with us—turns out it was "Changes," from our first album, which Jules had written and normally sang the lead on—but on Andy's show, Jules played backup and we let Andy realize his dream and sing the lead.

We would appear on *The Ed Sullivan Show* three times in less than one year: on December 8, 1968, and March 9 and November 9, 1969. "To a degree that young Americans couldn't comprehend today, *The Ed Sullivan Show* was American popular culture. More than fifty million Americans—over half of the TV-viewing audience at the time—tuned in to it on CBS every Sunday night."[69] Ed Sullivan was driven to the stage door in a limo, where he'd be handed a script for the show after he climbed the stairs, and then go onstage shortly thereafter. He was a very sweet man. On one of our three *Ed Sullivan Show* appearances, he patted me on the backside—like football players on the field sometimes do—as we exited the stage. The camera caught his sweet gesture. Regarding Ed, "Never before and never again in the history of our republic would so many gather so loyally, for so long, in the thrall of one man's taste."[70]

The first time we played New York, we did a concert at the Village Theatre (later the Fillmore East, the East Coast branch of the legendary Fillmore in San Francisco), and Bobby Kennedy and his family were in the audience. It was the same concert David Geffen writes about in the foreword for this book: concert promoter Bill Graham, whom I mentioned earlier, mistakenly billed both The Association and Janis Ian as the headliner, and David swooped in to solve the problem by assigning headliner status to each of us for

---

69   Kaplan, Fred. "Teen Spirit." *Slate.* February 7, 2014.

70   Leonard, John. *Smoke and Mirrors: Violence, Tension and Other American Cultures.* The New Press. April 15, 1998.

alternating performances. He later signed us to William Morris. Terry shares, "The demeanor with which he [Geffen] did it blew everyone's mind."

Pat Colecchio had grown up in a mob neighborhood in Jersey City and moved away from NY to be an independent bookie in Los Angeles and get away from the mob. But he still had all the friends he had grown up with, so inevitably, there were some…tangential connections of which we weren't too fond, including our mob-run booking agency. We wanted to work with William Morris, but had to relieve ourselves of our obligation to this booking agency first.

Some representatives from the booking agency asked Pat to meet them in the ice cream parlor downstairs in the Beverly Hills Hotel. Terry went with him. "They say to him [Pat] they're going to give him cash, tax free, $25,000, if he gets us to stand down from going with William Morris," Terry relays. "Pat says, 'What if I don't get them to stand down from William Morris?' And they say, 'It's going to be hard for them to *play* or *sing*.' Pat gets up and says, 'One second,' and he goes to the pay phone in the ice cream parlor. He makes a phone call, he hangs up, comes back, sits down, and they say, 'What happened?' The pay phone rings, he goes to it, answers it, hands it to the representative of the booking agency. After a short while, they hand the phone back and tell Pat, 'We're very sorry to have bothered you,' and left." Mayor Kenny had called. John V. Kenny had been the democratic mayor of Jersey City, New Jersey, from 1949 to 1953, but he was still very much in power. "If these guys called you," Terry said, "you did what they said." And just like that, we were released from our obligation to the booking agency and free to work with Geffen and William Morris.

I've mentioned Bill Graham several times without properly explaining how the evolution of the modern rock concert owes much to him. In the words of writer Andrew Grant Jackson:

On November 6 [1965], Graham arranged for the Airplane, the Fugs, and poet Lawrence Ferlinghetti to perform at a benefit[71] for Davis's[72] legal fees at the Calliope Ballroom. Experimental films were projected on bedsheets, colored light shows on the walls. Ginsberg was there, of course— and the line went around the block. When the police tried to shut it down, Graham told them Sinatra and Liberace were en route, so they let the show continue. Graham began to realize there was money to be made in the scene...In a year he would open the Fillmore ballroom and become the most famous rock promoter of all time.

Anyhow, during the concert Bobby Kennedy was at, at one point the electricity went out and I slipped into Los Angeles tourist guide mode, mentioning it was my first time in New York City, and then talking about Calvary Cemetery, the big cemetery you see in NYC as you're leaving the airport, and that the closest thing we had in Los Angeles was the Forest Lawn Glendale Cemetery, or "Disneyland of the Dead." That got a big chuckle.

I remember walking down Broadway for the first time, hearing the strains of "Along Comes Mary" blaring from a record store. The song "New York, New York" wasn't written until 1977, but its lyrics "If I can make it there, I'll make it anywhere" ring true. During that first trip on a hot summer night the whole band walked from the Barbizon Hotel downtown to Greenwich Village. As we stretched across the wide Manhattan avenues and passed through neighborhoods, several men called to us from their fire escapes.

"Hey, California!" one shouted.

"Hey, California!" another called out, a block or two later.

We all exchanged looks, but continued on.

---

71   That benefit made $4,000—a lot by 1965 standards.

72   Ronnie Davis was the director of the San Francisco Mime Troupe, which performed satirical guerrilla theater. When the San Francisco Parks and Recreation department deemed the troupe's performance of a sixteenth century play, Il Candelaio, to be in poor taste (it was a thinly veiled criticism of capitalism, racism, and more) and his troupe continued performing anyway, they were busted for obscenity and not having a permit. Ronnie was put on trial. I actually worked sound and lights for the San Francisco Mime Troupe when they did Tartuffe at the Pasadena Ice House on a Monday night in the new room.

"Hey, California!" This was still another stranger, shouting out atop a fire escape.

Curiosity got the better of me. "How do you know we're from California?" I yelled at him.

"Because you're so *clean!*" came the response.

Later, when we played New York again—this time our first concert at Madison Square Garden—we were staying at the Warwick Hotel, and at the corner of Fifty-Fourth Street and Sixth Avenue, I met Moondog, a six foot two blind composer and musician with a long beard and Viking hat, who was standing near the hotel's front door.

I remember the first time I heard his 1956 album, *More Moondog,* with my friend Morris Lafon at his house—I was probably sixteen or seventeen at the time—and I couldn't believe it when I learned he had recorded one of his compositions outside near the Hudson River piers! Moondog was legendary—he invented several instruments and essentially lived his life as a street busker, yet had developed legions of fans, including Janis Joplin, Frank Zappa (who credits him as the impetus for starting the Mothers of Invention), and composer Philip Glass, who cites Moondog's minimalism as inspiration for his compositions and says, "We took his work very seriously and understood and appreciated it much more than what we were exposed to at Julliard."[73]

"How do you make a living?" I asked Moondog.

"I sell songs and poetry," he told me.

I bought some songs and poetry from him—I still have them somewhere. Moondog recorded over a dozen albums, including one with Julie Andrews.

Another time, after performing our concert at Madison Square Garden, Ted and I took a cab downtown to just below Fourteenth Street and headed toward Greenwich Village. After we'd walked a few blocks, a homeless man called out to us from an alley, and then proceeded to eat an entire roast chicken while reciting what he

73   Scotto, Robert. Moondog: *The Viking of 6th Avenue.* Process Media. 2007.

professed was an original poem he'd written. He got only a few lines in before we immediately recognized it as an excerpt from Walter Benton's collection of poetry, *This is My Beloved*. We got a kick out of him claiming he was the author because it's the same poem we'd used as an introduction before "Cherish" at Madison Square Garden earlier that same evening. By the time the man finished his impromptu performance of the famous poem he was passing off as his own, he had devoured his chicken.

"What's that poem worth to you?" he asked us brazenly.

"I'll give him whatever you give him," Ted said to me.

I pulled out $100 and gave it to the man and Ted, always tight with a buck and not anticipating I would be so generous, reluctantly did the same. The man wiped his face with the bag he'd been using as his placemat and began a jubilant dance of joy down the street, waving the money. Only in New York!

One time we were in Chicago to play a series of concerts at the Opera House, a venue that could pack in an audience of about 2,500 people per concert. A voice came over the airport loudspeaker: "We have a call for Percy Curlman. Please proceed to the nearest desk to take the call." I turned to Terry and said, "Terry, that's for you." He looked at me as if I'd grown three heads, but I insisted he take the call. Turns out I was right! At one of those Opera House concerts, we had an issue when our plane landed and we realized our equipment hadn't landed with us. That was when we met our friend Marty Nicosia. Marty remembers, "They came to town and their equipment went to Omaha and you didn't have studio (equipment) rentals in those days. Through mutual friends, a panic call went out—it was on a weekend and somebody got a hold of me and I said, 'No problem.' From that point on I was like a prophet or something. I was a musician as well. That started the friendship and I was their hero through that." Our hero he was!

Yet another time on our way into Chicago in a limo from the airport, Brian spotted a lone fireman's helmet on the side of the highway. He picked it up and returned it to the fire department.

They were very grateful to have it returned to them. It was a third-generation helmet—the entire Chicago Fire Department became instant fans of The Association.

Chicago was good to us. Ray Staar remembers, "Chicago felt like going home because so many guys knew people there. It was like walking into a giant Mediterranean restaurant some place and everyone knew someone. These two muscle guys who drove limos, and I'm convinced were moonlighting as drivers, they knew everybody and they knew every trick in the book. I had a parking ticket once, and one of the guys took it away and said, 'I'll take care of that.' I don't know if he paid for it."

Our limo drivers were Doc and George. Doc was six foot four, 250 pounds. We called him Doc after Doc Savage, the fictional hero made popular by pulp magazines. George was only five foot eight or nine, and would later become a parole officer.

Once on a day off, we drove to Wheaton, Illinois, which is only about half an hour away from Chicago. We were going to the Theosophical Society[74] Bookstore. It was one of those rare times all six of us were together at the same time outside of a concert. There was no one else in the bookstore, and we all walked out with hundreds of dollars of books. It was the sixties, and we were all fascinated with the metaphysical.

Another time on the road near Virginia Beach, we stopped at the ARE (Association for Research and Enlightenment) bookstore, and it was run by Edgar Cayce's[75] brother. I had read maybe four or five books about Edgar Cayce, and the other guys were also familiar

---

74   The Theosophical Society formed in New York City in 1875. It's three objectives were 1) to form a nucleus of the universal brotherhood of humanity without distinction of race, creed, sex, caste, or color; 2) to encourage the study of comparative religion, philosophy, and science; and 3) to investigate the unexplained laws of nature and the powers latent in man.

75   Edgar Cayce, known as "The Sleeping Prophet," was a clairvoyant known to answer questions on anything and everything, including the future, while asleep! He wasn't conscious when he said the things he said—he just went into a sort of trance. He's also given credit for his theories on the therapeutic use of food and the alkaline diet. The bookstore was named after the organization founded to study his work.

with him. Again, we walked out with several hundred dollars worth of books and pamphlets.

And still another time in either Cleveland or Cincinnati, on one of my walks I loved to do around the places we toured, I saw a store selling religious supplies, and they had a great array of ecclesiastical appliques—crosses, birds, doves. I made a pile of things I liked on the counter. "We hardly sell these things," the guy running the place told me. So he gave a good price, and I bought more. I then went back to the hotel and showed the guys what I'd bought. They all said, "Wow!" and then they went back to the store to buy some.

Anyhow, back to 1966. Capitalizing on the success of our summer 1966 release of *And Then...Along Comes the Association*, in the mid-fall of 1966, we released our second studio album with Valiant Records, *Renaissance*. Jim's brother, Jerry Yester, produced it. The album had twelve tracks in total and peaked at No. 34 on the Top 100 *Billboard* albums in March 1967. You can hear the bass marimba on the album—we hadn't intended on using it, but some other recording artist had rented it and left it behind at the studio, so we took advantage of it. We doubled some of the bass lines on the album with the bass marimba. Our biggest successes on the album were "Pandora's Golden Heebie Jeebies" (written by Jules), which reached No. 35 in the late fall of 1966, and "No Fair At All" (written by Jim), which peaked at No. 51 in early 1967. Inspired by Sant Mat, a meditation practice on inner light and sound that came to the US in the 1930s, Jules wrote "Pandora's Golden Heebie Jeebies" as an exercise in meditation. The original demo of the song was stronger than the final recording of it—in truth, we should have released the demo; the interpretation of the other version just wasn't as strong; we couldn't replicate it. The unusual dissonance and chords caused Sam Riddle at KRLA to pan it because it "hurt his ears." I wrote and sang the lead on "I'm the One." I also sang the lead on "Looking Glass" and "Another Time, Another Place," both songs by Jules. "Looking Glass" was the B-side of "No Fair at All," but the single was remixed, and the other ones weren't released as singles, so they had no chance of making a dent in the charts. Jim was moved to write "No Fair At All" as homage to the 1940s ballad "Return to Paradise."

There are band members who will tell you that tensions sometimes ran high during recording sessions—that we were an exhausted group of performers who had just spent weeks and months at a time traversing the US, and during our only downtime back home with our wives, girlfriends, family, friends—our "normal home life"—we had to spend still more time together, ideally at our creative pinnacle, and cut an entire album in forty days. In recording an album, you are creating something new for the very first time, and that actually takes far more energy than performing the same material night after night—when you're touring, as you get more comfortable day in and day out, you learn just how much energy something entails and can then ration it over the course of the day to deliver for the fans at night, and yes, it's tiring, but recording exercises different muscles. In the studio you're on all the time, and if you're the songwriter, forget it, you're fighting for just the right note, the right sound, the right everything. If you're singing the lead, you feel the weight on your shoulders to bring the songwriter's vision to life with your interpretation. It could be easy to nitpick someone's voice or criticize someone's musical ability when you were at it for hours, when you can hear the sound in your head that you want to be able to hear on the record you're recording, and you're struggling to get there, but all you want to do is collapse for a three-day nap on the couch. Truthfully, I managed pretty well, on the road or in the studio, but there were others who had trouble. When he could, Pat made a point to be at our recording sessions to offer what he called "a modicum of stability" to help ensure the creative process was running smoothly and, as he alluded, to keep some of us from killing one another. I personally don't have any memories of people not getting along, but I know others do.

Less than a year later, we recorded our third album, *Insight Out*, which would be our first album with Warner Bros., who bought the Valiant label from Barry DeVorzon in 1967. As I mentioned earlier, the success of The Association is what made Valiant such an attractive purchase for Warner Bros. "When Valiant sold the label to Warner Bros. but still had an existing contract with the group, I fought for and got a larger percentage of the royalties before we went into the studio," Pat said. This was unheard of at the time. I always felt comfortable in Pat's more than capable hands.

Bones Howe, a legendary producer and recording engineer, produced *Insight Out*. In addition to working with us, Bones worked with The 5th Dimension, Tom Waits, The Mamas and the Papas, and Elvis Presley. *Insight Out* had eleven tracks on it, including three of our biggest hits, "Windy," written by Ruthann Friedman; "Never My Love," written by the Addrisi brothers; as well as the anti-Vietnam War anthem, Terry's "Requiem for the Masses."

The Addrisi brothers, Richard (Dick) and Don, wrote songs that felt as though they were crafted specifically for us. When we first heard "Don't Blame It on Me" (which was on our first album), we were excited about working on a tune where all we had to do was add the harmony. Dick and Don were also very funny and very Italian. Don passed on prematurely in 1984, but Dick is still around, still very funny, and still very Italian! "Never" was smooth as silk with (as Bones used to say) a shing-a-ling tempo. Once again, the tune and the arrangement were self-evident. All we did was add harmonies—we just made them thicker. Even the vocal fugue section is as written. Originally, Terry and I were to sing lead on the song, but I felt I had plenty of leads and that Larry, as the new guy, should have more, since it would help introduce him to our fan base. So Larry and Terry recorded the lead—at a studio in New York, strangely enough, since most of the album was done in Hollywood. But we were traveling so much of the time, we just did it where we could! I then did the same thing with "Windy," knowing that having Larry sing the lead with me would help to establish and integrate him right away. Larry was a really good singer.

Ruthann Friedman was a friend of the band who had spent time camping out on our couch on North Ardmore. While living at David Crosby's house on Beverly Glen in LA, she wrote "Windy." Bones and Wrecking Crew member Ray Pohlman, who was one of the musicians playing on the album again and also did some of the instrumental charts, sped up the original song. Ruthann and Birdie sang on the recording with us at the end of the song, along with Clark Burroughs and his wife Marilyn—our voices got so burnt out in a marathon recording session that by the end of it, the women were joining in on the tenor parts.

As I mentioned, the group voted on songs we would record for our albums. A song had to win a majority vote to make the cut—if it tied, it would fall to the wayside, never to be given a second thought. Pat, who in general stayed out of the voting process as per our group rules, remembered the unique case of "Windy": "The only reason I even listened to that song in my office…was because I was curious after hearing the name (of the song), even though it was about a guy. After listening, I heard a hit…when it was played for the group in that time frame, songs were voted in by private ballot by all and tallied by me…it lost in the voting, but I turned the negative vote around and announced it was in. That occurrence was the only dishonest thing I ever did as far as the group was concerned!"

Thank goodness for Pat's instincts on "Windy," which went on to hit No. 1 (and become our second No. 1 hit) on the *Billboard* chart in July 1967 and rank as the No. 4 song that year. In 1999, BMI ranked "Windy" as No. 61 in the Top 100 Songs of the Century—"Never My Love" was No. 2 and "Cherish" was No. 22![76] (Just in case you were about to fight me on The Association's place in American music history.) BMI wrote in their press release:[77]

---

76   See the appendix for this list of BMI's Top 100 Songs of the Twentieth Century.

77   "BMI Announces Top 100 Songs of the Century." December 13, 1999 (from the BMI online archives).

...The second, third and fourth place songs have all attained more than seven million airplays. They are: "Never My Love," written by Donald and Richard Addrisi; "Yesterday" by John Lennon and Sir Paul McCartney; and "Stand By Me" by Ben E. King, Jerry Leiber and Mike Stoller. Rounding out the Top 10 are the six-million-plateau performers: "Can't Take My Eyes Off Of You" by Bob Crewe and Bob Gaudio; "Sitting On the Dock Of the Bay" by Otis Redding and Steve Cropper; Paul Simon's "Mrs. Robinson"; "Baby I Need Your Loving" by the legendary Motown writers Brian Holland, Lamont Dozier and Eddie Holland; John Gummoe's "Rhythm Of The Rain"; and the evergreen "Georgia On My Mind" written by Hoagy Carmichael and Stuart Gorrell.

...John Lennon and Paul Simon each have four songs in the Top 100. Lennon's contributions are his Beatles' classics "Yesterday," "Michelle" (No. 42), and "Let It Be" (No. 89), all co-written by McCartney, as well as his solo outing "Imagine" (No. 96). In addition to "Mrs. Robinson," Simon is represented on the list with "The Sound of Silence" (No. 18), "Bridge Over Troubled Water" (No. 19), and "Scarborough Fair" (No. 31), cowritten by his long-time partner Art Garfunkel.

...The Association was responsible for three ("Never My Love," "Cherish" No. 22 and "Windy" No. 61), as were The Drifters ("On Broadway" No. 45, "Save the Last Dance for Me" No. 49 and "Up On the Roof" No. 92), Elton John ("Your Song" No. 37, "Daniel" No. 66 and "Don't Let the Sun Go Down On Me" No. 76), and Roy Orbison ("Oh Pretty Woman" No. 26, "Crying" No. 74 and "Blue Bayou" No. 85).

As you can see, the company we were keeping on this list is not too shabby. The only groups ahead of The Association are The Beatles (though technically we are tied with them, because "Imagine" was from John Lennon's 1971 solo album by the same name) and Simon & Garfunkel. With three songs on the list, we were tied with the Drifters, who would tour with us in Dick Clark's 1989 American Bandstand Tour; Elton John, who some of the guys in the band met backstage on our first and only tour to Europe; and Roy Orbison.

Both "Windy" (Best Arrangement, Best Contemporary Vocal) and "Never My Love" (Best Group Vocal Performance), along with *Insight Out* (Best Contemporary Album), were nominated for Grammys in 1968. Alas, we won nothing, losing to Bobby Gentry's "Ode to Billie Joe" for Best Arrangement, The 5th Dimension's "Up, Up and Away" for Best Contemporary Vocal and Best Group Vocal Performance, and The Beatles' *Sgt. Pepper's Lonely Hearts Club* for Best Contemporary Album.

Ruthann, who later lived in the group house briefly, wrote "Windy" in twenty minutes. "I was talking about me in that song, and how I wanted to be.[78] I had remembered my high school English teacher saying that if you wanted to catch people's attention in your writing, ask a question right away, and then people want to stick around to see the answer. So 'Who's peeking out from under the stairway?...Everyone knows it's Windy!'"[79] It might be worth it to mention that both parts of that quote are from two separate interviews she did in 2014, and a different sentiment than the one she expressed in decades prior, where she claimed the song was about a guy she knew! In the liner notes for the 2012 release of *The Association: The Complete Warner Bros. & Valiant Singles Collection*, Ruthann says, "It only took me twenty minutes to write, and I wrote it as an escape. There was a songwriter fellow who I will not name that was really... annoying me, and I wanted to think about somebody else. So I made up this other person."

With regard to "Never My Love," the rumor is that it was Paul and Linda McCartney's "song." We recorded a number of songs written

78   Pollock, Bruce, "They're Playing My Song: Ruthann Friedman – 'Windy.'" *Song Facts*. April 15, 2014.

79   Feuer, Daiana. "Ruthann Friedman: See Things as New." *L.A. Record*. July 10, 2014.

by the Addrisi brothers, who were always a hoot when they wanted you to hear a new song—ever the showmen, they'd pantomime or act out parts of the song or row an imaginary boat when you opened the door to welcome them into a meeting. Pat remembered, "When the song ('Windy') ran its course, the DJ at KHJ began playing "Happiness Is" on the album, which in my thinking could have been a bad single release if it had been continued. Bones and I decided immediately the next single release would be the wonderfully recorded and produced "Never My Love." I got on the phone immediately to Bill Drake, program director at KRLA...only a few weeks before I attended a small dinner party at his home and informed him that our next single release would be the aforementioned Addrisi song." A good manager is invaluable: they can push and press for you in a way the artist can't, or in some cases might not be able to (creative artistry and business skills take up different brain space), and Pat was our champion, through and through.

For some of our fans, "Requiem for the Masses" is one of their favorites. Terry was inspired by the call-and-response chorus structure throughout the lesser known Bob Dylan song "Who Killed Davey Moore" (based on the old English nursery rhyme "Who Killed Cock Robin?") wherein each chorus begins with "Who killed Davey Moore / Why an' what's the reason for?" and as each stanza progresses, leads with a "'Not I,' says..." and then a "'Not us,' says," and then a "'Not me,' says..." and so on and so forth. When we were in The Men, we performed "Davey Moore" with the requiem choruses—Terry's idea—and when The Men broke up, it just fell by the wayside. Later, at the group house, I told him he should write something with that structure, as it was very powerful.

So here's how "Requiem" came to be: When we were on tour with the Lovin' Spoonful, we all took off in their chartered plane from Milwaukee to Davenport one freezing winter morning. It was a four-engine prop plane, and they had to de-ice it before we boarded. We managed to take off, but due to the bad weather, were in the air quite

a while, circling and searching for a place to land. We blew the gig
and ended up in Minneapolis. The Spoonful had another obligation,
as did we, so we went our separate ways. We chartered a bus and
Terry, grateful like all of us to have cheated death and not been a
sequel to The Day the Music Died, climbed up into the luggage rack
of the bus to finish writing "Requiem for the Masses." He thought
about the last thing a guy would see before he was killed in a war.

> *Red was the color of his blood flowing thin*
> *Pallid white was the color of his lifeless skin*
> *Blue was the color of the morning sky*
> *He saw looking up from the ground where he died*
> *It was the last thing ever seen by him*

Powerful stuff, huh? And they call us a "sunshine pop" band
(and sometimes a psychedelic band, though that was mostly with our
fourth album, *Birthday*). Being labeled as "sunshine pop" pisses me
off. "Sunshine pop" bands aren't singing about marijuana or soldiers
dying. The term was clearly coined by people who are not musicians.
We made art, and we made it well. "Requiem for the Masses" was
no "sunshine pop." It was the B-side to the "Never My Love" single.
The government tried to discourage radio stations from playing it
because of the antiwar theme. New York DJ Murray the K would add
sounds of live combat before he played the song. Terry recalls that
soldiers listened to Association albums in their bunkers and shared
with him how much they appreciated the song. "I think the saddest,
self-serving contention that I've had is that had we already learned
and been able to perform 'Requiem for the Masses' and had we done
so at the Monterey Pop Festival, that we would have had an entirely
different career. I am really reluctant to say to anyone 'sour grapes,'
but…We would have blown everyone's mind." I happen to agree with
Terry's assessment. Associate Professor of History at University of
South Carolina Lauren Rebecca Sklaroff puts a song like "Requiem
for the Masses" into context:

...Vietnam was different. Unlike the 1940s—when Americans thought the Japanese bombing of Pearl Harbor and Nazi aggression in Europe justified the sacrifices of war—young people in the 1960s were deeply suspicious of the government's decision to go into Southeast Asia. As the military's commitment grew and the body counts piled up, many couldn't understand what they were fighting for.

Songs were able to express these feelings of anger and confusion with lyrics that could be abstract—like Bob Dylan's "Blowin' in the Wind"—or explicit, such as Phil Ochs's "I Ain't Marching Anymore."

Music also filled a void in the country's media landscape. Hollywood didn't release films that probed the complex nature of the Vietnam War until years after the fall of Saigon. While television news broadcasting became more critical after the Tet Offensive, the big networks were hesitant to promote entertainers who were vocally opposed to the war. Popular programs would censor artists who planned to perform protest music; for example, in 1967, folk singer Pete Seeger appeared on *The Smothers Brothers Comedy Hour,* only to discover that his song "Waist Deep in the Big Muddy" would later be cut due to its antiwar message.[80]

Because Vietnam-era musicians seemed to be the only people talking about America's failure to live up to its democratic principles, many young people viewed them as "their own."

Protest music took several forms. There was The Beatles' more tepid "Revolution" and Creedence Clearwater Revival's everyman anthem "Fortunate Son." Groups like the Grateful Dead and Jefferson Airplane excoriated the

---

80   Sklaroff, Lauren Rebecca. "During Vietnam War, music spoke to both sides of a divided nation." *The Conversation.* September 13, 2017.

hypocrisy of American values, shunned commercialism and supported anti-imperial movements across the globe. People chanted lyrics while marching, listened during gatherings like the "Be-In" in San Francisco's Golden Gate Park or simply absorbed the meaning and messages of these songs on their own.

Insight Out was released in the spring and we were still crisscrossing the country, touring and playing to packed houses. On one occasion, the six of us and our crew, Pete Stefanos, Steve Nelson, and road manager Lee Liebman, arrived at a small Midwestern airport, large enough to have a car rental, restaurant, and newsstand. Everyone who worked at this airport came out of their shops to look at us and comment on our clothes and our hair. It was uncomfortable, to say the least. So while the crew sorted out loading our equipment on the plane and returning our rental cars, I went to the restaurant, ate breakfast, and headed to the area where you watched the planes take off and land.

It was then that I noticed two men, probably in their fifties or sixties, standing together— one short and black, and one tall and white with faded red hair, both dressed identically in overalls, blue shirts, and short-brim straw hats. The tall one stood silently with a pipe in his mouth. I started talking to the short guy, whose name was Ed Hemphill (I only remember his last name because we'd worked with "The Pair Extraordinaire" with Marcus Hemphill on bass and Carl Craig on vocals).

Anyway, Ed was waiting for his son, who was in the army and returning from Vietnam. As we were talking, Ed revealed that he was a moonshiner and told me of his adventures with "revenuers" (tax men) and such. Eventually, the whole band and our road crew formed a semicircle around Ed, listening to his stories. Ed's redhead friend never took the pipe out of his mouth, or said a word.

"Have you ever been arrested?" I asked Ed.

"No," he said.

"How's that?"

Before he could answer, the tall, silent white guy finally took the pipe out of his mouth. "Because he makes the best 'shine in the county," he said.

We never did get to sample that moonshine. Ed's son arrived from Vietnam, and we boarded the plane to our next concert.

On June 16, 1967, we opened the legendary three-day Monterey Pop Festival. "Be happy, be free; wear flowers, bring bells," the brochure for the festival advertised. Allen Ginsberg had coined the term "Flower Power" and Abbie Hoffman capitalized on it in just one month before Monterey, at the Flower Power Day Rally, held in New York City and dedicated to honoring soldiers who had died in Vietnam. "The cry of 'Flower Power' echoes through the land. We shall not wilt. Let a thousand flowers bloom,"[81] Abbie said. That fall, an eighteen-year old actor, George Harris, would shove carnations down the rifle barrels of the National Guard at the Pentagon. In addition to the incredible music at Monterey, there were also, believe it or not, "Vocal and guitar workshops, theatrical lighting presentations, an East Indian dance seminar and an Oriental Mediation Room."[82] "At the time," Jonathan Gold wrote for *Billboard*, "Such festivals were commonplace for individual musical genres: Folk festivals were routine, the Newport Jazz Festival was long established, and even Monterey had played host to its jazz festival for nearly a decade. Monterey Pop, though, brought eclectic sounds together from across the country. Peace and harmony radiated from the Bay. A few had attempted it before—in fact, the Fantasy Fair and Magic Mountain Music Festival, which featured The Doors, Jefferson Airplane, and The Byrds, among others, had taken place just a week before—but with rock music in its relative infancy, never had such

81   Hoffman, Abbie. *Revolution for the Hell of it: the book that earned Abbie Hoffman a five-year prison term at the Chicago Conspiracy Trial.* Thunder's Mouth Press, 2005 (edition).

82   Elwood, Philip. "Monterey Festival Starts Popping." *The San Francisco Examiner.* June 16, 1967.

different sounds from such different places come together for the common cause."[83]

Amazingly, the festival was organized in just six to seven weeks. The organizers took their advice and cue from Bill Graham, that concert promoter (remember him from earlier?) who had fled Nazi Germany (where he lost his entire family) and singlehandedly ushered in the era of rock concerts as stadium-sized events with incredible sound, a line of merchandise, and massive audiences, from his beginnings with the Fillmore in San Francisco to the 1985 Live Aid concert.

Monterey Pop Festival tickets ranged in price from $3.00 to $6.50 for the day and though estimates vary, it is thought 200,000 people attended. Dunhill Records executive Lou Adler, who along with John Phillips of the Mamas and the Papas organized the festival, shares, "...rock 'n' roll was not considered an art form the way that jazz was...With the possibility of doing something at Monterey, the same place as the jazz festival, it just seemed like a validation to us."[84] The festival almost didn't happen. Locals were nervous about their town being overrun by a bunch of longhaired hippies. To ease their concern and detract attention—or perhaps I should say attract (more desirable) attention, John Phillips wrote "San Francisco (Be Sure to Wear Flowers in Your Hair)" in about twenty minutes. It was released on May 13, just one month before the festival, and hit No. 4 on the *Billboard* chart every week in July that year.

We were the first of thirty-two musical acts to appear over those three days, and nearly all of the artists, including us, worked for free, with only our lodging and transportation paid. Most of the money from ticket sales went to charities—a Harlem music education program, a minority scholarship system for broadcasting students, and free Los Angeles and San Francisco clinics. Monterey

83   Gold, Jonathan. "How Monterey Pop Set the Stage for Festivals to Come." *Billboard*. June 16, 2017.

84   Sisario, Ben. "Monterey Pop, the Rock Festival that Sparked it All, Returns." *The New York Times*, April 14, 2017.

was unusual in that many of the performers stayed or arrived early to watch their peers perform over those three days. I remember meeting Jimi Hendrix while we were in line to get some grub, before we'd all even heard one another play. At that point, I had no idea who he was or what he did. And so imagine when I first saw and heard him play! I'd never seen an act like Jimi Hendrix—and they were just a trio!—drums, bass, and guitar. He blew my mind—he was spectacular. When he lit his guitar on fire during his performance, it was obviously show biz, but it was still great art. "Cass Elliott and I sat together and watched Hendrix together," Terry recalls. "We were about sixty to seventy feet from him, the second or third row, maybe."

Henry Diltz

Birdie and I sitting in the audience seats at Monterey Pop before sound check for The Association. She's not taller than me—I'm slouching in my chair. We had no idea that that festival would go down in rock history.

"Terry?" Terry recounts Cass asking him.

"Yes, Cass?"

"Is he fucking his guitar?"

"I think so, Cass."

Everyone always talks about Janis Joplin, The Who, and Jimi Hendrix, the three acts most etched in the minds and post-dialogue of the Monterey Pop Festival experience. Monterey was where the rest of the world first witnessed the raw, sexual vocal talents of Janis, the guitar smashing antics of The Who, and that sacrificial offering Jimi made when he gave his guitar up to fire. The only act missing from the lineup was The Beatles. They had stopped touring in 1966 but were kind enough to send along an illustration for the program (Paul sat on the Board of Governors for the festival, along with Mick Jagger, Brian Wilson, Paul Simon, Donovan, and Smokey Robinson).

I remember hearing Ravi Shankar, who was first up on June 18, the last day of the festival. The kid in me was so excited to see him perform live—I had first heard his "Morning Raga" at a party in San Diego when I was just seventeen or eighteen, and his music knocked me out. I went out the next day and bought my first two Shankar albums. Anyhow, just before he began his performance in Monterey, he asked that no one smoke during his segment—so no one did. He actually performed on this long runway that extended out into the audience from the regular stage. The audience response was tremendous. I'm sure most of them had never heard him before, and certainly not live. In looking back on his contribution to the rock and roll canon, *Rolling Stone* wrote of that Monterey performance, "Shankar's elegant and blazing Sunday afternoon set and the sudden, volcanic applause at the end, by a truly stunned audience....an extraordinary moment in his life—and rock's expanding consciousness."[85]

I also have memories of Moby Grape—helmed by Peter Lewis, actress Loretta Young's son—performing. Their music was something else and they moved with so much ease. Their first album was produced by Columbia in 1967, and the label would release five of their songs *at the same time* (as I shared earlier, artists didn't often have control over these decisions)—as a result, none of them made it into the Top 40...and they should have, their music was great! But it just goes to show that it can really be a gamble when it comes to

---

85   Fricke, David. "From Monterey Pop to Carnegie Hall: The Best Recordings of Ravi Shankar." *Rolling Stone.* December 13, 2012.

making the right decision for what songs to release in what order and when. Sometimes it works out, other times you hold your breath and hope for the best, and still other times you make a stupid decision that only becomes clear in twenty-twenty hindsight! At Monterey, for some reason, Moby Grape denied the festival permission to film their performance, so only those of us who had the pleasure of seeing them live can carry the memory of it with us.

Documentary filmmaker D. A. Pennebaker, who'd gained popularity through his 1967 film *Don't Look Back*, which followed Bob Dylan on his 1965 tour of England, was given a $200,000 advance to film the Monterey Pop Festival with a crew. Originally the film was intended as a ninety-minute ABC special for their new "Movie of the Week" series, but when sponsors weren't interested, it was released theatrically. "*Monterey Pop* never aired on ABC, the network that bankrolled it—a decision made by Tom Moore, the head of ABC at the time and, according to (Lou) Adler, 'a very conservative Southern gentleman.' We showed him Jimi Hendrix fornicating with his amp and we said, 'What do you think?' Adler recalls. And he said, 'Keep the money and get out.' He said, 'Not on my network.'"[86]

Even though we kicked off the entire historic, legendary weekend, The Association was not featured in the original release of the film. John Phillips introduced us, and we opened with our "Machine" bit, always a bit of a thorn in the side of some band members, followed by "Enter the Young," "Along Comes Mary," "Windy," and likely "Cherish" and "Never My Love," though all of the official set lists out there are somehow "incomplete" when it comes to The Association. We did for free what we were paid big bucks to do all over the country: wear our smart ensemble (at this point in time it was sports coats with shirts and ties), sing our six-part harmonies, and entertain. This is part of Terry's beef when he says he thinks history may have played out differently had we sung "Requiem for the Masses." In opening the festival, we were setting the tone for the entire weekend—we just

---

86   Ingles, Paul. "A Look Back at Monterey Pop, 50 Years Later" on *All Things Considered*. NPR. June 15, 2017.

had no way of knowing that what we were putting out there would be so drastically different from all of the other offerings, or that it would be easier for journalists and history to write us out of their accounts. One reviewer, looking back in 2015, wrote, "The opener, however, was already a successful AM pop act. Known for their beautiful harmonies and radio-friendly melodies, the Association were quite an interesting choice to begin a show that would also feature the likes of Country Joe and Paul Butterfield, and their inclusion signaled a sort of a changing of the guards in popular music. But in spite of the competition, the Association held their own, opening with a great rendition of their first hit, 'Along Comes Mary.'"[87,88]

We had, as I mentioned, recently finished recording *Insight Out* and Jules, though he was back in the US, was not yet performing with the band again. He did, however, perform at Monterey Pop with another band that called themselves The Group With No Name. "We had just started rehearsing, and one of the guys in the band was friends with Lou Adler," Jules explains. "(Lou) asked, 'Do you guys want to play?' And he said, 'Yeah, sure, we'll come play.' We had rehearsed three times at the most. It was terrible, it was awful... That was it. We didn't do anything else." One reviewer who was there wrote of The Group With No Name's performance at Monterey that they "may well not last long enough to get a name." "No one seems to have recognized, recorded, or recalled anything they played. The band was led by Cyrus Faryar, a founding member of the Modern Folk Quartet who had also played with the Whiskeyhill Singers."[89] Still looking back, *Rebeat* reflected, "The Group With No Name is arguably the greatest mystery of Monterey Pop. It's essentially impossible to find anything about them, other than that those who heard them play reported they were terrible...nobody seems to have

87   Unico, Gretchen. "Jukebox: Down in Monterey." *Rebeat*. June 19, 2015.

88   We actually opened Monterey with "Enter the Young," which I just shared, but this song isn't included in the CD box set or in the film.

89   Marsh, David. "'This whole weekend was a dream come true'...Monterey Pop Festival, day three (Sunday).'" *And And And*. June 19, 2017.

recorded them, but unlike anyone else on the bill, their set list is completely unknown." Jules didn't even watch us perform. "I knew what they were going to do," Jules says with a smile.

On Friday night, June 16, we opened the festival. We were followed by The Paupers, Lou Rawls, Beverley (Kutner), Johnny Rivers, Eric Burdon & The Animals, and Simon & Garfunkel.

In a recent article commemorating the fiftieth anniversary of the Monterey Pop Festival, *The Santa Cruz Sentinel* wrote, "We can look back now," said music journalist Joel Selvin, "and see an entire kind of music onstage that was over by the time that weekend was done. Look at Friday night—The Association, Johnny Rivers, Lou Rawls. For the most part, they were never heard from again."[90] Ouch! Really, Joel Selvin? We have a song that is No. 2 ("Never My Love," remember?) among three of our songs listed on the most played hundred songs of the twentieth century, and we're still playing concerts to this day, but we were never heard from again?

In the early nineties, Rhino Records released a thirtieth-anniversary boxed CD set, "The Monterey International Pop Festival Box," in which we were included, but only "Along Comes Mary" and "Windy" made the cut. *The Salina Journal* of Salina, Kansas, wrote, "We discover, perhaps for the first time, that the baroque pop-vocal group known as The Association was no mere recording studio contrivance, but rather a well-prepared stage act that could make breakthrough hits 'Along Comes Mary' and 'Windy' sound as convincing in a live setting as they could within the sheltered confines of a studio. Here is an Association performance from a time when many critics were dismissing the band as a collegiate knockoff of The Beach Boys, and the ensemble proves to hold its own nicely in the company of such rowdier, born-to-the-stage acts as Canned Heat, Jimi Hendrix, and Janis Joplin."[91] I'm glad you tout our musical

---

90   Baine, Wallace. "The 1967 Monterey Pop Festival remains the cultural high point of the Sixties." *The Santa Cruz Sentinel*. June 14, 2017.

91   Price, Michael H. "'Monterey Pop Festival' album a treasure." *The Salina Journal*. January 13, 1993.

capabilities, but we never would have had the success we had if we weren't the real deal and we didn't have the fan base to support us. *The Orlando Sentinel* wrote in their review of the CD box set, "The biggest shocker is pop group The Association. Its lush harmonies weren't just the product of studio tinkering, it turns out, and aggressive bass lines and a sharp-edge Rickenbacker guitar sound make 'Windy' and 'Along Comes Mary' sound like more than moldy oldies. (The guys still look like goofballs in the photos, however. Everyone else is pictured wearing beads and colorful scarves or at least turtlenecks—they're wearing suits and ties.)"[92] First of all, we were actually in sports coats, shirts, and ties at the time, not full-blown suits. Secondly, those suits are *exactly* what helped set us apart when we got our start. (Yes, I know I've told you that already, but since you weren't there and you don't know, or if you were there but you can't remember, I want to make it clear so there's no confusion.)

Ironically, one night after we opened Monterey Pop, just two hours away in San Francisco, The Kingston Trio, after nine years of touring and making nineteen hit albums, gave their final performance in their two-week stint at the hungry i nightclub. You have to understand—The Kingston Trio was really a supergroup. Music historians will analyze the symbolism of The Kingston Trio playing their final concert the same time the one and only Monterey Pop Festival took place, and use it as a platform to insist that bands like us and The Kingston Trio were beginning their decline, their phasing out, to make way for a new era of rock and roll. I call BULLSHIT. All of us who didn't die from a drug overdose are still touring today—The Association and The Who, for example, to name two in a long list of many.

Regarding The Who, we did several concerts with them— when they first began touring the states, they would open for us and we would be the headliner. Believe it, it's true! Their popularity skyrocketed after they performed live at Monterey on Sunday,

92   Gettelman, Parry. "Monterey Pop." *The Orlando Sentinel.* p. 75. January 22, 1993.

June 18, 1967. They finish their concerts in uniquely The Who fashion—with Pete Townshend standing on top of four speaker cabinets, Godlike, before then proceeding to jam the neck of his guitar directly into one of the speakers while Keith Moon trashed his drum set. Equally fascinated and full of horror, the audience couldn't take their eyes off the spectacle. The first time we saw The Who perform, Terry and I were standing to the right side of the bleachers on a football field at the Illinois State Fair, where they were opening for us. Pete stood atop those large speakers, raised his guitar to the heavens, and then shoved the neck of the guitar directly into them.

After he was done, Terry turned to me and asked, "How are we gonna follow that?"

"No problem," I said, "we do what we do, and they do what they do."

We got our usual standing ovation and everything was right with the world. That whole finale to their gigs began in a concert they performed in London, where Pete lifted his guitar over his head and it accidentally went through the ceiling of the Railway Hotel. Ever the performer, Pete just passed it off as though he'd intended it to go that way and kept jamming his guitar into the ceiling. The press promised to put it on the front page if he did it again, so at another concert, Pete repeated the show and it became a permanent part of the act. Terry remembers, "They invited us for tea back at the hotel. [They were] apologizing for still blowing up...their instruments, which they were trying to shake. They were embarrassed that they were still doing it, as opposed to just getting up and being a great band...Everybody had to have shtick in England because there were only twelve major performance places. So in order to get hired in a big draw venue, you had to have shtick. You either had to have Beatles hair, you had to dance The Freddie, you had to have outrageous outfits with big glasses, you had to blow your instruments up." We never did have tea with The Who; likely we had to get back on the road for our next concert.

On more than one occasion, there was a time when "special guest stars"
The Who opened for us. The Who's finale was a tough act to follow, but our
sound blew audiences away every time. This advertisement was for a concert
on November 18, 1967, at the San Francisco Cow Palace.
We played The Hollywood Bowl the next night.

If you want to know the secret behind The Who's finale of destruction, their crew would hit pawn shops in whatever town they could and purchase playable cheap guitars so Pete could easily sacrifice one at the end of each show. As for the stacked speaker cabinets, only the bottom one actually had speakers in it, so Pete would always be sure to shove his guitar into the top speakers only.

The remaining cabinets were empty and covered with speaker cloth, which the crew replaced after each show. No one could move like Townshend and Daltrey, and Moon and Entwistle were no slouches, either. Their calculated act of destruction was rock and roll showmanship at its best.

I recently celebrated the fiftieth anniversary of Monterey Pop (along with Ted) at the Grammy Museum in Los Angeles in the spring of 2017. Nothing makes you feel old like celebrating the fiftieth anniversary of something you remember like it was yesterday. According to *Billboard* (and I agree), "Monterey Pop was seen as one of the first breakthroughs of the counter-culture movement. During a time of tremendous political unrest, Monterey Pop was not just a music festival, but a moment in time."[93] Monterey is credited as ushering in the Summer of Love and its popularity has escalated to mythological status, likely because not only was it a pioneer rock festival featuring iconic superstars, some of whom later met their tragic death, but also because there never was another festival. In a laugh-out-loud 1968 article debating whether or not there would be another festival, Jann Wenner, cofounder of *Rolling Stone*,[94] wrote:

> One of the City Council members who is for the Festival—in reply to the anti-Festival attacks of Monterey's mayor—best summarized the illogical outcry: "The real problem is that the young people it attracts have long hair and funny clothes and are somehow different and we don't understand them so we don't want them. Isn't that right?"
>
> The local newspaper—the *Monterey Peninsula Herald*—carried two stories last February 19, one with the news that the festival would probably happen again, and another next to it which began: "Almost like Horatio at the Bridge,

---

93   Gold, Jonathan. "How Monterey Pop Set the Stage for Festivals to Come." *Billboard.* July 16, 2017.

94   Wenner, Jann S. "A Bloody Battle over Monterey Pop Festival." *Rolling Stone.* April 6, 1968.

Monterey Mayor Minnie D. Coyle symbolically stood at the city gates last night ready to protect the citizenry from the 'flower children.'"

… Monterey Mayor Minnie Coyle is a heavyset spinster with tinted hair whose attacks against the Festival do not seem to be from fear of the unknown but from a curiously personal motive. Last year she asked to be put on the Pop Festival's all-star Board of Governors. Phillips turned her down. This year she seems to want her revenge on Phillips and all the beautiful people who left her behind. Around her rallied the opponents of the Festival.

Jann is about the same age as I, and *Rolling Stone* just celebrated the same milestone birthday as Monterey Pop. Jann, in an interview for *AARP The Magazine*,[95] said on the founding of *Rolling Stone*, "I wanted my generation to have a say in the national conversation. And I think we got there really quickly. We've had crusades on drug legalization, the environment and drug control. We've helped move the needle. Our generation hasn't won every issue. But we've moved the conversation along." I agree with Jann. Rock and roll was and is more than just something you listen to for pleasure— the social conscience fueling it and influencing the political and social landscape, especially back then, cannot be ignored. We haven't yet made it into the Rock and Roll Hall of Fame, but the rumor is that's the result of bad blood between Jann and Terry Kirkman, the details of which have never been disclosed and are only known by the parties involved. I would say, however, that The Association more than fits their criteria: "Artists—a group encompassing performers, composers and/or musicians—become eligible for induction twenty-five years after the release of their first commercial recording. Besides demonstrating unquestionable musical excellence and talent, inductees will have had a significant

---

95   "What I Know Now: Jann Wenner" *AARP The Magazine*. p. 16. October/November 2017.

impact on the development, evolution, and preservation of rock and roll."[96] We should be in there—we had chart-topping hits that have some of the highest airplay in the world today, we opened Monterey, and we opened many venues whose doors had previously been shut to rock and roll.

Sometime shortly after Monterey, we went to rehearse for our appearance on the weekly TV variety show, *The Hollywood Palace*. Bing Crosby was the host and guests included Diahann Carroll, Joey Heatherton, comedian Milton Berle—the original "Mr. Television" beginning in the late 1940s, affectionately known to millions of fans as "Uncle Miltie"—and beloved singer/comedian Jimmy "Schnozzola" Durante. Ravi Shankar, whom I loved at Monterey, was also on the bill, but we didn't see him perform.

I went back to Durante's dressing room as I wanted to meet him, but at least twenty people were in there milling around. A few moments later, the crowd parted and I was able to enter. Durante was sitting in a tall chair in the middle of the room, and as I approached him, I was only able to utter, "Mr. Durante—" before he grabbed me and hugged me. He was a warm, genuine man.

My experience of Milton Berle, on the other hand, was not enjoyable, but it was memorable. When he first met the band, he greeted me by sticking his tongue down my throat. I didn't miss a beat—and stuck my tongue back down his throat. He really didn't like that and it obviously bothered him that my mind wasn't blown by his action. At any rate, we continued our rehearsal.

During a break in the taping of the show the following day, we were standing onstage with Crosby, Durante, Carroll, Heatherton—and Berle. I was directly behind Durante. An announcement came over the loudspeaker that some technical adjustments were being made. The performers' microphones were live and Berle began making rude comments about a lady in the audience a few rows back. He kept at it, and the comments grew more and more rude.

---

96   Critera for inductees, according to the Rock & Roll Hall of Fame website.

I don't remember what his remarks were, but that gentle gentleman Jimmy Durante was appalled. He bowed his head and shook it as I heard him say quietly to himself, "God have mercy on his soul."

Milton Berle and me minutes after our saliva exchange at the Hollywood Palace. Brian is on the right and Terry is in the background.

At the end of the summer of 1967, we continued playing major venues that had never before been open to rock and roll acts, one of those being the iconic Cocoanut Grove, which was part of the Ambassador Hotel in Los Angeles. The Ambassador Hotel was the location of the second and twelfth Academy Awards, but would become probably most famous for the June 6, 1968, assassination of presidential candidate, US Senator, and former Attorney General Robert F. Kennedy. (Incidentally, when Bobby Kennedy was assassinated, Pat Paulsen was running for president and hosting a huge victory party at what was known as the Earl Carroll Theater at the time on Sunset Boulevard—he was always pulling some crazy stunt—and the FBI showed up to ensure something didn't also happen to Pat.) The Ambassador was a stately grand hotel with incredible landscaped grounds, bars, restaurants, and shops. Pat Colecchio said, "Who do you think got the group to play venues never before considered in rock and roll circles?…Only after relentless prodding by me, Tanglewood, Saratoga Performing Arts Center, Cocoanut Grove…" Pat was like a dog with a bone on the phone with William Morris and the concert halls, negotiating the best and most for us. Not every band could have bridged that cultural gap in audience demography to play those houses, but we could, and that was the combination of everything working together—our sound, our harmonies, our routines, and our wardrobe choices. (Take that, Monterey Pop selective history omitters!)

We played the Cocoanut Grove September 5–8, 1967, and during one of those concert nights, Joey Bishop presented us with a gold record for "Windy." Opening night was packed and as the lights came up, I spotted George Burns and Carol Channing at the front center table. As I mentioned earlier in the book, we had guest-starred in a TV special we'd recently taped with both of them, the one where Carol sang and danced a shortened version of "Along Comes Mary" as "Along Comes Carol."

After the first few songs at the Cocoanut Grove I said, "Ladies and Gentlemen, I'd like to take this opportunity to introduce the man who taught us everything we know about singing: Mr. George Burns. And of course, the lovely Miss Carol Channing."

The audience cracked up as Carol beamed and George stood to wave his cigar in greeting. Some of the guys in the band confessed they had romantic liaisons at the Cocoanut Grove Hotel, but I never did.

To give you an idea of our journey up until that point, and the significance of opening at the Cocoanut Grove, take a read of what *Cash Box* had to say in their September 16, 1967 review of our performance:

> It has taken the Association machine approximately twenty-two months to travel the twenty-two mile route from a Salvation Army building on Brand Blvd. in Glendale (the Ice House where they debuted in November of '65) to the considerably more fashionable and lucrative surroundings of the Cocoanut Grove, their first major nitery engagement.

En route and somewhere along the way they have divested themselves of their six button vested hopsack ivy league haberdashery (supplanted by bizarre gray-on-blue Beau Brummel uniforms ornamented with black satin lapels), disassociated a manager, three record producers and one lead composter-guitarist (Gary Alexander, replaced by Maui marauder ex-Christy Minstrels banjoist Larry Ramos). They have also basked in the bulleted warmth of three prodigious LP's, a quartette of top ten singles and in the sale of Valiant Records, their former logo, to Warners for an estimated $1,000,000, a considerable source of this revenue for their contract.

The Association is a big business machine. But too, they are among the most competent, concise and harmonious folk-rock combos on record...

In reviewing their Ice House debut almost two years ago we noted that "if musical merit is any indication, they should prosper wherever they are."

Hal Bates wrote of those concerts in "Association Sounds Win Grove Fans" for *Valley News* on September 8, 1967, "Relying on all the objectivity I could whip up, I saw them as typically rock, typically noisy, yet atypically entertaining...They created interesting harmonic qualities greatly enhanced by excellent orchestrations. These arrangements are their biggest asset." Pete Johnson wrote "Association Opens at Cocoanut Grove" in the *Los Angeles Times* one day earlier:

The Association ended a two-year trek from the Ice House to the Cocoanut Grove Tuesday night, simultaneously marking their total absorption by the establishment and the Grove's total conversion from the champagne to the Pepsi generation...They are polished performers, confident of their vocal and instrumental abilities, with bright comic

routines (which, unfortunately, change insufficiently between appearances)…All are good singers, enabling them to
achieve a varied array of solo and harmonic combinations, a
flexibility which combines with the span of their material—
hard rock, ballads, folk songs and humorous numbers—to
keep the act consistently interesting…Their instrumentation ranged from the simplicity of two soft guitars to the
massive sound of three guitars, an organ, a recorder, a trumpet, tambourine and drums (not all at once, but in combinations of six). Vocals spanned all the combinations from
solos (alternated through the group) to a total choral blend.

In 1968 we received the Bill Gavin Award for Best Pop-Rock
Artists of 1967—the runner-up was The Beatles—and we tied with
The Doors' "Light My Fire" for first place in KHJ's Million Dollar
Battle.[97] I can't even remember exactly what that award was, but hey,
we won first place! We wound down the year with more touring and
TV appearances and were back in the studio yet again, working on
our fourth album, *Birthday*, which was also produced by Bones Howe
in multiple recording sessions held throughout the fall and winter of
1967 and early 1968. *Birthday* had eleven tracks, two of which were
hit Top 40 singles for us: "Everything That Touches You," written by
Terry and sung by Terry and Jim, hit No. 10 on the charts, and "Time
for Livin'," another Addrisi brothers song, reached No. 39. I wrote
and sang "The Time It Is Today" while staying at the Warwick Hotel.
Birdie was with me and I wrote it while she went out to grab lunch. It
was later released as the B-side of our "Goodbye, Columbus" single
in January 1969.

Sunrise, sunset
What you're born with is what you get
Let your fear just pass away, then your love will fill your days
I know

---

97   "Association Opening Stand at Maryland." *Progress Bulletin*. May 26, 1968.

I need so little, yet so much
Child's sweet laughter, woman's touch
I can't say just what is real, all I know is what I feel
I know

The time it is today, and we must find our way
My heart it clearly states, the answer's not in hate
I once believed that life was but a dream
But now I know that love's a flowing stream
They're lying, killing, they're pushing their rules
They tell you the prophets all are just fools
But I know different and I won't be used
It's they that are lost, it's they are confused

Sunrise, sunset
What you're born with is what you get
All your worries, all your fears
They don't change the passing years
I know

My favorites on that album are "Everything That Touches You,"
"Come On In," and "Like Always."

The album peaked at No. 23 on June 15, 1968. My friend Randy
Sterling, a musician who became a music engineer, created the
bass line for "Everything That Touches You" in five minutes. We
had actually worked together before when we were hired to play a
graduation party while I was still working at The Ice House. The bass
line in "Everything That Touches You" was challenging to play, so
when it came time for the recording and Joe Osborn had to play it, he
did the same thing Randy did! He said, "Give me five minutes." We
took a break, returned five minutes later, and Joe had it all figured
out. The result is what you hear on the recording.

In May 1968, not long after *Birthday*'s release, we kicked off our
five-week (first and only) European tour (and promotional album
tour) at the First International Pop Festival at the Palazzo dello Sport

in Rome, held May 4 through 7. The Move, a lesser known British rock band (among American audiences) that enjoyed enormous popularity abroad but never made it in the States, went onstage before us, and the Italian audience hated them with a passion. They booed and booed, but the band wouldn't stop—so the audience stormed the stage and began destroying the microphones and set. They had to pause the show for at least thirty minutes while the crew scrambled to find enough replacement microphones. The audience grew restless, clapping and chanting, "Boom! Boom! Boom!" Jim Yester recalls, "We started with 'Enter the Young' and as soon as we got the first big vocal break, they all stood up and applauded." Ray Staar, who was on our crew and traveled with us, remembers, "They would hit harmonies and the audience didn't know what they were saying by and large, but they were responding to the sound—howling with approval at the chords." That was a far cry from another memory of Ray's from a time we performed in Texas. "Russ sang 'Blistered,'" says Ray. "The audience reaction had been tepid. They were polite, but (there was) no real enthusiasm. At some point I thought something's gotta give. The song ends rather quickly. No big buildup and no indication it's going to end. They got to the end and nobody clapped. It was dead silence. I was running the lights and had a headset on, I was with a kid from the AV department from the college—this kid was trying to be my friend. When the crowd didn't say anything, he said out loud, 'These uncles don't know shit from a tree!' Heads snapped around at the light booth where I was and people started coming toward us and a couple of security guys took me by the arm and led me out and I don't know what happened after that. Most of the time the audience was very engaged. That was the only time I know (of that) they didn't get a great response."

The festival wasn't well reviewed by *Billboard*, and The Association wasn't even mentioned. US newspapers ran headlines like "Europe's First Pop Festival Lays An Egg."[98] In "Europe Music Festival Gets Financial Aid," *The Shreveport Times* wrote:

---

98   The newspaper that ran that headline was Fremont, California's *The Argus*.

Europe's first pop music festival seemed like a bad dream Sunday to the men who planned it. The organizers agreed it was a disaster in every way.

But the festival, which began ninety minutes late Saturday night before a jeering, whistling crowd of two thousand, was not closing down until Tuesday, as scheduled.

The reason for holding out was money. A West German television company purchased film rights—and thereby guaranteed the bills would be paid for musicians from the United States, Britain, France, Italy, Czechoslovakia, Yugoslavia and Japan.

"Sure, we'll complete the festival," organizing secretary Alan Zion told newsmen. "We're going to learn a lot from our mistakes."

The mistakes ranged from mechanical breakdowns in the sound system to rebuffing the few movie stars who turned up with free tickets and then were shunted into the bleachers of the glass domed Sports Palace. None of the stars stayed around long.

Two of the scheduled groups begged off, to be replaced by others, including one led by an Indonesian girl folksinger who was booed offstage after one number.

"It is impossible to be an artist here," a member of the band shouted to the longhaired, hippie-dressed crowd.

Most of the crowd stayed around to see the festival star, British pop singer Donovan, who appeared in loose white suit and gold braid.

During his forty-minute appearance, the twenty-three-year-old composer of such hits as "Sunshine Superman," "Mello Yello" and "Jennifer Juniper" had trouble tuning his guitar.

"Be cool," he said when the booing began. "It is essential."

Much of the trouble plaguing the festival—advertised as the first of its kind in Europe—was attributed by Zion to lack of time to organize.

The festival was postponed once after financial and managerial snags. Only with the signing of a key television contract seven days ago did things finally get moving.[99]

Whatever the press was back home, I was there, and I can tell you that overall, European audiences were delighted by our sound and welcomed us with open arms. We went on to play the New Musical Express (NME) Festival at the Tottenham Court Royal in London, appear on *Top of the Pops*, and perform in concert with the Rolling Stones, Dusty Springfield, Status Quo, Amen Corner, the Herd, the Move (again!), Cliff Richard, Scott Walker, and the Love Affair as part of the NME Winner's Concert at Wembley Empire Pool. The *New Musical Express* declared, "…the astonishing music and vocalizing of The Association was pure mastery."[100] At the taping for *Top of the Pops*, we had to rerecord our instrumentals for "Time for Livin'" and then sing along to them live. That's how they did it there. "For over forty years, everyone…stopped by the BBC's weekly *Top of the Pops* to perform their latest single as either a lip-sync or sing along with a prerecorded backing track. It was a tradition: rite of passage. You went on the UK equivalent of *American Bandstand* and pretended to perform live."[101] During that recording, Terry recounts, "Elton John fell in love with Ted so hard, he didn't know what to do with himself. Little Richard was pounding on Ted's door (later, in Vegas). Ted had gay guys in airports follow him into the restroom and try to peer through the booth."

At Wembley, Mick Jagger burst through the door to our dressing room, very polite and complimentary of our sound, declaring, "I've

---

99   "Europe Music Festival Gets Financial Aid." *The Shreveport Times*. May 6, 1968.

100   "'Six Man Band' to Appear." *The Baltimore Sun*. March 18, 1969.

101   "15 Most Outrageous Faked Musical Performances." *Rolling Stone*. February 6, 2014.

never heard anyone sing like that." My buddy Howard Kaylan of the Turtles was interviewed in a recent book where he recounted a meeting with Brian Jones of The Rolling Stones, where Brian admitted he was a fan of The Association!

On the Turtles' first trip to England in 1967, we met the Beatles. Graham Nash took us to the Speakeasy Club. Lennon and McCartney sang "Happy Together" at the table. Paul and I also traded verses on Don and Dewey's "Justine."

I met Jimi Hendrix. He got me so high on grass in a club that I puked on his suit. But he did come to see our show that the Turtles did at the Speakeasy. I left the club and wanted to go back home. "I gotta get out of this country. I gotta go back home where somebody is waiting for me and they know who I am."

Brian Jones then asked me for an autograph, and I signed it. I didn't really look up when I did it. I almost did one of those double takes where you look behind you to see who he was really talking to, 'cause I didn't think it was me. He was so sincere. I was very shocked. I didn't realize he was a fan of West Coast pop music, or that he cared at all about harmony stuff, let alone that he was a collector of it. And really big into the Mamas and the Papas and the Association. Anybody on the West Coast singing harmonies—he knew their stuff backward and forward.[102]

We made brief trips to Belgium to appear on their TV shows, *Vibrato* and *Tienerklanken*, as well as to the Netherlands to appear on *Twien*. It was in Antwerp, Belgium, that we started doing high kicks at the end of "Windy." Larry and I began doing the high kicks again in the 1980s. I also distinctly recall a stop in Bremen, Germany, where we had taped an appearance on a television show called *Beat*

---

102   Kubernik, Harvey. *Turn Up the Radio—Rock, Pop & Roll in Los Angeles 1956-1972.* Santa Monica Press, 2014.

Club, in an episode with Julie Driscoll, Brian Auger & The Trinity. Later that night, we convinced a guy who was closing his restaurant to open it back up for us and feed us because we were starving. "If you feed us," we told him, "we'll tip you very well." He did, and we did (tip well), and we were very grateful. The restaurant was on multiple levels, and filled with music boxes—he ran around the restaurant turning them on.

Whenever we were on tour, I packed a Frisbee in my luggage, which helped in passing the long periods of hurry up and wait time that come with lots of travel. Remember, this is pre-electronic devices. So water balloons, water rockets, balsa wood planes sent soaring off hotel balconies, spinning Frisbees... We were creative in keeping ourselves entertained. By the time we would get back together (I'm getting to that), water rockets were taken off the market, likely as a result of the danger they posed. So later, in the 1980s (still largely before the cell phone era), and ever in search of entertainment on the road, Larry launched a boat-building competition, which kept the guys occupied in their spare time as they tested out models out in hotel bathtubs. Joe Lamanno, who played with The Beachwood Rangers and then The Association in the 1970s and on the first Happy Together Tour, remembers that it was "a contest to build some type of model boat, but you couldn't buy a boat kit. You had to make it out of available materials you could find and there would be a boat race at the end of the tour. [The race] happened at the fountain—above the grassy knoll where JFK got shot [in Dallas]. [There were] Rube Goldberg-type boats made out of soda cans. Larry and Jules were the most creative— the process of them going through that and trying to hide from one another what they were doing..." He laughs. "They had to be self-steering—they had to go in a straight line down this pond. I think Larry won, if I recall. None of them tipped over!" I didn't participate in the contest, but Ted remembers it was a boat festival with rules the band created, including "you can't spend any more than $1 or $1.50 on the parts. We all started making one. Larry and his brother Del—there was a strange boat on their bed—'Does this thing float?' [you wondered]. Meanwhile, back in their bathtub was the real boat—a catamaran with coke bottles and 7-Up cans. They used dry cleaning bags for the sails. Scotch tape to tie them all together. Most money we spent was to make the mast. When we had the big regatta, a couple of the boats sank, but the rest of them were self-steering and went across…That's how we entertained ourselves!" I remember while at a concert at the Executive Inn in Owensboro, Kentucky, we made a boat out of cardboard and filled it with lit fireworks and sent it out to float. Less than two minutes later and much to our surprise, the boat came back…*and the fireworks exploded!* Needless to say, we made ourselves scarce pretty quickly.

But that time in Rome when we landed at the airport, we got two limos and at some point we had to stop in front of some building or another so our manager could take care of some paperwork. So what did I do? I broke out my Frisbee. Steve Nelson and I were tossing it back and forth when we looked up to see about a hundred people hanging over the railings of the building, watching us play. Perhaps the Frisbee came late to Rome? Another time we played Frisbee on the tarmac of the Pittsburgh Airport, and the airport cops, lights flashing, made a beeline toward us in their vehicles to tell us that what we were doing was too dangerous.

We were supposed to perform in Paris on that trip, too, but that leg of the trip was canceled because of the violent unrest that had just exploded there, escalating with rioting university students on Monday, May 6 (the violence would continue for over a month). "It was not a political revolution in the way that earlier French revolutions had been, but a cultural and social one that in a stunningly short time changed French society…Both the women's liberation movement and gay rights movement grew out of the 1968 upheaval and the intellectual ferment of the time. The night of May

6 was particularly violent, with 600 people wounded and 422 people detained...The protestors...set fire to cars and confronted the police. By the time the bloody fighting ended, hundreds of students had been arrested and hundreds more hospitalized..."[103] Pat Colecchio, who was with us on the tour, and the promoters were worried about our safety. We wanted to do it anyway because we'd never seen Paris, but they said no. And so our European tour was cut short and we returned back to US soil sooner than scheduled.

It's no wonder France was undergoing its own social unrest; with our European tour sandwiched in between the Martin Luther King Jr. and Bobby Kennedy assassinations, we were no strangers to unrest. But we never returned to Europe again. "It was probably shortsighted on our manager's part," Jim says. Maybe, but rock and roll touring and especially international rock and roll touring was still in its infancy. Pat likely weighed the costs of ten guys traveling in the US (the band and our crew) against the costs to travel in Europe, and decided against it.

Birthday, meanwhile, hadn't climbed above No. 23 on the US charts, even though reviews tended to be positive, like this one in *The Honolulu Advertiser*:

> The Association's newest album, *Birthday* (Warner Bros.-Seven Arts WS 1733) is no party pooper.
>
> It's a lively outing in the folk bag, and everyone in the sextet gets his chance to show off. Terry and Russ mix voices on an inviting opener, "Come On In." From then on, the candles are alit and aglow.
>
> "Rose Petals, Incense and a Kitten" is folk-oriented, sung with candor by Jim. Larry, the Hawaii-born member, solos on a moving, grooving rock ballad, "Like Always." Ted's outstanding effort is "Hear in Here."

---

103   Rubin, Alissa J. "May 1968: A Month of Revolution Pushed France Into the Modern World." *The New York Times*. May 5, 2018.

The Association's recent chart-topper, "Everything That Touches You," is a psychedelic journey that epitomizes the Birthday party. Outasite, indeed—so far out, it's in.[104]

Terry's "Everything That Touches You" hit No. 10 on the singles chart. We'd collaborated with Bones Howe again on *Birthday* because we'd had such a successful experience on *Insight Out. Renaissance*, our second album, which Jerry Yester had produced, hadn't performed as well. Ted remembers of Bones, "Bones was on the telephone all the time we were trying to record. We'd finish our take and he'd wave his hand and just say, 'Do it again.' We played back the album with just the voices and it sounded fantastic. Of course, Bones took it and mixed it down where you couldn't even hear the voices. I said, 'Are the rest of the voices there?' He said, 'Oh, yeah, I put it in harmonic layering.' So we stopped doing any more albums with Bones. Bones had all kind of projects. He was in it for the money." It would be our last collaboration with Bones until the 1980s after the band got back together. We were, however, still getting plenty of press, such as the journalist who claimed, "Their songs are of love, not only as a replacement for war, but as a way of life. They speak of the inner satisfaction one must find before he can really begin to live. They are lyrical liberators using the musical structure as a means of getting their message across."[105]

So we went on to do what any successful band would: make financial investments.

104 Harada, Wayne. "On the Record." *The Honolulu Advertiser.* May 2, 1968.

105 "Association to Sing of Love, Inspiration." *Abilene Reporter-News.* September 22, 1968.

When Good Groups Make Bad Investments
1968 (continued)-1970

TOURING LIFE WAS NOT without its magical moments. Sometime around 1968 or so, while we were on the road in Chattanooga, Tennessee, we were transferring in Cincinnati, Ohio, and then flying from there to Detroit, Michigan, where we were doing the usual: renting two station wagons and driving to our next gig, this time at a Methodist college near Battle Creek.

The first plane in Chattanooga had a flat tire on the nose wheel, so everyone's luggage was loaded on a different plane. Lee Liebman, our road manager, found a pay phone and called the college we were scheduled to perform at to tell them we might be late. We landed in Cincinnati, changed planes, and then sat on the tarmac for what seemed like forever. The captain then told us we were returning to the gate because something was wrong with the plane, so we'd have to board a different one. Once more, Lee headed to a pay phone to call the college and tell them we were further delayed but still en route. Pete Stefanos and Steve Nelson (that's right, *our guys*, not the airline employees—times were simpler) transferred our gear and luggage from the one plane to the other.

We flew to Detroit and rented two station wagons as Lee called the school yet again—this time with the news that we were wheeled and on the way. At last we arrived at the gig—amazingly only thirty or forty minutes late. The audience had been told of our plight and waited patiently. The auditorium was round with a large balcony, many wood pillars, and trim throughout the room. An old wooden theater organ was behind the stage and it actually looked as though the building had been built around it. With the help of some students, we set up the drums, amps, guitars, and sound system in about eleven minutes.

Our entrance to the stage itself was actually through a door in the cabinetry of the organ. The applause was tumultuous and we performed a wonderful show to an appreciative audience. After the concert, we exited the stage, packed up the two station wagons, and set off into the night on a hundred-mile journey to another town, another hotel, another plane, and another gig. (This was the life, as I told you—pack up, travel via plane, occasionally bus and/or automobile, unpack, perform, eat, smoke, and repeat. I loved it, but if you were a complainer or hated mornings, this life was not for you.)

Anyhow, it was nearing midnight as we cruised through miles of pitch-black, flat Michigan farmland when I noticed colored flecks of light dancing off the inside of the windshield. I signaled to the other station wagon to pull over to the side of the road with us so we could better examine the source. Terry remembers that a radiator had blown, though for the life of me, I can't remember that happening because after the incident, we just continued on. I do remember that we thought the lights were reflecting off of something shiny inside our vehicle, but it was pitch black inside the car. We then realized that we were privy to the rare treat of seeing the northern lights live! Spectacular is a mild word for the light display of the aurora borealis. We could even hear it crackling and popping—like fireworks—only better. I felt like it was the reward for a hard-won day. After some time, we got back in our station wagons and continued our journey.

In 1968, with four albums under our belt and six hit singles, we were still busy as ever, touring. By this time Lee Liebman was working with Pat Colecchio in the office in Los Angeles, Pete Stefanos was now our road manager and Pat's son, Rick, was doing lights. "I had a boutique dress shop [in New York City]," Rick remembers, "and the wives would come into the store and the guys, when they were in town, would come in and say, 'What are you doing here? Come

to California and go on the road with us.' I said, 'Hey, do you realize
I have a boutique on Madison Avenue? Who are you guys? Get lost.'
Then 'Cherish' hit No. 1 and I said goodbye! That's how I got started,
and I was with them until 1974. Because of The Association, I'm a
little bit deaf...I was on the road with them for six years. I set up
the stage, I was their lighting director—which I had no idea about!
They just threw me into a booth the first show. Lee Liebman was our
[road] manager at that point. We were in a huge college arena and
the lighting booth was at the top of the dome in a little booth and
you actually had to walk across a grated walkway to get to the booth.
I'm afraid of heights. When the elevator door opened up, I said, 'Lee,
I can't do this.' He said, 'Close your eyes, hold my shoulder, you have
to do this. He gets me out there and he opens the door to this booth
and it's like Star Trek Enterprise!...Six spotlights—three on each
side—he said, 'Now just tell them what you want to do,' and he leaves
me and goes downstairs. And that was my introduction to lighting!"

We had no problems filling up our calendar or the venues in
which we were booked. Tensions in the group would occasionally
flare, but they tended to bubble far below the surface and band
members would look past the bones they wanted to pick when the
time came to focus on the music. In Terry's eyes, beginning with
the lack of coverage and attention paid to The Association when
we opened Monterey in 1967, the nail in the coffin came after we
recorded *Birthday* in the fall of 1967/winter of 1968 and we had
to determine which song to release as a single off the album. We
released "Everything That Touches You" in January and that was a hit,
reaching No. 10 on *Billboard* Hot 100. The lyrics of the chorus were:

You love for real
You show the feel
Of everything that touches you

We also released "Time for Livin'," another song from the Addrisi
brothers, who of course had given us a No. 1 record with "Never My
Love." Larry and I sang the lead on it. The lyrics of the chorus are:

Time for livin', groovin' on everything
Life is givin', from now on I'm taking
Time...
For life

If it were up to Terry, we'd have been making socially relevant music only. "I've been a civil rights activist since 1963," Terry says, "and I wanted to write about other things than love you, love, love you, baby, baby, baby, have a malt with me." According to Terry, he did everything he could to get us to move in this direction; the rest of us were content to keep doing what we were doing: recording songs we liked, regardless of how one might want to categorize them, and making a good living getting paid to sing our hits.

"For both Pat and me, the turning point was when the band decided to release 'Time for Livin',"" Terry shares. "Going into that album, Pat and I both sat and begged the rest of the guys that if you record that song, Warner Bros. is going to want to release it and if they release it, we're done. It was a catchy tune, it sounded like The Association; but it was this insipid, meaningless piece of froth lyric. I was looking at the market, Pat was looking at the market—you don't want to do this song. We did, they did, and that was it. [George Michael, the WFIL program director out of Philadelphia] called me up and said, 'Wow, you are never going to be able to turn the corner of this. No disc jockey working at a Top 40 station is going to look at The Association for anything other than soft bubblegum rock and roll.' He said that to me when we released 'Six Man Band.' 'Six Man Band' had a little more burn to it and his response was, 'Love the song, it ain't gonna happen.' The lyric," Terry continued, "in the context of the times, in the context of what the market was perceiving as more important than other things, the 'Time for Livin'' lyric was essentially so sophomoric, not to everybody, but to anybody who was at all current, literate, really aware of the war, civil rights, and how pop and rock were being looked at to be a provocative voice, even though the disc jockeys didn't give a shit, couldn't care less, or the record company, for that matter. As a matter of fact, Warner Bros. was very afraid of political commentary. CBS FM NY didn't play us," Terry adds. "They totally looked at us as just white, middle-of-the-road, inconsequential fluff. Nice music, well done, but just not the image that they were looking for."

Rock and roll could live and die by the whim of disc jockey personalities. George Michael was "the music director at WFIL as well as the 6:00 to 10:00 p.m. disc jockey. He was named *Billboard*'s top radio personality several times, as well as picking up numerous awards as Music Director of the Year. He was nicknamed 'King George' Michael because he 'ruled' evening radio." A promotional leaflet for him boasted, "Radio listening in the early evening belongs to the Young Adult. As a group, they have strong interests, desires, and loyalties. They insist on knowing what's happening while it's happening. George Michael is tailor-made for this audience. He's the 'much more music' man with savvy for picking and playing the hits. He's a sports buff who knows virtually every college and high school coach, cheerleader, and star player from Trenton to Wilmington and from Reading to Atlantic City. His regular newspaper column carries the fast-breaking news from all corners of the entertainment industry. The key word for George Michael, then, is involvement. The result has been instance [*sic*] acceptance and a strong rapport with listeners..."[106]

If these guys were the so-called "chefs" of rock and roll, they were plating up which songs to dish out to their public—in deciding what to play, they demanded their audiences fall in love with their selects—and they did. So long as the material was fresh and it helped sell advertising and keep their target market tuning in, the disc jockeys kept playing it. If your record wasn't being played, it dropped lower and lower on the charts, until it fell into oblivion. In fact, the

---

106   https://www.broadcastpioneers.com/bp4/georgemichael.html

influence of the disc jockey can be traced back many ways, one of which will take you right back to 1942, the first year of Capitol Records' existence. "With this new company struggling to survive, and unable to press up records because of a wartime shellac shortage (a ship carrying huge amounts of the stuff had just been sunk), Capitol's chairman, Glenn E. Wallichs, looked to the DJ to keep the company's music in people's minds. A list was drawn up of the country's fifty most influential jocks and they were each personally delivered a special vinyl sampler of Capitol's output. 'It was a service that created a sensation,' said Wallichs. 'We made the jock a Big Man, an Important Guy, a VIP in the industry. And we published a little newspaper in which we ran their pictures and biographies.'"[107]

In opening those venues that were previously closed to rock and roll, in that exposure we got, not only through the venues but also through repeat appearances on shows like *The Ed Sullivan Show*, *The Smothers Brothers Comedy Hour*, *American Bandstand*, and *The Andy Williams Show*, we were then thought of as sellouts, even though an appearance on *The Ed Sullivan Show* could help you sell an additional hundred thousand records alone. And let's be clear—The Beatles, The Rolling Stones, and Elvis Presley were three separate categories apart from the rest of popular music, and immune to any of the "rules" the rest of us had to follow. There was a bias against us, however subtle. Not enough of the "right" people took us seriously.

...readers of a certain age may recall a seventies publication *Dark Star*. In 1976 Steve Burgess offered this explanation in its pages as to why The Association never, in his opinion, achieved the cult status or hit parade longevity of harmony outfits like CSNY,[108] The Byrds and The Beach Boys: "Probably the reason why they failed where The Beach Boys made it into mythology is that their songs never related to

107   Brewster, Bill and Broughton, Frank. *Last Night a DJ Saved My Life: The History of the Disc Jockey*. Headline Book Publishing, 2006.

108   Crosby, Stills, Nash, and Young.

anything much other than themselves...they never touched on the turbulent traumas endemic in The American Way of Teenhood."[109]

Time would prove that this guy had his head up his ass—obviously one of the "tragically hip."

"Had we launched in the early seventies," Terry surmises, "we might have had an entirely different career because people were really hitting the mark of exhaustion where they *wanted* good time music, where all of a sudden you had disco, where all of a sudden you had John Denver, who could not get arrested in the sixties." Sure, Terry has some valid points and God love him, but he's often singing that one note about The Association on repeat—that we weren't respected the way we should have been and that we went in the wrong direction with our music and if we had listened to him, things would have been different. Maybe, maybe not. "Everything That Touches You," which Terry wrote, is a really great song. But it's not trying to save the world or make a big statement with its lyrics. It's not bringing about world peace. It's just a damn good feel-good song. End of story. Not every song can be a "Requiem for the Masses"—I mean, we don't want our fans to feel like slitting their wrists after listening to our albums. There is a responsibility on the part of the fans as well, to open their minds to the fact that a musician or a band can encompass many different sounds—often one song brings the fame, but it's possible to demand your audience open their ears up to other ways of making music; you just can't control the results. It's not often you can have your cake and eat it, too. No one and no band, certainly, is ever all one thing. Or if they are, they usually fall off the radar. You have to take some risks; it's not always going to pan out the way you envision or land with an audience, but you have to try.

If you haven't guessed by now, I maintain that people get far too obsessive about assigning labels and categorizing things under the false pretense that in doing so they will thus be able to *understand*

109   Pearson, David. "Roots and Branches." *Shindig!* Issue 78. May 4, 2018.

it better. Whatever. It's bullshit. Either you jive with it (in this case, a particular song) or you don't. It's perfectly okay to jive with one song or some songs and not others. In the end, though, we were never quite "hip" enough for the history books, even though, Terry says, "we had a long, sustainable shelf life with people who liked our harmonies and liked the musicality of the songs." True enough. For the past several years, The Association has performed over fifty-five concerts per year—not bad for a group that started over fifty years ago!

Had we recorded Jimmy Webb's "MacArthur Park," we might have had a chance to take the band in a radical new direction, not only for the fact that all whopping seven minutes and twenty-one seconds of it made it on DJ playlists (a song that long had never made it onto a playlist before), but also because in six-part harmony, it would have been something else. Jimmy actually wrote the song for The Association. But it was presented to us in the middle of a recording session for the *Birthday* album (that we were paying big bucks to record), as something like an eighteen-to-twenty-minute piece (Terry and I differ in our memory of just how long it was, but the point is that the original version was long) and Bones told us that it couldn't be cut down in length, or broken up. "It was issued as rather a challenge to me from Bones Howe…that I could do an extended, classically oriented piece that could be played on the radio,"[110] Webb recalls. He (Bones) "…asked me to create a pop song with classical elements, different movements, and changing time signatures. 'MacArthur Park' was more of a suite than a song, was everything he wanted, but when we presented it to…The Association, they refused to record it."[111] We were just finishing the album, and because the song was so long and we were told it couldn't be cut, we just didn't

110   Fallick, Allan H. "Jimmy Webb discusses famous lyrics in 'MacArthur Park.' *Newsday*. October 8, 2014.

111   Simpson, Dave. "How we made MacArthur Park: Songwriter Jimmy Webb recalls recording the somewhat infuriating suite with actor Richard Harris, and the real story behind leaving that cake out in the rain." *The Guardian*. November 11, 2013.

have room for it, so we didn't record it. Yet when we were on the road three weeks later, we heard the shortened version by Richard Harris on the radio! So let it be known that we didn't refuse the song—we were going off the information we were given. Waylon Jennings and the Kimberlys won the 1969 "Best Country Performance by a Duo or Group" for their version of "MacArthur Park."

In 1968 we also released our *Greatest Hits* album, which peaked at No. 4 on the *Billboard* charts in February 1969, on a Top 10 list that included Blood, Sweat & Tears, Glen Campbell, Cream, Iron Butterfly, Elvis Presley, Diana Ross and The Supremes, and of course, The Beatles. Jim Metropole shot the cover for the album at Descanso Gardens. He also shot a bunch of our PR shots and even toured with us to Florida, New York, San Francisco, and Chicago.

The album became our biggest seller. Fans sometimes criticize us for the fact that Jules's "Pandora's Golden Heebie Jeebies" didn't make it onto the album, since it did chart as high as No. 35 in 1966. Truth be told, Pat picked the tunes that went on the album, and because Jules had left the band and then came back, I think Pat may have been trying to spread the money out among all of the guys, so he attempted to distribute the songwriting spectrum that our works on that album represented as equally as possible. Our *Greatest Hits* album went gold and then platinum while I was in the band, and then after I quit, it went platinum again! It seemed, to some degree, that our music was infiltrating a wider audience. The *Courier-Post* in Camden, New Jersey, wrote:

> How many singers and musical groups have really been able to bridge that great divide commonly called the generation gap?
>
> There's Sinatra of course. There's Simon & Garfunkel (thanks to *The Graduate*). And to a lesser extent there are The Supremes and Tom Jones, both of whose music now

seems to be more popular among the older generation than among the younger ones who "discovered" them.

And now there is another group attempting to narrow the gap—musically at least. Enter the Association.

THE ASSOCIATION, of course, is not a new group. Terry Kirkman and the group have been performing together for around five years now. But thanks to their Warner Brothers-Seven Arts album, they are beginning to reach new listeners, and doing it not with any new-type songs but rather the great hits that made them the popular group they are today.

"The Association's Greatest Hits"—a thirteen-song repertoire is beginning to reach some of the older inhabitants of the generation gap, causing them to react as much as they did when they "discovered" Simon & Garfunkel via *The Graduate.*

"What beautiful music for such a new group."

Simon & Garfunkel, new? The Association, new?...

LISTEN, OLDER GENERATION. Listen to some of the best music written in the last few years. Listen-up and welcome to the club that enjoys the music of The Association.

Here they come. With the bouncy, lively music of "Windy" and "Along Comes Mary."

Here they come. With the beautiful music and lyrics of "Cherish," "Never My Love," and "Everything That Touches You."

Here they come. With deep views on today's world in "Enter the Young" and "Requiem for the Masses."

This is an album that all should like. For those who have listened to the group in the past, here are their hits together in one package. For new listeners of The Association, what better way to initially find the group than by hearing them at their best?

OF ALL THE SONGS written the past couple of years, including Lennon and McCartney's "Yesterday" and "Michelle"; Simon & Garfunkel's "Sounds of Silence"; Burt Bacharach's "Look of Love" and Jimmy Webb's "By the Time I Get to Phoenix," "Cherish" may indeed be the most beautiful.

Musically and lyrically, it is a difficult song—not too many singers or groups have tried to do it—but it is a song that, like others mentioned above, hits home at that inner something and makes listeners glad to hear it over and over again.

And then there's "Windy"—the wispy tune about a woman-of-the-night—which has been mimicked by Sinatra, Andy Williams and many others.

There's "Everything That Touches You," slightly reminiscent of "Cherish" (both were written by the group's Terry Kirkman) and "Never My Love," two best-selling singles in their own right.

"Along Comes Mary," one of the group's early songs, is the most bouncy in the album, and provides good contrast with the slower songs.

ALMOST ALL GROUPS and singers today put out a "greatest hits" album. Some make for enjoyable listening; others do not—especially if the listener never liked the songs in the first place. Still other groups, who may have had but a handful of great hits, have to struggle to find enough material to fill the album.

This is not the case with The Association. This album is not comprised of just "THEIR" great hits; it is comprised of great hits. The Association's hits are great, by anyone's standards.

It is an album to be listened to, savored—and saved. It is an album for both sides of the great divide. For the music is just plain great. There is no better way to describe it.[112]

Another reviewer who saw one of our November 1969 concerts at Xavier University admitted:

I went to an Association concert last week at XU to see what was new in the world of lollipops.

I must admit I went into it with a negative attitude, having seen the group several times before, and having suffered a diabetic reaction each time.

Everybody said it would be different, that they had something new on the ball. I scoffed.

But then I got there and guess what? It was really nice. I could hardly believe my ears.

The Association has grown some guts.

Not only are they doing all sorts of new things, but they've also redone some of their most "saccharine-ish" oldies and come up with a really hard-hitting show. Nowadays, Terry Kirkman spends a lot of time out front—a lot more than ever in the past, and that is a gigantic improvement.

His voice, which used to be buried in harmonic acrobatics, skillful but trite, is now the backbone of the group. His sound adds gravel, a range that the group has never had, and an intensity that previous to this, they could only flirt with.

KIRKMAN has also mastered the art of the flute.[113] If you'll recall, in past days, various group members would goof

---

112   Bitman, Terry A. "Everybody's Association?" *Courier-Post*. March 29, 1969.

113   Nobody in The Association ever played the flute (the recorder, yes; the flute, no)... don't believe everything you read.

around with a flute and sound not unlike the pied piper on a bad trip.

Now, it's all Terry Kirkman, and he's very serious about it. He has a variety of flutes, which he toots on when not strumming away on his guitar.[114] To really appreciate the added dimension, you have to hear it—maybe even see it.

But all the credit shouldn't go to Terry Kirkman, even though he's the group's backbone.[115]

In early 1969, Jules returned from India. He came to an Association rehearsal and rejoined the group, making us now a seven-man band. That year, we were invited to do the music for *Goodbye, Columbus*, a Hollywood movie based on a novel of the same name by Philip Roth, and starring newcomer Ali MacGraw. The film was finished and the music was one of the last elements they needed. Following a concert we did in Chattanooga, we flew directly to New York City for a private screening—we sat down, watched the movie, and then had something like three days to go away and write any songs we wanted to pitch to them for the opening and closing of the movie, as well as the love montage between the characters of Brenda, played by Ali MacGraw, and Neil, played by Richard Benjamin. I wrote a song called "I'll Still Love You," but the studio executives didn't select it. In the end, they took three of our songs—the lead theme, "Goodbye, Columbus," was written by Jim (there were two versions, one with lyrics and one instrumental); "It's Gotta Be Real" was written by Larry but never released as a single (I always thought was a hit); and Terry wrote Brenda's theme, "So Kind to Me." Reviews were mixed.

Two of the most beautiful tunes to climb to the top of the pop charts were issued by The Association in 1967—"Cherish"

114   Excuse me, Mr. Reporter, Terry doesn't play the guitar. Never did. He must have gotten all of us guys mixed up…I get it…there are a lot of guitars up on that stage!

115   Knippenberg, Jim. "He went to scoff—but found The Association had changed." *The Cincinnati Enquirer.* November 1, 1969.

and "Never My Love." The tunes were soft and deep, like a pillow and sincere, polished goblets from careful craftsmen. Nothing prominent has been done by the seven men since. Now we have their soundtrack from *Goodbye, Columbus* adapted from the book by Philip Roth. The collection isn't bad. It doesn't fail in singing the mood of the story. In fact, it sells the theme so well it is commercial. The Association writes everything it sings. For this collection the smooth, relaxed, well-paced style has been kept. But next to its fine-spun hits with subtle lyrics and voices used as instruments, the soundtrack merely has no personality. Love is the hidden theme, but there is nothing loving in the treatment. Come back old Association.[116]

Ouch! *The Akron Beacon Journal* reported:

If *Goodbye, Columbus* doesn't do for The Association what *The Graduate* did for Simon & Garfunkel, it will be the group's own fault. Their songs are so good, they blend in perfectly with the film—so perfectly that sometimes you aren't completely conscious of the music. They are credited for three songs in the movie, all of which were written for specific moods and scenes...

Before the group went on the road, I visited with Terry Kirkman and Jim Yester, who talked about the film and their music. They seemed to feel that with more time they could have produced even better songs and would have preferred working on the music while the film was in production rather than after it was completed. With more artistic control, they could have been more creative and their biggest complaint was that the incidental music didn't pick up on their themes as they hoped it would. But they admitted the end result was more than satisfactory for their

---

116   Jennings, Elaine. "Record Previews: Back to the Blues by Don Lass." *Asbury Park Press*, July 27, 1969.

first film and they are looking forward to working with film more in the future.

I have always felt that film producers overlook a tremendous wealth of talent by ignoring pop musicians, and Paramount really deserves a cheer for having enough foresight to include The Association in *Goodbye, Columbus*.[117]

The New York *Daily News* reported, "Paramount feels the appeal of the Association is so great that the execs are hustling to shape up a three-picture package deal that will present the musical group in much the same way the Beatles moved into motion pictures."[118] Ultimately, there wouldn't be another movie with music by The Association or any movies starring us as characters—even though much was made of it. "There's a good chance you'll also be seeing them on the big screen. They've been approached to star in two films (one of which would star them only), and these two offers are only the beginning."[119] The closest we would get to extending our brand beyond the music and now film mediums would be the 1969 revised edition of *Crank Your Spreaders*. *Goodbye, Columbus* made $10.5 million at the North American box office alone, which was a heck of a lot of money in 1969, and it was one of the most popular movies that year. *The New York Times* wrote, "…at its center, *Goodbye, Columbus* is sharp and honest…is so rich with understanding in more important ways that it is a thing of real and unusual pleasure."[120] We released Jim's song as a single, and it peaked at only No. 99 on the *Billboard* Hot 100, but reached No. 22 on the Top 40 Easy Listening. We also received the 1969 Outstanding Achievement Award from Loews Theatres for our "outstanding contribution to the field of popular

---

117   Orloff, Kathy. "Association 'Arrives.'" *The Akron Beacon Journal*. Akron, Ohio. March 23, 1969.

118   Muir, Florabel. "Hollywood." *Daily News*. New York, NY. June 16, 1969.

119   "Association of Road Runners." Publication unknown. From author's personal collection.

120   Canby, Vincent. "Screen: A Vivid 'Goodbye Columbus.'" *The New York Times*. April 4, 1969.

music and better understanding between generations, resulting from the three songs penned for the Paramount film"[121] and Jim received a Golden Globe nomination. Ali MacGraw also won several awards for her performance.

The same year we cut our fifth album in the studio, *The Association*, with producer John Boylan, who would later go on to win the 1999 Grammy for "Best Musical Album for Children" for the ABC-TV Primetime special *Elmopalooza*, as well as produce albums for Linda Ronstadt, the Chipmunks, and Muppets. "We were growing apart [from Bones Howe]," Jim said in a recent interview for *Shindig! Magazine*, and "...we wanted to try some different genres of music and Bones wanted us to stay where we were, as did the program directors of most radio stations. Once we started releasing things that weren't 'rich warm brown' so to speak, of love songs, they backed off from playing us...John had a better idea of what the group really was than any other producer we ever worked with."[122] In that same article, Jules shares, "Bones Howe never produced The Association. Bones Howe produced Bones Howe, his concepts and his sound. I didn't mind coproducing his sound but it became tiresome when I found that Bones Howe had essentially one sound and stayed pretty much in his comfort zone."

It would be my last studio album with the group before I left. *The Association* album is often referred to as our "Stonehenge" album because of the cover art. The artist who did the album cover art was William Crutchfield, from whom I'd bought eight hand-colored lithographs, and I recommended him to Pat to hire to design our album cover, which ended up being a photograph of two paintings he did—one for the inside of the album, and one for the cover. There was a Sunset Strip billboard of the cover art, which went up in August 1969, and it was terrific. Crutchfield's friend, sculptor Claes Oldenburg, happened to be staying at the Chateau Marmont

---

121   Orloff, Kathy. "Association Cops The Loew's Award." *The Akron Beacon Journal.* April 27, 1969.

122   Pearson, David. "Roots and Branches." *Shindig!* Issue 78. May 4, 2018.

hotel right next to the billboard, and was impressed. I later learned from Crutchfield that the billboard had to be revised—his original painting included constellations representing the astrological signs of each band member, but they were omitted from the billboard version, so they had to be added.

William Crutchfield's Sunset Strip billboard (upper right) of the artwork he did for our album, The Association, often referred to as our "Stonehenge" album.

The album was critically well received but didn't perform well. We played a lot of our own instruments on it, more so than other albums, and it would be the first album Brian received a songwriting credit on for "I Am Up for Europe." The first stanza was

I am up for Europe or any other place
Where I do not speak the language or recognize a face
But the clouds are gathering before me
What else in such a case?
And I am up for Europe or any other place

And a song I wrote, "Broccoli," was also on that album.

Broccoli—I really dig it steamed
Broccoli—just plain, with cheese or creamed

I like to eat it with my mouth
It tastes so good
I like to eat it with my mouth
It's my favorite food

Broccoli—it grows right from the ground
Broccoli—I even dig the sound
A favorite Atlantean dish
They thought it was the end
I'm a-turnin' you on my friend
I'm a-turnin' you on my friend

Broccoli—I really dig it steamed
Broccoli—just plain, with cheese or creamed

I like to eat it with my mouth
It tastes so good
I like to eat it with my mouth
It's my favorite food

Wait! Don't shut the book! You're probably wondering what possessed me to write that song and chalking it up to drugs, but no. You're wrong. I just wanted to sing about something I loved (other than women), so I wrote a silly song about one of my all-time favorite foods. When I first presented it to the group to record, the vote was a unanimous "yes." It was the same response when the group voted on Mike Deasy's "Wantin' Ain't Gettin'" in 1967 on *Insight Out*. That wasn't a love song, either, but it was unique and the lyrics and beat interested us. Don't remember that ditty? Here it is:

...a fat hog log in a bog
Knucklebone and a hairless dog[123]
Tryin' to get away
From a two dollar cop

But wantin' ain't gettin'

---

123   The original lyric was "hair lip dog." I think we changed it because no one understood it.

And gettin' ain't got
And I'm gone
Have mercy, baby

A runaway mule, pig in a poke
TV screen and a bullfrog croak
Tryin' to find a way
To get a bottle of pop

But wantin' ain't gettin'
And gettin' ain't got
And I'm gone
Have mercy, baby

Horse's ear, hoot and a holler
Midriff bulge and a righteous squalor
Tryin' to find a place
Where nothing's hot

But wantin' ain't gettin'
And gettin' ain't got
And I'm gone
Have mercy, baby
The cock's crow, hole in the wall
Man sayin' God is a cannonball
Wanna fly high
So my head won't rot

But wantin' ain't gettin'
And getting' ain't got
And I'm gone
Have mercy, baby

But wantin' ain't gettin'
I still ain't got
And I'm gone
Have mercy, baby.

Every now and again, when we were performing, I'd hear someone in the audience scream, "Broccoli!" all the way up until the time I left the band in late 2013. We were never able to honor those requests, considering "Broccoli" is a tune we haven't done since 1969.

Interestingly, Terry was quoted that same year in an interview with a reporter: "The best concept is to go into recording your first album and do two while the group is fresh and you're writing and creative. Record twenty-four songs and make two good albums out of them and hope one or the other hits. Otherwise, you can only think of so many things to write and go on the road 365 days a year and perform. Your head starts to get fried." In that same interview, the reporter also shares Ted's perspective. "Ted Bluechel, the drummer, says that the way the Association did it, with one album, then being in demand to appear, their second album was a 'don't cop out' type thing. We didn't want to use our old formula sounds but we hadn't gained experience in new sounds, we'd been so busy working. It was do or die, a challenge to the quality of the music, a compromise between business and art. The reason for our problem, it is called time."[124]

Ted, Terry, and all of the other guys are certainly entitled to their opinions, but I never felt the way they did on these matters, ever. See, I wanted to be a singer on the road most of my life. I can hardly remember a time where I didn't want that. So the road never bothered me. Pat Colecchio always said to me, "The guys always want to be on the road *less* and make more money—except you." We made money from record sales, of course, but being on the road increased our record sales and kept the money rolling in. It was a great feeling, knowing you were blowing the audience away with stuff they hadn't yet heard. I remember back when I was still working lights at The Ice House, some of the entertainers would whine about how boring it was to be on the road, playing little cities and towns night after night. I had a different experience. I found *all* of it interesting. There's this

---

124   Campbell, Mary. "The Association Gets a Hit, Takes Time Off For New Ideas." *Nashua Telegraph.* April 5, 1969.

old saying that really resonates with me: "No matter where you go, there you are." At the end of a concert, I always rated our shows on a scale of one to ten. We were almost always at a ten, and occasionally an eleven or twelve. I made the most of my time, wherever I went. Marty Nicosia describes me as a "…little bit of a loner, [Russ] kind of liked to be by himself—he'd get up at 7:00 a.m. and hike all over whatever town we were in and no one else wanted to do that."

Marty's right about that. I'm definitely an early riser. No one ever wanted to join me on my crack-of-dawn walks. I also liked to take in the sights whenever possible. There was one year we spent Thanksgiving at the top of a restaurant overlooking Chicago during a series of dates at the Chicago Opera House. Over the years through various gigs in Chicago I would take in whatever exhibition was at the Art Institute—my favorite was one on Andrew Wyeth. I spent hours there. An interview I gave in the 1980s best explains my attitude:

> But while some musicians are content to remain in their hotel rooms when they're not onstage, Giguere prefers to get out and see the sights, smell the flowers, and tune in to whatever else the area has to offer.
>
> In Texas, for instance, Giguere saw a restaurant advertising a "Quail Special"—all the quail you can eat for $4.50.
>
> "I just couldn't pass that up," he says. "Actually, I can't pass up anything that sounds interesting and out-of-the-ordinary. I'm one of those guys who'll go out of his way to see the world's largest ball of twine, the deepest crater—you name it…"[125]

Ted recalls that Terry found out about the opportunity to write the music for *Goodbye, Columbus* a few days before everyone else and that he had a chance to write and submit material before the rest of us. I'm not sure if that was true or not—we're all fighting memories

---

125   Faris, Mark. "The lights go on again at Peninsula Nite Club." *The Akron Beacon Journal.* February 12, 1987.

that are fifty-plus years old now. Ted says, "I never had a thing that 'this would be good for me' or 'I hope I benefit from this.' The group was laying the golden eggs. You don't kill the group and expect to get more eggs." I would agree with that. The group was the animal putting money in our bank accounts. Ted also refers to the band as the "six-headed monster" no one wanted to deal with—meaning six distinctly different male personalities was a lot for anyone to contend with and make consistently happy. "Oh, God, I need to get away from the group," Ted explains the inevitable thought that would cross individual band members' minds from time to time, some certainly more frequently than others. "Everybody carried that football at one point or another." Lord knows I did; I left in 1970. But more about that later.

Even if we weren't yet replicating the success of "Along Comes Mary," "Windy" or "Cherish," we were still very much in demand and playing to sold-out audiences. Another time in New Orleans around 1969–1970, for some reason, the whole band and our equipment guys—so probably about nine of us total—were walking down Bourbon Street, stretched out, meandering and taking in the lively scene that is Bourbon Street in New Orleans. I remember it vividly because we seldom walked together in a group. In general, outside of singing onstage together, we weren't really group-oriented guys. We loved each other, we got along well, there were arguments here and there, and sometimes we would go places together or be invited to a party, but a lot of times, everyone had their own friendships, friends, lovers, whatever they had going on. Anyhow, on that walk in New Orleans, Brian carried a cane. I'm not sure why, but he was a character. It was an accessory; he didn't need it for any other reason. As we walked along, Jim spotted an ocelot on a leash in an alley. Only in New Orleans do you see (literally) wild things like that and people don't even blink an eye. Shortly thereafter, I noticed that there were two plainclothes cops up ahead of us, and don't ask me how I knew, but I *knew* they were talking to a hooker. All of a sudden, one of the cops noticed that Brian has a cane. Before we knew it, the cops were swarming around Brian, asking to inspect his cane. Instinctively, all nine of us gathered around Brian immediately, so then the cops were surrounded by all of us. Needless to say, they were surprised. New Orleans is famous for sword canes, which, if you don't know what a sword cane is, it is exactly what you think it is—a cane concealing a big ol' sword. The cops checked his cane, discovered it wasn't a sword cane, and we continued on our way.

In general, we weren't paying much attention to any of the specifics involved in the band's finances—we had a team of lawyers we gave power of attorney to, and they handled our affairs. The objective was to track the money that came in, keep the money (except for any necessary expenses), distribute the money, and, ideally, help us use the money to make even more money to protect the personal futures of all band members, regardless of what might happen. (Music is, after all, an unpredictable business.) The money was flowing, and no one had any complaints. Yet the more success we had, the more it became clear we actually had to do something with our money—having it sit in an account wasn't doing anyone any good and was subjecting us to bigger tax bills. At first this led our accountants to encourage us all to invest in real estate by buying a home if we were only renting—everyone did that. I never really had the "must own property" bug, but I had bought a house in Beachwood Canyon that I lived in with Birdie. After we separated en route to divorce in 1968, I sold that house and went back to renting a large apartment on Silver Ridge Avenue.

Ted got a place up in Laurel Canyon. He got a pair of sibling otters to go with it: Toots and Otto. Ted then moved from Laurel Canyon to a house with several acres on Mulholland Drive, where he fenced in the property with an electric gate to keep in his otters, but they had other ideas. The electric gate had a switch you'd flip inside a wooden box attached to power cords that ran up into it from the ground, but Toots and Otto discovered how to open the gate by reaching between the cords to the switch box. The "fugitive" otters were always eventually found—usually in a neighbor's swimming pool—and Ted kept "Missing!" signs on hand to post each time they vanished. They were smart, playful, high-energy animals and Ted had to make sure each door and window of the house was securely locked—otherwise they'd get inside, open up the refrigerator and cabinets, and eat everything. Otto's luck ran out in the early 1970s when a coyote killed him, and Ted got another otter pair to keep Toots company—Geyser and a female named Sam—but after Geyser bit Ted, he gave him to a friend. When Ted moved again, to an ocean-view house on the Pacific Coast Highway at County Line Beach, Toots and Sam went with him until they died peacefully of otter old age. (In captivity, an otter can live fifteen to twenty years... in case you didn't know...)

And now I'm finally getting around to those bad financial investments. At some point in late 1969 or early 1970, Larry came to the group with information about two guys in Costa Mesa who were developing the Box, a car that would revolutionize the automotive industry. Ted remembers it as a "car that would drive on water...it would be taken worldwide—appeal, production, sales." The bottom of the car was made of two layers of fiberglass that had been poured into a mold and separated by end-cut balsa wood, and then the top was interchangeable. If you wanted to have a sports car one day or a truck another day, you could do that—the heaviest part of the car was the bottom, which would always remain the same, while the interchangeable top might be only 150 to 200 pounds. *Popular Science* reported:

> Racing car? Economy car? Dune buggy? Off-road vehicle? The answer, every time, is yes; the Box is all of these. It began life as a multipurpose car suitable for street, track and off-road use; but because it even converts to an amphibian when paddles are fixed to the wheels.

The designers, Dan Hanebrink and Matt Van Leeuwen of Costa Mesa, Calif., aimed for aircraft lightness…

…There is no separate frame. The body structure is what holds the parts together. The body is made in two sections, a top and bottom, bolted together. The Box is a two-seater. You step into it through a single front door, which also serves as the windshield.

The Box is made of balsa wood (the ultra light stuff you build model planes of) and fiberglass (the kind used in big aircraft). The balsa, end-cut into small pieces, is fitted between layers of fiberglass…

…You steer with your feet. It sounds weird, but really isn't.[126]

When you read it in print, it seems pretty clear our investment was a gamble…and especially when you see a photo of it—it looks like a life-size version of a toy with which a child might play. Somewhere, there's a magazine photo of all of us lifting the Box over our heads. Bruce McLaren, who was the number one race car driver at the time—he'd recently won the 1968 Spa in Belgium—had ordered three of the Box. The car was featured on the cover of one or two major car magazines. There were two versions of it; one that would be mass-marketed to the public, and then one that race car drivers like Bruce would like, where the car would be steered with your feet, which would redistribute the strain driving causes in the body. At an April 1970 concert at Purdue University, a reporter printed our conversation about it:

EXPONENT: Have you guys got a goal? Are you guys going somewhere or just kind of grooving along?

LARRY: We're grooving along going somewhere, working toward something.

---

126   Davis, Jim. "'The Box'—All Wheels Steer." *Popular Science.* November 1970.

TERRY: Well, we're going toward a lot of things, because our interests are very diversified. We're hopefully going to manufacture a car (for which we have the prototype done), and we're hoping to be a major contender in utilitarian vehicles through that.

LARRY: The big commuter car market.

RUSS: We hope to compete with Chevrolet, in fact, we hope to destroy Chevrolet. And General Motors.

LARRY: This is the honest truth. It sounds like a big shock, but we are. We have two aerospace engineers; we are in the business. We've already been on the March cover of *Design News*, and the vehicle is called the Box. Like shoe box.

RUSS: Or lunch box.

LARRY: And the company is called Monocoque Engineering, that's a type of structure which is like an airplane, where the strength of the structure is from the skin, from the outside. It's a new concept in manufacturing, and I know we're the first rock-and-roll group to go into manufacturing, automobile manufacturing.[127]

Had the car made it to the public (spoiler!—now you know this ends badly), the United Auto Workers would likely have objected pretty loudly, as their very livelihood would have been threatened—as I mentioned, the bottom part of the car was a mold, which meant that anybody could be taught how to pour the mold; thus making the car cost less and capable of being mass-produced more easily. Yet as it turns out, no one had to worry about that because somebody broke into their shop, busted all of the molds, and we never heard from them again. We'd invested something like $150,000 of our money in the venture, which was a heck of a lot back then, but we never saw a penny of it and no one ever heard about the Box again. To hear Ted

---

127   Ziegler, David S. "The Association is manufacturing." *The Purdue Exponent*. April 22, 1970.

tell the story, he says the guys skipped town with the money and they were no longer reachable by their phone numbers, but I don't know what happened. I did see the head honcho of the Box at a wonderful outdoor concert in Big Bear, California, in the mid-1980s.

"Hey! Whatever happened to those several thousand bucks I gave you to put a Box body on my Porsche?" I asked.

He didn't answer me—and that was the end of that conversation. Terry thinks they legitimately spent our money on the product they were building for mass production and then vanished when the mold was vandalized and they were left with nothing. It's one of those mysteries we'll never get the full story on.

A loss of $150,000 was painful, to be sure, but it didn't break our stride. We were even inadvertently involved in Washington, DC, politics and ended up in the *Congressional Record*. Thomas H. Rees, the forty-four-year-old US representative from California, addressed Congress's Speaker of the House, seventy-seven-year-old John W. McCormack, on April 15, 1969, as follows:

> Mr. Speaker, we of Southern California are keenly aware that most non-Californians believe we are a little odd. I would like to risk proving this thesis by taking this opportunity to honor seven young men who wear their hair long and who sing and play in a pop music group. I refer to The Association, a band that makes its home in the Los Angeles area.
>
> It is not unusual for Congress to pay tribute to an organization such as this, but I would like to take a moment here to explain why I believe The Association is an unusual group, earning unusual attention. Perhaps then you will not think me so odd.
>
> The Association is a band that was formed three [*sic*][128] years ago in a small coffee house in Pasadena. Since then, The Association has become one of the most widely recognized

---

128   Correction! That would be four years ago, Congressman Rees.

and commercially successful young folk-rock bands in the history of popular music. And while accomplishing this, the individual members of The Association have acquitted themselves in a manner that brings credit to young people everywhere.

The Association has received nearly every award to be won—several "gold" records certifying at least one million copies of a record sold and no less than seven Grammy nominations—for best vocal group, best contemporary rock and roll group performance, and best contemporary album. The Association also has won the applause of fans throughout Europe and the Orient.[129]

Perhaps the most important thing The Association has done is span the generation gap, linking young and old. In the pleasing melodic sound of The Association, parents have found something in pop music that they can share with their children. The Association's most ardent fans are young people, of course, and hundreds of these teenagers write The Association each week, asking personal advice. Every letter is answered and always the advice is good: Stay in school, always give your parents a chance to explain, listen to all opinions—not just those of friends—and then make up your mind. As a result, many parents have written The Association to thank them for giving their time and the Association has, in turn, written parents, giving them some advice.

Young people are grateful The Association exists and so, apparently, are their parents. So, Mr. President, I think we should express our gratitude, too. And say "Welcome" whenever The Association comes to town—your town, my

---

129   I don't know about that...We would later learn that we had legions of fans in the Philippines and would play several concerts there decades later, and while I appreciate the reference, I don't think our reach had extended to the Orient at that point in time.

town, any town. We need people who can communicate, and in the field of communication, The Association excels.[130]

I have no idea why Congressman Rees felt compelled to mention us in Congress that day, but we thought it was cool. While album sales past our *Greatest Hits* weren't exactly stellar, we still continued selling out concerts, even on the night that man walked on the moon for the first time on July 20, 1969. The day before that concert, we'd performed two shows at Convention Hall in Asbury Park, New Jersey. The reviewer wrote:

...The Association. Are they barbershoppers? angelic chorusters? Actually, they are neither, although their music is built soundly around vocal harmony...

...Bluechel is one of the best drummers on the rock scene for his absolute understanding of what's going on within the group and his ability to provide the necessary rhythms and colorations. The rhythm is usually there with rock drummers. The coloration isn't.

One of the most interesting and appreciated offerings was "Enter the Young."[131] This song was released in December or January, and was written for submission as a new national anthem.[132] Copies were sent to every member of the national government, from representatives to cabinet members, to the

---

130   "The Association and the Generation Gap." *Congressional Record.* April 22, 1969. Page 9,997.

131   The journalist didn't do her homework. Terry's composition, "Enter the Young," was actually Track One on our first album, released three years earlier in 1966.

132   *The Christian Century Magazine* had put out an article in fall 1968, calling for a replacement of the national anthem, citing "the common people can't sing it...the very fact that the anthem is typically reserved for solo performers testifies to the fact that it isn't an anthem at all...the words are troublesome...the most vivid imagery has to do with the weapons of war—rather than with the heritage of our people or our pilgrimage through the generations or the beauty of our landscapes." Many people jumped on this bandwagon, but you know how it turned out...we still have the same national anthem!

presidential staff.[133] There's been a lot of talk lately about the need for a new national anthem for the US. This probably won't be it, but wouldn't it be a blast if it were?

"Enter the Young" is a call to self-realization embedded in a solid rock foundation. It doesn't advocate rebellion and it doesn't reflect the absurdity of life. What it does do, with a good, hard, steady beat, is suggest that it isn't enough to only think, one must also dare.

That seems to be very much in keeping with the traditional (verbal, if not actual) bedrock of American Democracy. Even so, it doesn't stand much of a chance to replace the "Star-Spangled Banner." But it's a good tight composition.[134]

Barbershoppers or angelic chorusters...another journalist who knew one label wouldn't suffice. The day before that concert a Michigan reporter had written, "Many people have tried to describe the Association, but they are so versatile no one description fits them for very long. Perhaps the one and only description that fits them is 'the famous seven-man band...' 'The intelligence that they display is sugarcoated with humorous finesse. Fun and frolic are their passwords.' 'Musical harmony mixed with hues of the rainbow; with a flare of showmanship!' 'They strive for total involvement of the audience and certainly they achieve this.'"[135]

Oh, and about that new national anthem we were lobbying for? The newspapers covered it.

The Association, which made news as the first rock combo to play the Tanglewood Music Festival, is now shooting for a place in our history books.

---

133   I don't remember copies being sent to every member of the national government, but that's not to say it didn't happen.

134   Pikula, Joan. "The Pop Box: Skillful Association." *Asbury Park Press*. July 21, 1969.

135   Knapp, Jan. "Seven talented young musicians." *Battle Creek Enquirer*. July 19, 1969.

And how, you ask? Several weeks ago, Terry Kirkman, their songwriter, read a new attack on an ancient sore subject, our national anthem, by no less an authority than the opera's George London. London joined the chorus of those who through the years have called "The Star Spangled Banner" virtually impossible to sing.

Kirkman has come up with a replacement, waxed by The Association, which will be sent to every government VIP, from the President down. The five hundred advance singles will be accompanied by a copy of the London piece from *Life Magazine* and a personal letter from the rock group urging adoption of "Enter the Young."

Sample lyric: "Enter the young yeah / Yeah, they've learned to think / Enter the young, yeah / More than you think they think."[136]

(Note how the article also mentions we were the first rock band to play Tanglewood.) Incidentally, the lyrics to "Enter the Young," which Terry originally wrote as "Beware the Young," came to him as he was opening a can of creamed corn. Clearly nothing came of that lobbying for a new national anthem, but imagine if it had!

On July 20, 1969, the day of the first moonwalk, we had a concert in Bridgeport, Connecticut. It was supposed to be held at Kennedy Stadium, but we got rained out and the venue was moved to a tent theater in Seaside Park. Sundance, an unknown band from Amherst, Massachusetts, opened for us. The stage crew had a portable television in the orchestra pit with the sound turned off (because we were performing), so we watched Neil Armstrong walk on the moon that night *during* our concert. That might explain why the critic for the Bridgeport concert wrote, "The seven man group...seemed to please most of the audience, in all respects except one, their on-stage positioning. For the better part of the short show, the Association

---

136   Haber, Joyce. "Joyce Haber's Column." *San Francisco Chronicle*. October 16, 1968.

had their backs to the audience, on occasion they moved around to face their fans."[137] I really can't be sure if that was the way the stage and sound equipment were positioned in the tent or because we were engrossed in Neil setting foot ON THE MOON (if you weren't alive then you probably can't wrap your brain around just how huge that was, but it was HUGE), but assuredly having our backs to the audience when we were performing was not typical. I do remember the sound was perfect at the show, and when Armstrong finally set foot on the moon, we all cheered and informed the audience of the historical news.

Shortly before I grew disenchanted with the group and left to release my first and only solo album in 1971, the band made another set of investments. There was a tax shelter—if you bought a large piece of property or invested in anything, what you paid, what you bought first, so long as you were paying the interest on the loan for the property, you could deduct all of the interest—a win-win when it came to taxes. So our lawyer took our band and a number of other largely successful entertainment industry clients they had at the time, and formed us into a cartel—we weren't connected in any way beyond the fact that we shared the same lawyer. They told us what amount of money to put in, and bam—we were all investing in the Shenandoah Apartments somewhere near Las Vegas, Nevada. There were also some apartments in Houston, Texas. I never saw them—I knew what they were—a large set of apartments built in the 1950s and made of cinder block—working-class apartments, you know, nothing fancy, but there were a lot of them. The shelter was like solid gold, particularly for someone like Terry, who had significantly more revenue as the songwriter on a number of our successful hits. The idea was also that no matter where you were, whether you were a member of The Association or not, you were still a part of the collective group making this investment and would reap the benefits. It was a smart long-term plan for our money. You

---

137   "Music and Comedy Combine In Show by 'The Association.'" *The Bridgeport Post.* July 21, 1969.

could deduct for wear and tear, a lot of things—and before you knew it, you could make a $50,000 investment and get $200,000 back. The benefits lasted for many years, until one day they didn't.

Ted remembers, "We were picked clean by people handling our money. I got called up to our lawyer's office and all they wanted me to do was to sign a document giving them the right to sell all of our apartment units in Las Vegas. They just wanted their money. They said, 'We can put a lien on your equipment and if you don't sign this we will lock you down until you can't see light anymore.' We got a letter that said the units were sold and 'this is what you will get when you pay the taxes.' We were told there wouldn't be taxes… The jaws of doom are always waiting to get you if you don't have someone looking out for you for every step." One night we went to bed and everything was fine; the next morning we woke up and had a whopping big tax bill. It's exactly the sort of thing you hear about what happened to Billy Joel and Leonard Cohen or other artists on those *Behind the Music* television shows. In some cases, those are stories about the people they trust embezzling money or stealing from them (and we'll get to those stories with The Association later, in a different decade), but at any rate, as Terry says, "You're not about money, you're about your art, you trust these people, they realize you're not about the money and the next thing you know, it's all gone." On the other side, sometimes those people—in this case, lawyers, but sometimes also managers or agents—they think you're working for them because they're running your life and without them you'd be "nothing," but the fact of the matter is, it's the opposite. Their job wouldn't even exist without the success of the very artist that lawyer, agent, or manager is representing.

There were also some grumbles in the group about how Pat was managing us, though I never supported any boo-hooing about that. Pat was the best thing to ever happen to The Association. Pat said, "When the contract [with Warner Bros.] expired…and we were devoid of hit records, I negotiated a deal with Clive Davis at

Columbia again for an unheard of $100,000 bonus for signing, much to the surprise of all in the biz. Ahmet Ertegun[138] actually called me to congratulate on that coup because at the time he had some interest in the group." Some people in the group thought this was measly, as there were other bands getting three-million-dollar signing bonuses. I'm not sure that's true, either—that sure does seem like a helluva lot for the 1960s and '70s, and maybe it was true for The Beatles, but didn't I already mention they have to be considered separately? (Remember, not that far into their US debut and Beatlemania, The Beatles stopped touring…because they *could*. Because they were making so much money, they didn't need to tour. Everyone knew their music already and they were adding fans to their base without needing to fill up stadiums.)

It's a bitch, really; you can't be successful in art without considering the financial aspects; you have to be involved in the decisions and on top of the people handling them for you, as the risk of what can happen when you're not is far too great. (Case in point: The Association. We didn't lose our shirts, but it wasn't pretty.) And let me tell you, you ain't heard nothing yet. But that's still a ways down the road in my tale…This money talk is making my head spin. Why don't we take a break and talk about the ladies, all the beautiful ladies….

I'm smiling already.

---

138 Ahmet Ertegun was the copresident and founder of Atlantic Records.

Cherish the Women
1943–(do I ever stop cherishing the women)?

WELL NOW, I KNOW you picked up this book about my band and me because you love our music and/or you're jonesing for a trip (perhaps literally) down nostalgia lane to the 1960s, but don't think I don't know you're holding out for some good gossip to fill in the "sex" part of the sex, drugs, and rock and roll equation. (You're only human.) While I can't say I've had the juiciest love experiences on the same level as, say, Elizabeth Taylor, I can say I've loved well and been loved, often. Isn't that what we're put on this earth to do? Isn't that what we sing songs about?

I've already shared a lot about Birdie, as she really was my first love, my first wife, and figured so largely in the beginnings of The Association. My life experiences to date have taught me that I'm not much of a marriage kind of guy—the piece of paper isn't so important to me. Either the relationship is working and you're devoted to each other, or it's not. No document is going to make it otherwise. Birdie and I were going to get married anyway, but ended up marrying earlier than we'd originally planned so my number for the draft wouldn't skyrocket to the top. The marriage didn't help or hinder our relationship one way or the other—we were meant to be together for as long as we were, and no shorter or longer—we simply drifted apart. Me being away so much of the year took its toll on the relationship, and when I was on the road, she was ostensibly a single mother to our daughter, Jill. We were married just under three years. At one point we separated, and then we got back together, only to divorce later. I sure am thankful we got Jill out of the marriage. Jill is like her mother; she has perfect pitch! Anyhow, I had my fun on tour, which I'll tell you more about, but never when I was officially married. Birdie would eventually marry a project manager for a construction firm and have another child. She was also a great songwriter—she was prolific in writing fun, educational songs for children to learn about the world, and she taught them in the Laguna school system. But enough about Birdie now, may she rest in peace.

Here I am with my daughter, Jill, on Catalina Island in the mid-1970s.

In between my first and second marriage, I spent something like ten or eleven years as a single man. Single only meaning that I wasn't married, *not* that I was without the pleasure of the company of women. The most significant of the parade of women in the late 1960s and through the 1970s—"significant" meaning the women you want to read about—were Helen Mirren and Linda Ronstadt.

I met Helen Mirren—I'm sorry, that would be *Dame* Helen Mirren—long before she was a dame, or I should say long before she was recognized as a dame by the British monarchy in 2003—I knew she was one helluva dame the moment I saw her!

It was early spring 1969,[139] and The Association was booked in Detroit at the same time she was touring the United States with the Royal Shakespeare Company's (RSC) production of *Much Ado About Nothing* in the role of Hero, the second female lead. She'd also recently filmed the role of Hermia in the RSC's production of *A Midsummer Night's Dream*. She was twenty-three years old and her star was on the rise—she was getting much attention for her role in Michael Powell's movie *Age of Consent*, in which she had something like three nude scenes. But I didn't know any of this when I met her—all I saw was a beautiful woman across a room. I was recently divorced, and I was instantly captivated.

The band had a few days off and Pete Stefanos, now our road manager, and I had gone out to dinner at a local restaurant at the top of a Detroit hotel with a great view. When we finished dinner, we went to the bar for cocktails. It wasn't crowded, but the place was large—it was on two levels. We were at the bar and there was a group of fifteen or twenty people, all obviously together, laughing and enjoying themselves, occupying the tables about forty to fifty feet from us. These people turned out to be the members of the RSC. The moment I laid eyes on Helen, I told the bartender to buy her a drink on me. She later joined me at the bar. We got to talking, and before I knew it, we found ourselves spending most of our spare time together over the next few days. She invited me to see the Shakespeare play the RSC was rotating in rep with on the tour—she wasn't in that one. We sat right in front and she made little comments to me as we watched the play, and I was just so taken by her; she was so bright. Helen was devastatingly beautiful, not to mention wickedly talented—it's no surprise she's achieved all the success she has.

In a March 30, 1969, *Detroit Free Press* article, Helen gave Lawrence DeVine her opinion on the character of the wronged and

---

139   In Helen's book, *In the Frame: My Life in Words and Pictures*, she mentions that she went to Detroit (which I'm about to tell you about) in 1967, but she's actually off by two years, as newspaper interviews with her at the time and reviews of her performance with the Royal Shakespeare Company prove. But don't blame Helen—she's trying to put together the puzzle of decades-old memories, just like me, and it ain't easy!

later redeemed Hero in *Much Ado About Nothing*, one of Shakespeare's most acclaimed comedies: "Of course I don't like her, I hate her, she's so spoilt and she always has nothing to say. We had an awful opening night, positively disastrous, we all felt. I don't think we're perfect, but I think the audience was very cold to us."[140] DeVine had reviewed the same production two weeks earlier and written in his review, "Well, now as ever, Claudio and Hero are two nice enough young sorts—played here by Bernard Lloyd and Helen Mirren—and both are about as exciting as Cream of Wheat."[141] Ouch! I know what it's like to be on the receiving end of a review like that. The Association had its fair share of critics who liked to put us in our place. In fact, Mike Gormley reviewed our show in Detroit on that tour and wrote the following:

> The highly successful singing group opened their show with, appropriately, their first hit, "Along Comes Mary." It was acceptable, but not great... But it wasn't until half way through the second set that The Association put across their feeling. They did it with the masterpiece "Requiem for the Masses." The tune, though never released as a single, gained international acceptance because of its greatness... They hung onto their reputation as one of the best singing and instrumental groups around.[142]

Apparently we started off lukewarm but went out with a bang. Well, a critic's opinion is only ever one person's opinion. We once had a show in the early 1980s at the Fairmont in San Francisco that got panned, and the maître d' told us the reviewer had slept through the whole thing—passed out at his table the entire time! It was bullshit, because we did nothing but stellar concerts during our engagement

140   DeVine, Lawrence. "Royal Shakespeare's Helen Mirren Makes Film Debut in Nude Scene," *Detroit Free Press*. March 30, 1969.

141   DeVine, Lawrence. "Much Ado About Nothing Done with Style and Color," *Detroit Free Press*. March 13, 1969.

142   Gormley, Mike. "The Association Concert-A Display of Fine Talent," *Detroit Free Press*. March 24, 1969.

at the Fairmont. Later, that same reviewer was fired for reviewing a dance show he hadn't attended—in fact, it had never even *happened*—and he gave it a poor review! How's that for unbelievable? This isn't to say all critics are bad. It's just that every critic is influenced by his or her own personal taste, or in the case above, alcohol. I never saw Helen perform live when I met her in 1969—her performance times conflicted with The Association concerts—but she didn't win an Oscar for nothing.

Anyhow, back to Gormley's review of our Detroit concert. I would agree with him about "Requiem for the Masses," as would Terry, I'm sure. The song had social and emotional impact that hit you right *there*; it was a crowd pleaser because of what it stirred deep inside, and it differed from the rest of our repertoire and image. In fact, in another article Gormley had written just three days earlier, prior to reviewing our concert, he wrote:

> The Association is a strange group. They are definitely a "commercial" group but at the same time respected by fellow musicians…It takes a while to get into the type of music The Association puts out. Heads obviously wouldn't like it. As a matter of fact, just before talking to Terry, Bing Crosby had mentioned The Association as a very good group. Terry wasn't sure if that was bad or good.

> But there is something good there. They are a good group and deep down, and you don't have to dig too far to find it, there is meaning and deep feelings. Remove the whipped cream topping of The Association and there's a lot of guts.

Terry told Gormley in that same article:

> When we got started, the so-called underground sound was just forming. We weren't part of it therefore or [sic] music didn't go at all in that direction. We came straight out of folk and our music was just a projection of that part of our lives.

Speaking for myself, I get a little bothered with the way our music has been accepted. Through our production techniques using so many voices, etc., people have missed the lyrics, which are deep in terms of poetic content. [143]

I wasn't in Terry's head at the time, but if I know Terry, he was probably thinking specifically of "Requiem for the Masses" and its lyrics:

Requiem aeternam, requiem aeternam
Mama, mama, forget your pies
Have faith they won't get cold
And turn your eyes to the bloodshot sky
Your flag is flying full
At half mast, for the matadors
Who turned their backs to please the crowd
And all fell before the bull
Red was the color of his blood flowing thin
Pallid white was the color of his lifeless skin
Blue was the color of the morning sky
He saw looking up from the ground where he died
It was the last thing ever seen by him
Kyrie Eleison
Mama, mama, forget your pies
Have faith they won't get cold
And turn your eyes to the bloodshot sky
Your flag is flying full
At half mast, for the matadors
Who turned their backs to please the crowd
And all fell before the bull.

You read lyrics to a song like that and realize we were a band singing songs as diverse and incomparable as "Requiem for the

---

143   Gormley, Mike. "The Association Changes After Working Holiday," *Detroit Free Press*. March 21, 1969.

Masses," "Along Comes Mary," and "Cherish," you wonder how anyone could ever try to put us in a box with a "sunshine pop" label.

There isn't much more to say about Helen—a gentleman kisses but never tells. A few days after I left to Detroit, I flew her in to see another concert we had somewhere else in the Midwest, I can't recall—she loved it and spent the night, and then flew back to Detroit the next morning to honor her performance commitments on tour. I sent her a postcard from Griffith Park Observatory with a bunch of stars on it, and that was pretty much it. I have nothing but fond memories of the short time we spent together.

Helen did an interview with the *Los Angeles Times* in February 1969, which would have been a month before she went to Detroit. In it, the journalist writes, "Between performances, she's exploring America with great glee. An orange Peanuts sweatshirt she bought for her English boy friend hangs over a chair..."[144]

Whether that was a boy friend or a *boyfriend* or Helen had broken up with him before we met or she made me her "road husband" for those few days, I'll never know. Helen didn't meet her husband until her late thirties and didn't even get married until she was something like fifty years old. (Smart lady!) She was quoted in a November 29, 2016, Kendall Fisher article on *E! Online* about her marriage to director Taylor Hackford as saying, "We got married in the end because we realized that we were going to be together forever. We got married, ultimately, for legal reasons more than anything else. Estate planning and other complicated things like that. And our families, we sensed, wanted us to be married." Though Helen and I didn't have an opportunity to get to know one another at length, reading that statement—and who knows, I mean it's just an interview with a journalist for crying out loud—makes me think we each recognized a kindred spirit in the other.

The Association had done a few shows with Linda Ronstadt, so I had met her in passing and we were friendly. One night at the

144   Smith, Cecil. "A 'Dream' Worth Staying Awake For." *Los Angeles Times*. February 6, 1969.

Troubadour bar later in 1969, I asked her if she would spend some time with me, and she said she would. We were together for a few months, shortly after my final separation from Birdie. Now, Linda and I never spoke of the relationship or attempted to define it with labels. We never said, "Let's go together" or "We're going steady, here's a ring." We just liked being together, and so we were.

She was on the road, and I was on the road, and when we were in town, we'd see each other when we could—we'd go to restaurants, she'd come to my house. That was when I had an apartment up on Silver Ridge Avenue between Echo Park and Silver Lake. There was never a harsh word between us. She was far more politically active than me. I had opinions and I wasn't shy about them, but I wasn't politically active.

One rainy night we had dinner at a little restaurant on Melrose, a couple of blocks east of The Troubadour, called The Black Rabbit Inn. Co-owner Billy James, who was also a music executive and band manager, greeted us at the door. It was a beautiful wood-paneled room and not crowded that night, and we ate at a table near the roaring fireplace. I was a vegetarian at the time and while I don't remember what we ate, I do remember it was an excellent restaurant with great food.

One evening, I went to pick Linda up at the Troubadour and as I walked into the bar, I spotted her sitting with a group of people at a table in the southwest corner. When she saw me, she stood up and we left together. I learned later that a journalist who was also at the table did not recognize me, asked who I was, and was told "Russ Giguere." She misheard it and printed in her publication: "...Linda Ronstadt left with Rusty Gear." I don't know the name of the journalist or the publication and have searched for it to no avail—but I thank them for this lovely name, which has stuck with me to this day.

Linda is an incredible singer—she's half-Mexican, so she did albums in Spanish in addition to making her chart-topping hits in English. She reminds me of the Mexican singer Estela Núñez, but

Linda is her own being—she is so intelligent and so beautiful. (I always go for the combination of beauty *and* brains.) All the women's libbers loved Linda. Bill Martin, whom I had a comedy duo with a few years after I left The Association, once called her "a teddy bear with tits." He played keyboard in one of her early bands and had a huge crush on her. (With a phrase like that, he wasn't disguising his affection.)

Once the band was doing a large indoor concert in either Phoenix or Tucson, Arizona—Tucson was Linda's hometown—and Linda was visiting her parents, so she came to see us. Planning to watch the show from the side of the stage, she wore a white Mexican blouse, somewhat sheer, with flowers embroidered at the neckline— and no bra. One of the security guards found her braless appearance too provocative and said she'd have to watch the concert from behind the stage, out of sight of the audience. We both thought it was silly, but she complied with his request. It was a great show, and I was so pleased that Linda was there to see and hear it.

There are stories out there about how Linda snorted coke, and it's just not true. She didn't snort coke, and she didn't smoke pot. (She was allergic to weed.) She may have had a glass of wine occasionally, but I don't even remember that. The relationship just sort of phased out, and we moved on. There was no definitive thing or event that ended it. Later, when we were both seeing other people (specifically when she was with singer/songwriter/actor J. D. Souther who was in a pre-Eagles duo with Glenn Frey, called Longbranch Pennywhistle, and cowrote several Eagles hits including "Best of My Love," "New Kid in Town," and "Heartache Tonight"), we went on double dates, so everything was always very friendly between us. It still is. I recall one game of Monopoly at JD's house, between him, Linda, me, and my lady at the time, Jayne Zinsmaster. Another time we went to a drive-in movie theater in JD's car—a Studebaker. JD was interviewed as recently as 2015 about his then-new album, *Tenderness*, and he confessed Linda is still his first listener on any album. "She's always the first to hear a new album…she's the greatest listener: an astute, well-read woman, as well as musical."[145] I was blown away when I called JD up to ask about interviewing him for my book and lo and behold, he turned around and *wrote* something! Here it is.

Rusty Gear
By J. D. Souther

I met Russ Giguere in Los Angeles in 1972, or so I remember now because that year viewed through the sweet tea glass of retrospect was my complete immersion in the baptismal of New Life in Southern California and Russ was pure California to me. He had a great singing group called The Association and besides beautiful love ballads like "Cherish," they had a verified big hit about marijuana, "Along Comes Mary." He lived on the top floor of a cool old house in Beachwood Canyon, biked everywhere, seemed completely unselfconscious, and was outrageously tan and happy. He had a big shiny smile and laughed often, loudly, and is to this day the only person who can laugh himself breathless at his own jokes without embarrassment or any need of it.

I know a few good Russ Giguere stories, mostly told by him at our sunset toasts, often following an afternoon movie at the Chinese Theatre on Hollywood Boulevard. We would wind up the hill to Yamashiro,[146] a famous restaurant and gorgeous Japanese temple where Russ, Bill Martin, and I would order vodka tonics and watch the sunset from the southeast corner while we reviewed the film and generously applied the lubricant of humor to the squeaky wheels of contemporary life in LA. We were part of a loose coalition that came to be known as the Beachwood

---

145   Cordova, Randy. "JD Souther talks 'Tenderness,' Ronstadt, 7/10–11" *The Republic.* www.azcentral.com. July 3, 2015.

146   You can still find me there occasionally.

Rangers.[147] I love Beachwood Canyon, less famous than her sisters Laurel, Coldwater, and Benedict, each successively tonier and further west than the one before. The Rangers also included Harry Dean Stanton, Kris Kristofferson, and Linda Ronstadt, with whom I shared the first of my three Beachwood Canyon houses. Sometimes Harry Dean would join and Linda would come with me as we lived on the same property; Harry Dean in the garage apartment behind the main house (more like a lanai than anything else), Bill and Lois Martin in most of the downstairs, and Linda and I perched in the upper floor. Either Linda or Bill introduced me to Russ and my second Beachwood house was directly across the street from Russ. It is the scene for this little tale.

It was ten or eleven in 1971 or 1972, the very shank of the evening on one of those hallucinogenic nights in the Hollywood Hills and Bill Martin and I were smoking and drinking our way toward the midnight hour, alternately laughing and playing music and listening to great records. My driveway was just below a balcony and we heard a scuffle outside and some yelling. I hauled open the heavy Spanish-style front door and Russ, somewhat rumpled and out of breath, shouted that some guy had tried to break into my car, just below us. Russ had stopped him and tried to make the collar himself, but the guy squirmed away and ran down Gower Street toward Franklin Avenue and was disappearing into the hedges by the time we'd fully grasped the situation. Another petty crime prevented, this time by my friend Russ.

It was over just that fast. We thought. Back up the stairs we went, poured another round and stood around the fireplace. We were strong and happy and toasted the success of our Unofficial Beachwood Ranger Crime Prevention Task

---

147   This would actually become the name of a short-lived band I formed after my first time with The Association, though JD was not in that band.

Force. Soon the music was again shaking the glasses on the mantle and all were back to our previous good humor. The night was cool and Ray Charles was killing it with "Lonely Avenue." As Ray and the Raelettes were holding the last notes I heard two quick pops, a clink of larger glass and heard a bullet whiz past my head and spit into the adobe wall above the fireplace. I just remember barking, "Get down, get down...," and thinking some fool is shooting up my house. Then four more shots flew almost softly through our buzz and the heavy curtains that draped the windows. The street was at a fairly steep angle below and the shots were mostly too high to hit anyone on the far wall of the room, where we all were. Lucky, I suppose, that neither Bill nor I were sitting at the piano, which, as all Hollywood Hills pianos must, overlooked the street. I remember either Jimmy or Waddy Wachtel (or both) as being there too that evening, but I can't be sure how long they stayed.

This became part of the Beachwood lore and was toasted roundly whenever the council gathered. Russ (or Rusty Gear as Linda affectionately renamed him) is a man whom everyone is delighted to see coming through the door. His speaking voice is hoarse and gruff, like a favorite uncle, but his singing is silky and beautifully complex, that of a natural-born harmony singer. He can be loud and positive to the point of exasperation, but the room is always missing some zest when he leaves it. He has a rejoinder to any observation contrary to his choices but they are always good-natured and usually followed by that beautiful toothy laugh. We ate regularly at Nucleus Nuance, a "health food" eatery on Melrose that featured date shakes, a favorite choice of Linda and me, and best of all, a waiter named Prince who made the plain tables and little chairs in this, our family joint, seem like the best place in the world to start an evening.

Once I chided Russ about his devotion to iceberg lettuce, claiming it had no real food value compared to the spinach and arugula in our salads. He leaned forward, widened his eyes behind his glasses and boomed, "...Washes the blood, my son, washes the blood!" and reared back in his chair and cackled until he was holding his sides and the whole room was smiling. Unlike Will Rogers or new wave positivists of any stripe who may never have met anyone they didn't like, almost everyone I know has disliked at least one of us for some reason at one time...All but Russ Giguere.

—John David Souther

Bill Martin, JD, and I were movie buffs, and in the seventies we frequented all of the Los Angeles Japanese movie houses and art theaters. We saw every Kurosawa movie we could—*Seven Samurai, Yojimbo, Rashomon*—all of them. One of our haunts was the Toho LaBrea theatre (now a Korean Presbyterian Church). We also saw many of the Zatoichi "Blind Samurai" films. They weren't full-length—they were more like serials with titles like *Baby Cart in Peril, Inevitable Swords*, and so on. And I hardly remembered that night at his place where the gunshots rang out until he sent me the story!

Anyhow, that was Linda and JD—I couldn't speak of Linda without also talking about JD.

I would say I've been married four times—three times legally (I'm getting to those!), and once in my heart and soul to my late wife, Noma. Though we never made it official at a courthouse, I was devoted to her, and she to me, and no piece of paper or lack thereof would ever change that. The third time is the charm, so they say, and being that we were together later in life, after I'd worked through all the bullshit of my youth, fame and some fortune, well, it worked, until she was taken from me far too soon. But before I get into my time with Noma, since I'm cherishing the women here, I suppose I should talk a little more about that ten- or eleven-year gap between my marriage to Birdie (late sixties) and my marriage to my second wife,

Penny Dovey (early eighties), where I dated Helen (a tour dalliance) and Linda (for a few months), both of whom I've mentioned, as well as Caroline Walton-Howe, whom I dated and lived with for several years before we both took other lovers and split, and Jayne Zinsmaster, whom I met while she was in high school and then began dating (but never lived with) after she graduated college—Jayne and I are still friendly to this day. There are others, but I'd say these were the most significant women I had the pleasure of dating. And I'll say this—never once in my life have I dated a woman who was anything less than super smart. As I mentioned, I like them beautiful, and I like them smart. Anyhow, this list is starting to make me seem like I'm a lothario, which isn't quite the case, but I suppose it's safe to say I was never lacking for female company.

Caroline worked for one of those studios that put out TV dramas that were based on old horror films. She had to put up with a lot of crap from me. I left The Association for the first time in 1970, and I spent the better part of the decade defining myself through other forms of artistic expression, albeit all of them musical. But I remained on good terms with the band and still went to see their concerts whenever they were playing in the Los Angeles area.

In the summer of 1967, we had become the first rock and roll band to play the Greek Theatre, an outdoor venue in Griffith Park in Los Angeles. We would then play it two more times, once in August 1970, when B. B. King opened the show (this was right after I left the band), and with the reformed Mamas and Papas in July 1985. The reformed band consisted of original members John Phillips and Denny Dougherty, Elaine "Spanky" McFarlane replacing the late Cass Elliott, and John's daughter, Mackenzie Phillips, replacing his ex-wife, Michelle. Spanky was an old pal of ours from her "Spanky and Our Gang" hit-making days in the sixties. We'd met her at Western Studios when they were cutting their first album (we were impressed by their sound and work ethic—*and* they smoked dope, so we were like peas in a pod). If you only knew Mackenzie Phillips as an actress from her hit TV show *One Day at a Time*, her singing would bowl you over. She was one of those people who appeared real "straight" off stage. But once she set foot on the stage, she became electric—it was incredible to watch. Now, I know no one wants to hear this, but the John-Denny-Spanky-Mackenzie lineup sounded as good, or *even better*, than the original Mamas and Papas, whom we played with many times—more times than any other band they played with.

Elaine ("Spanky") recalls, "I grew up with five brothers, so when I met The Association it was like finding my family in a recording session. Such incredible voices and harmonies. They all seemed to know their value to the group. They were cute, they were funny and they were arrogant as hell. Not without something to be arrogant about—I mean my band was listening to their records. We loved them. Every once in a while one or two of them would slip away from their own sessions with Bones Howe and sit in on a 'Ba Ba Da' or two. I'm sure I was a little in love with a couple of them. Sometimes we would see other bands in different airports around the country. One time The Association had some fans following them through the airport. They were sort of running away, but took enough time to drop all the change from their pockets to leave behind them a trail of coins that I guess were meant for the pitiful people following them. They were pretty crazy—but fun."

But back to my musical experiments post-Association. There was my 1971 solo debut album, *Hexagram 16*, and of course the adventures with the Beachwood Rangers and Hollywood, as well as my time with Bill Martin as a comedy duo. There were also a couple of other bands I struggled to get off the ground that are too inconsequential to mention.

I am, however, trying to stick to just the women at the moment— I'll return to the music shortly. Back to Caroline and how she had to put up with my crap. As I mentioned, my preferred drug of choice for a long time was marijuana. Then there was coke in the eighties (let's be clear—there was always cocaine, but it enjoyed a popularity surge in the eighties). And my preferred drink these days is bourbon. But I gave up the coke decades ago and quit drinking for the most part after my 2014 cancer diagnosis, limiting it to a weekly happy hour drink. A couple of times it was two drinks and that was one drink too many—my physiology has changed. I occasionally drink coffee, and a cappuccino once in a blue moon. Pot, however? I still smoke that daily. Though it's stronger these days, so I don't need as much.

In the early seventies, though, I went through a methedrine phase. I thought that with each new band I formed that struggled to get off the ground, the struggle meant I had to work that much harder and longer. And so that, in turn, meant I needed help staying awake more hours so I could be more productive. Enter the Judy Garland problem. (You know, MGM supplied her with speed while she was shooting *The Wizard of Oz* so she would slim down and have enough energy to get through the grueling, long shoot days. This ultimately set up the lifelong drug habit that killed her.) Slimming down was never my problem, but hours in the day? I wanted more time to accomplish what I needed to get done. And so I took methedrine. Methedrine is a white crystal powder that is pure, unadulterated speed. I started taking it when I was with Caroline, not every day—but that didn't matter, it really screws up your body. Even after Caroline moved out and I was living alone, I was still taking it. "Methedrine is the devil," Caroline told me. But I didn't listen. I had to discover it for myself.

Thankfully, I was able to get off of it. If I was taking a drug, I wanted it, it was my choice, but if I wanted to quit cold turkey, I had the constitution to do just that. (Yes, I'm fortunate—I know that's not always the case for everyone.) The last time I ever took methedrine—we're talking a little over forty years ago now—it put me in bed for over a week and I never had a desire to touch it again. In fact, that time I spent laid up in a bed from nearly dying of speed led me to give up music altogether for a few years, but more on that later. I was so incapacitated, people had to actually bring me food—I couldn't even go out to get it. It hit me when I was up on a ladder, working on hanging the acoustic baffling from the ceiling of a rehearsal hall I was working in on another one of my new band ventures that never really took off. I somehow woke up on the floor—I must have fallen—I have no memory of how I ended up there, I just woke up. I was so weak, how I managed to pull myself up off the floor, lock the place up, and get into my car to drive home—it's amazing I even did that, really. Thank God I didn't hit anyone driving home. I slept for twenty-four hours straight and stayed in bed for more than a week—my own version of a rehab, I suppose. I came damn close to dying that night and never touched speed again.

Years later, I had minor surgery and before I had the surgery, I had to have a physical, which included a cardiogram. The results came back and the doctor said, "Well, you've had a myocardial infarction before." I said, "What's that?" And he said, "A heart attack." I said, "No, I've never had a heart attack." But driving home from the appointment I thought it about it some more, and I realized that whole episode in the early seventies, with waking up on the floor of the rehearsal hall, probably *was* a heart attack. And that heart attack probably saved my life because it made me drop speed like a hot potato.

Penny was my second wife. She was a blackjack dealer in Tahoe, and I met her while I was on tour with the band when we got back together in the early eighties. I saw her walking across the room (yes, I know it sounds like a pattern here between Helen and Penny, spotting attractive women across the room), and she was so strikingly beautiful, I just started walking in the direction she was walking. As it turns out, she was walking up to one of the guys in the band. I was actually going with a lawyer at the time—we had no promises or anything, but we were seeing a lot of each other. However, once I met Penny, the lawyer and I split. We married in 1984 and divorced in 1986. She must have walked out on me at least six times before we ultimately divorced. I didn't know what PMS was until I was married to Penny. Thanks to her, I learned the real cause of PMS: *me*. We had passion, but we drove each other crazy.

Several years ago, Penny died. A few months before she died, she called me. I hadn't talked to her in something like fifteen or twenty years. She called to tell me she loved me, she'd always loved me (not that she told me that often when we were together...), that she had terminal cancer and would be gone in four to six months. Birdie then died in 2010, about two years after Penny. When the women you've loved in your life start dying, it puts your own expiration date into perspective.

Which brings me to Noma Paulsen. If we had married, she would have lost all of her retirement and benefits. She'd been in the music talent management business (and before that she'd been a pilot, a real estate broker, had owned a clothing shop and a temp agency, and sold airplanes, all at various points in her life). She had so many benefits and I didn't want her to jeopardize them, so we never made it official. But I'd be lying if I didn't say I considered Noma to be my wife and if she hadn't died, we'd still be together. With Noma, everything just clicked—by far, she was my most successful marriage. Whether that's due to my maturity or our compatibility, I'm not sure—it's likely a combination of both.

She once said to me, "This relationship has lasted two times longer than any other relationship I've had."

"That's funny," I told her, "It's *three times* longer than any relationship I've ever had!"

Noma and I were officially together for about twelve and a half years. The first ten years I basically lived at her place but continued to hold on to mine. That's not because I had a foot out the door or anything; it's because when you've lived in the same apartment since the 1970s, you don't give up the rent-stabilized deal too easily. The last four years of our relationship, Noma sold her house and moved in with me. We actually got together in the first place because of Pat Paulsen, God bless him. Noma had been married to Pat and following his death, as we spent time together, we grew closer.

Pat's last concert was in Lancaster, California, with The Association. That's when he told me, "Russ, don't tell anyone, but I'm fighting cancer. I think I'm going to win." This was the same concert Pat was scheduled to perform after us. He said, "I can't follow you guys." So he went on first! Sadly, he didn't live long past that concert. When he died, they shut down The Ice House and had a gathering of everyone who knew him and loved him. Tommy and Dick Smothers' manager, Kenneth Fritz, gave a speech about how much Pat Paulsen had meant to him. Kenneth was always wearing strange coats, and that night was no exception.

"Where'd you get that coat?" Tommy yelled from the back of the room. "Carpeteria?"[148] The crowd roared.

After Pat died in 1997, I invited Noma to lunch. A couple of weeks later, I called her and we had dinner. I would see her every two to four weeks, and then I was seeing her every week, again, just for a meal and company, and nothing happened for a couple of years. But somehow gradually we became involved. It developed slowly. I was sort of afraid of relationships. Why, I don't know. Noma was so smart, I never could figure out what she was doing with me.

It might be hard to believe coming from someone who has spent his life in show business, but I'm actually pretty reclusive. Noma was very social. She loved me dearly, and I loved her with all my heart. We were celibate the last few years of her life, because before she was diagnosed with cancer, she had developed a rare skin disease where she couldn't really be intimate. She lived with it for over five years. A couple of doctors she went to didn't know what it was, and the third doctor she went to diagnosed the condition and told her, "It won't kill you, but you'll wish you were dead." He was right. She never told anybody, never whined or said a word about it. She kept it to herself. It was uncomfortable most of the time, and sometimes it was extremely painful. She had blisters just about everywhere but her face. She kept them covered so no one would know. She said the skin

---

148   Carpeteria sold carpets. Kenneth Fritz's jacket looked like it should be included in the store's inventory.

disease was more painful than the cancer. Six months after the cancer diagnosis, she was gone. I feel like I was robbed of the twenty-plus years I expected to be able to share with Noma; her mom had lived until her late eighties and her father was ninety-three when he passed away, but clearly with life you never know what hand you'll be dealt.

Noma died in 2012; I kept to myself and hunkered down to mourn, venturing out for daily walks with my dog, Annie, and still touring with the band, but otherwise laying low. Just over a year after I made it through radiation treatment for my own cancer in 2014 (I'll get to that story later), I reconnected with Valerie Yaros, whom I went with for several years in the 1990s. An historian for SAG-AFTRA and a member of the National Film Preservation Board of the Library of Congress (I told you, I go for brains), she's my honey, my friend, my companion, and my wife. I'd like to thank Ted Bluechel, who is also an ordained minister, for marrying us. We got married at Valerie's birthday party at a ranch in Acton, California. I'm grateful to have a special lady in my life again who, when she's not around (which thankfully isn't often), I miss something fierce.

I can't really talk about all of the muses in my life, though, without mentioning another lady I thought I would one day grow old with, Judee Sill. Judee and I were never a couple—we were never linked romantically—but I loved her, like a friend, a sister. She was a helluva songwriter and a great human. I encountered her music before I ever met her. After my marriage to Birdie ended and I moved out, Jules moved into my apartment on Silver Ridge Avenue. The apartment was three stories tall and in the middle story, there was a kitchen and living room/dining room. There was a Hammond organ, and a cross and a candle hanging from the ceiling. One day I walked through the door to hear Jules singing, "One star remains in the false darkness / Have you met my man on love?" It was haunting. I stood at the door to listen until the song was over.

When it ended, I said, "Jules, did you *write* that?"

"No," he said. "Judee Sill wrote it, and she has a shitload of others."

The song was "My Man on Love."

Jules was dating Judee at the time. I met her in the kitchen one morning—we were both stark naked and padding into the kitchen to get something to eat when we ran into each other. "Hi, I'm Russ," I said. "I'm Judee," she said. And then we just went about our business. (It was the sixties. No one gave a crap about nudity.) We became friends; Jules and I even bought her a Martin guitar.

In a 2004 article in *The Guardian*, "The Lost Child," music business lawyer Bill Straw told Barney Hoskyns, "Judee was so different from everybody. Everybody was writing oblique lyrics back then, but her oblique lyrics had a character of their own." Judee played in a music festival in Barnsdall Park the summer I met her. I went to see her perform and was impressed.

I called up David Geffen. "David," I said, "you've got to hear this lady's music. Songs like I've never heard before."

"What she's like?" he asked.

"She's influenced by gospel, but there's gospel, folk, country western, and rock and roll."

I took David to see her perform at a Troubadour hoot. We stood on the stairs and watched her through the railing. "Wow, I've never heard anything quite like this," David said. He was knocked out and signed her to Asylum Records instantly. I think she may have even been the first act he signed for the label. She used the handsome advance to put a down payment on a house in the Valley.

Judee had a colorful background. Her father had died when she was eight, and her brother had been killed in a car crash. She had an alcoholic mother. She had been a prostitute, she'd done jail time for armed robbery, and she'd been addicted to heroin. She lived a lot of life in her far too short thirty-five years. She also dated J. D. Souther at some point (who, as I mentioned, went on to date Linda Ronstadt, which really pissed Judee off), and he broke her heart. (The music industry was small; some might say incestuous. We all dated each other.)

But Judee's talent was something else. JD remembers an audience member at one of her gigs requesting her to play and sing a Judy Collins song.

"I don't know that song and if I did, I wouldn't play it," Judee said.

She believed in her talent, as right she should have. Judee cited her three major influences as Bach, Pythagoras, and Ray Charles. (She even had a cat she named Pythagoras—he had a hole in his ear—and one Christmas, Caroline and I got her a tiny earring for the cat.)

Judee always looked so serious in her photos, including this autographed one she gave to me, but she was one of the funniest people I've ever known.

There was something between us that I've never experienced with any other relationship, and I'm not talking sexual. It was built out of mutual respect, to be sure, but there was also something unexplainable about it. When I met her she was no longer a junkie, but she still did heroin now and again. I didn't know it at the time. She started recording her first album and had a date at Western Studios with an orchestra and she stopped by my house on the way down to the studio. While she was visiting me, she had parked her rental car in my parking spot and when she went to leave for the session, a Mercedes-Benz had blocked her in. We knocked on the doors of several houses to see whose car it might be, but no one knew.

"What am I going to do?" she asked.

"Nothing to do but ram him out of the way," I said. She couldn't leave all those musicians waiting for her at the studio rates. So she rammed that Mercedes owner's car out of the way. I never heard anything about it.

Judee toured with Crosby, Stills & Nash. David Crosby was so stunned by the quality of her music that he gave her his guitar. "Jesus Was a Cross Maker" is about JD. She also wrote a song about me called "The Vigilante," which she sang on her second album, *Heart Food* (1973). The opening lyrics are:

> *I see the vigilante watchin' in the deep o' the night,*
> *I always find him where his heart is, he's fightin' the good fight,*
> *He smells the scent of trouble and prepares to leave,*
> *He's got his eyes on the horizon, reachin' higher,*
> *He's got his eyes on the horizon, and his boots on his feet.*

I didn't learn I was the subject of that song until years after she died, and a writer who was going through her journals told me. Judee did the vocal arrangement for one of The Association's songs, "Michelangelo," which was a funny song that Mason Williams wrote. In 1972, I joined The Association onstage (I wasn't with the group at the time) for their encore in a double billing with Judee at the Troubadour, which *Cashbox* reviewed:

> Summer solstice brought rain, Judee Sill and the Association
> to Los Angeles, each in a particular way, welcome and
> refreshing.

Given a choice between hearing Judee Sill talk or sing, I would have to cop out and ask for a generous measure of both. Unfortunately, her Troubadour set was limited to six songs, two from her first Asylum album, four new, each introduced with a rap so memorable as to suggest a volume of collected phrases. A performer/writer of enormous intensity and intimacy, she treats her audience to slices of life and soul-deep insights. Melodically fresh and exciting, lyrically profound, hers is music that melts with familiarity.

Introducing "Jesus Was a Cross Maker," she simply said: "A song about unrequited love turned to forgiveness." A new song, written "for Grover...a writer who has an honorable loneliness" called—"There is a Rugged Road"—was typically Sillsian: more words to the phrase than could possibly fit, but did. Musically and philosophically, Judee Sill is a force and a presence, creating and sharing in a very special way, and with her own very personal truth.

With a new Columbia album on release and a total body count of eight people[149] and enough instruments onstage to warrant the placing of a sign saying, "Guitar Sale," the Association is swinging out once more. Their fourteen-selection set (including two encores, in which they were joined by founding member Russ Giguere) displayed their tremendous versatility and excellent intra-group rapport. The Troubadour stage was barely large enough, but the lack of ambience did not dim enthusiasm; old Association standards gave way to material from the new album, and a fine—if somewhat homogenized—time was had by all. Original material by Jules Alexander—"Please Don't Go (Round the Bend)" and "Kicking the Gong Around"—

---

149 I believe the reviewer is referring to what would have been Terry, Jules, Ted, Jim, Larry, Richard Thompson, and Maurice Miller (on drums), plus me in the encore that night makes eight.

provided high points of the set, as did their classics, "Along
Comes Mary," "Windy" and "Cherish," though the familiar
vocal harmonies were somewhat obscured by ornate
instrumentation.[150]

I still frequented the Troubadour often. I remember one night in
the seventies, I was sitting at a table in the bar with singer-songwriter
Tom Waits, who looks like he's been drinking and smoking all his life.

"I'm going out to the alley to smoke a joint," I said. "You want to
join me?"

"Well, I don't smoke weed," he replied, "but I'll share the alley
with you."

And so we did.

One evening in 1971, I was sitting with Glenn Frey at the
Troubadour when he introduced me to his new drummer from
Texas, for the as-yet-unnamed band he was putting together. The
drummer's jaw hit his chest, "You're from the Association?" It was
Don Henley and the band would become The Eagles.

On another night right around that time period, I was at the
Palomino, a wonderful country-western music club/venue in North
Hollywood (Jim Yester's dad, Larry Yester, had played there with
musician Hank Penny, who cofounded the club in 1949). As I sat
there listening to the house band on a slow night (there were maybe
thirty or forty people there), Merle Haggard, one of my favorites,
stood up from the audience. The house band's leader gave him his
guitar and Merle did a twenty-five- or thirty-minute set. Only at the
Palomino did things like this happen. Another time, I was sitting at
the Palomino's bar having a drink with a woman I was seeing when
I heard the deep distinctive voice of "Francis the Talking Mule"
(from the 1950s film series) behind me.

"Howdy, Mabel. Say, Mabel, we were wondering if we could
buy you a drink." My hair at the time was long and wavy down to
my shoulders, and I knew he meant me. I turned around and there

---

150   Ms.c.b. "Judee Sill The Association." *Cashbox*. July 1, 1972.

stood the *Francis* voice actor, Chill Wills. He invited us to join him
at his table where motorcycle daredevil Evel Knievel and two blonde
women were sitting. I told him we already had drinks and thanked
him for his offer. A few minutes later he came back and repeated
the invitation, so I got off my barstool, walked to their table, and
thanked them. I took no offense at the "Mabel" comments and was
mildly amused.

Another time Judee came by my house—Caroline and I were
going to go with her to see the new Ingmar Bergman film, *The Silence*,
down on Franklin and Vermont. I was feeling depressed that day.
"Why don't you guys go? I'm not feeling up to it." Judee talked me
into going. The movie was so dreary and so dismal, it actually made
me feel better.

Judee would call you on a Saturday morning, early, and say, "Let's
go to Chinatown and have dim sum." She would bring all these weird
people together. She particularly loved El Coyote, a Mexican restaurant.
She'd order a Bishop's Cap, which was brandy, a slice of lemon, and a
sugar cube with bitters. She'd eat the bitters, bite the lemon, and toss
back the brandy. She also had a birthday party at El Coyote once—her
party took over the whole outdoor patio, turned it all into one long
table. Someone broke out cocaine, laid it on the table, and passed it
down; you took a bump and slid it down to the next person.

She is the one and only person in my life who ever set me up
on a date; no one had ever dared. That date and I spent the whole
evening talking about Judee. If you knew her, it was hard not to think
highly of her. The most important thing I learned from Judee is most
darkness we experience is false darkness. That has always stayed with
me and really helped me out.

Judee's downward spiral began when she badmouthed David
Geffen onstage. It's never a good idea to bite the hand that gave you
your first meal. She was going with a guy named David Beardon at
the time, and he was a bad influence. It was poor judgment on her
part to badmouth Geffen—very unprofessional. It essentially ended

her recording career. Word got back to Geffen, and he cut her off immediately. Without his support, she floundered.

She died in November 1979. It used to be that she had all the lost souls over for Thanksgiving dinner, but she was gone before Thanksgiving that year. It was a real shock to me. She was such a sweet, tender soul. I really looked forward to being friends with her in my old age. I'd visit with her at her house, and one of the women she was living with, Donna Todd (whom I was seeing at the time), had a parakeet—that bird once landed on my teeth and stuck its head down my throat to see where the loud sound of laughter was coming from (my mouth). Later, Judee had a pet slow loris named Lazlo. When I first met Lazlo at a party, he sauntered out from behind the refrigerator, leaned against a wall, and inspected me with giant eyes.

"What a beautiful animal," I said.

"Oh," she said. "That's Lazlo."

One evening I went over to Judee's house to pick up Donna. The bathroom door was open and Judee was in there, uncharacteristically putting on makeup, so I had to find out why.

"Why are you getting all dolled up?" I asked.

"I'm giving a lecture," she said.

"To whom?"

"The Rosicrucians in Bakersfield."

"What's the lecture on?"

"Rosicrucian humor."

To this day, I can't be sure if she was joking or serious. You never knew with Judee.[151]

If I keep talking about these women I'm bound to bore or depress you, but a rock and roll guy is nothing without women to have inspired him to play music, to sing songs, and to love.

---

151   According to the website for the Rosicrucian Order, AMORC (www.rosicrucian. org), "The Rosicrucians are a community of mystics who study and practice the metaphysical laws governing the universe."

Ridge Riders and Stopping the Motor
1970–1972

B Y THE TIME 1970 rolled around, we'd had six gold records and a platinum record (that would then go platinum again), I'd been married and divorced, had a child, dated, traveled around the country, and made more money than I'd ever dreamed. (Let's not go wild—I wasn't making Jagger or McCartney kind of money, but I was doing all right.) That year in Salt Lake City, Utah, we recorded *The Association Live* album, which peaked at No. 79 on August 22, 1970.

I hadn't even turned thirty yet. While 250+ days on the road per year wasn't getting to me, the people were. I have a crystal clear memory of one of the band members criticizing me at a business meeting at our lawyer's office.

"Russ," he said, "you shouldn't wear shorts in first class!"

I can't adequately express the ridiculousness of the observation. I was wearing tailored shorts—they most certainly were not raggedy. I looked like I was ready to hit the tennis court. I just felt like the little things—little things that, when they became too many, added up to big things—had become so contentious, and I couldn't take it. I do music because it's fun to do music, that's what I like about it. Performing music is doing something beautiful for people. You're making them feel better, you're adding to their lives, it's a very positive thing. *This* was not positive. It was, as they say, the straw that broke the camel's back. My shorts? Are you kidding me? There's a war going on, and you're talking about my shorts. Come on!

"You have to give a six-month notice for leaving, correct?" I asked.

"Correct," our lawyer answered me.

"Well," I said, "you just got mine."

I did the unthinkable. I quit.

With all of those creative, independent minds spending time together in close quarters, it was inevitable we wouldn't agree on everything all the time. There was just no way. Rick Colecchio, Pat's son who worked on our crew, shares one of his experiences: "I was very seldom down by the stage, but for some reason I was walking in front of the stage, I can't really remember, but Russ was up there and he looks down and I have a whole auditorium of people behind me and he looks down at me and goes, 'Where is my tambourine?' When I tell Jim this story he rolls on the floor. I pointed to the tambourine on the stool next to him. 'You mean that tambourine, Russ?'" Now I have no memory of this, but I'm willing to admit I got on some people's nerves sometimes. But getting emotionally invested in the shorts I'm wearing on the airplane? Get over yourself.

Rick also remembers a time we did "Requiem for the Masses" in Texas. "At the end," Rick shares, "Terry plays a solo trumpet. Lights go down and the spotlight is on the trumpet. A lot of times I didn't have a big enough spotlight, but I would always try to get just the trumpet—that was what I wanted for that song. (I told) the Texas spotlight guy, 'Zoom down on the trumpet.' He zooms down on *Larry*—the rest of the stage is totally black. Larry is just standing there. No one is doing anything but Terry. I'm screaming at the guy to shut it down, but no matter what I said, he didn't give two craps about us. Finally I said, 'Move it over, move over to the guy with the trumpet!' He finally did. After the show, Terry just started screaming at me, 'What the hell do you think you're doing up there?' If that were to happen the first two or three years on the road, it would have been fine, but because of where we were at that point in time, it wasn't funny to Terry. It wasn't funny to me, either. At that point, family started going out the door." Rick likely felt the contrast further since he'd previously described being on the road as "going out on a vacation every day."

Aside from Jules, who'd taken a two-year leave of absence to travel to India, I was the first to leave. The band was now back to just six members. My absence was made note of in the press at another appearance at the RKO Orpheum Theater in Davensport, Iowa:

> Unmistakably missing last night was the explicit voice of Russ Giguere, one of the six young Californians who originated the group more than five years ago, who retired just three months ago. The absence of his lead singing in a couple of the songs has caused a variance in the sound, a sound which is still good but somewhat different from the original.
>
> His retirement from the group, apparently permanent, will cause some changes in the arrangements of songs in which he had the lead.[152]

Another reporter wrote, "He (Richard Thompson) is now replacing original member, Russ Giguere, who felt he'd earned a vacation after five years."[153] I didn't have a plan for what was next. I left the band because I couldn't take the petty disagreements anymore, not because I had a grand vision for what I wanted to do with my life. But as it turns out, all I knew was music—I certainly wasn't trained to do anything else—and so the first thing I ended up doing with the sudden time on my hands, and the ability to stay in LA for more than just a week or two at a time, was put together a solo album. Pat called up Joe Smith, President of Warner Bros. We—Pat, Joe, and I—had dinner and I told Joe I wanted to do an album. Joe gave me the green light. Coming straight from the hits and success of The Association, I didn't have to jump through any further hoops to get the album done—he simply waved his hand and it was done; Warner Bros. foot the bill to record it and I produced it, following my musical whims and making the most of my artistic freedom.

---

152   Bergstrand, Tom. "The Association Presents Unique Talent—Harmony." *The Dispatch.* July 22, 1970.

153   "'The Association' At Mac April 27." *The Jacksonville Daily Journal.* April 18, 1972.

The album was called *Hexagram 16*. The title is an ode to my affinity (at the time) for the *I Ching (Book of Changes)*. That might sound corny in a twenty-first-century frame of reference, but in the early seventies, many musicians and artist types were familiar with the *I Ching*. Heck, even Steve Jobs read it while backpacking through India, in the period he first experimented with psychedelic drugs and before he *became* Steve Jobs. In a 2016 article, "What is the I Ching?" in *The New York Review of Books*, Eliot Weinberger wrote:

> The *I Ching* has served for thousands of years as a philosophical taxonomy of the universe, a guide to an ethical life, a manual for rulers, and an oracle of one's personal future and the future of the state. It was an organizing principle or authoritative proof for literary and arts criticism, cartography, medicine, and many of the sciences, and it generated endless Confucian, Taoist, Buddhist, and, later, even Christian commentaries, and competing schools of thought within those traditions. In China and in East Asia, it has been by far the most consulted of all books, in the belief that it can explain everything. In the West, it has been known for over three hundred years and, since the 1950s, is surely the most popularly recognized Chinese book. With its seeming infinitude of applications and interpretations, there has never been a book quite like it anywhere. It is the center of a vast whirlwind of writings and practices, but is itself a void, or perhaps a continually shifting cloud, for most of the crucial words of the *I Ching* have no fixed meaning.
>
> The origin of the text is, as might be expected, obscure. In the mythological version, the culture hero Fu Xi, a dragon or a snake with a human face, studied the patterns of nature in the sky and on the earth: the markings on birds, rocks, and animals, the movement of clouds, the arrangement of the stars. He discovered that everything could be reduced to eight trigrams, each composed of three stacked solid or

broken lines, reflecting the *yin* and *yang*, the duality that drives the universe. The trigrams themselves represented, respectively, heaven, a lake, fire, thunder, wind, water, a mountain, and earth.

From these building blocks of the cosmos, Fu Xi devolved all aspects of civilization—kingship, marriage, writing, navigation, agriculture—all of which he taught to his human descendants.

Here mythology turns into legend. Around the year 1050 BCE, according to the tradition, Emperor Wen, founder of the Zhou dynasty, doubled the trigrams to hexagrams (six-lined figures), numbered and arranged all of the possible combinations—there are sixty-four—and gave them names. He wrote brief oracles for each that have since been known as the "Judgments." His son, the Duke of Zhou, a poet, added gnomic interpretations for the individual lines of each hexagram, known simply as the "Lines." It was said that, five hundred years later, Confucius himself wrote ethical commentaries explicating each hexagram, which are called the "Ten Wings" ("wing," that is, in the architectural sense).

You haven't heard of it? (I'm talking about my album, not the *I Ching*.) That's okay, I don't take offense. It wasn't exactly a smash, but that's not for lack of talent—I'm not even talking about me; I'm talking about the incredible team with whom I put the album together.

There are ten tracks on the album, some of them written by my close friends; I wrote two, Bill Martin wrote two, and then Judee Sill, Jim Spheeris, John Boylan, Berry Gordy, Smokey Robinson, Randy Newman, and Jules (see? I left The Association on good terms and of my own accord, and Jules is always happy to contribute) wrote one song each. Randy Newman was at the beginning of his career—this was prior to his twenty Academy Award nominations in the "Best

Original Score" and "Best Original Song" categories. The Smokey Robinson song was my cover of "Shop Around," which he'd recorded and released in 1960 with The Miracles, when it hit the top of the charts, and my rendition was before the 1976 cover by Captain & Tennille that also went to the top of the charts.

I recruited some of my close friends and other musicians I loved to play on the album, handle arrangements and/or do backup vocals: Bernie Leadon, Larry Knechtel, Chris Ethridge, Judy Henske, Jerry Yester, Spooner Oldham, Herb Pederson, Merry Clayton, and too many more to list here. Merry had recorded "Gimme Shelter" with the Rolling Stones. I'm not gonna lie—it was fulfilling to own the full process start to finish on the album, and not to have to contend with five or six other guys chiming in with their opinions. Even though I was doing my first solo production, I remained true to my philosophy of what I'd been practicing and preaching in The Association all along—my goal was the same as always: to create beautiful music but not feel like I had to be a slave to any one style, type, or sound. And so what I ended up with on the final cut of the album is everything from the folk- and country-influenced "Let It Flow" (Jimmy Spheeris) and "Rosarita Beach Café" (Bill Martin) to the more progressive rock melodies in "My Plan" (Bill Martin) and "Pegasus" (Jules Alexander). Judee wrote a beautiful song, "Ridge Rider":

> He rides the ridge between dark and light
> Without partners or friends
> He's courageous enough to be scared
> But he's too humble to win
> Bless the ridge rider
> The ridge he's ridin' is mighty thin
> I guess the ridge rider
> Forgets he's travelin' with a friend
> He comes from under the cryptosphere,
> Where the great sadness begins

And he doesn't pretend to be brave
Tho' the road's dusty and dim
Bless the ridge rider
The ridge he's ridin' is mighty thin
I guess the ridge rider
Forgets he's travelin' with a friend
Since the great fall he's been travelin' hard
Thinkin' bondage is sin
Hopin' someday the path'll turn gold
And the weight'll turn into wind
Bless the ridge rider
The ridge he's ridin' is mighty thin

I recorded the album before Judee died. She played the guitar part on the original track for "Ridge Rider." I tried other studio guitarists, but they couldn't play her chart. If I listen to the song now, or even in looking at her lyrics on the page, it's haunting, knowing how she ended up (dying from a cocaine overdose). It's almost like she could have been writing about herself. It puts a lump in my throat. Up until I was finished playing with the band in 2013 (yes, not to give it all away, but I did end up joining The Association again, but more about that much later...as in another decade later), I would occasionally still sign an album for a devoted fan of *Hexagram 16* (much to my surprise, Real Gone Music had put *Hexagram 16* on CD for the first time in 2013—they did a nice job, too, with the liner notes). Reviews were few and nothing to bowl you over. *The San Bernardino County Sun* reported, "The album's distinction is in the continuity of taste and sound Giguere produces here. The selections offer a wide variety of rhythms and styles which Giguere handles equally well...A nice voice and some excellent musicians put this together. But it's all too smooth and too sweet, lacking vitality or excitement..."[154]

Incidentally, the original release of *Hexagram 16* (1971) was the same year The Association's sixth studio album, *Stop Your Motor*,

154 "Great Music: Seals, Crofts." *The San Bernardino County Sun.* December 22, 1971.

was released, and it was the first Association album I was not on. *Stop Your Motor* was also the last album the band did with Warner Bros., and it was self-produced by the band. All but two of the tracks on the album were written by band members. None of the singles, however, made it to the charts, and it peaked at No. 158 on *Billboard* on August 21, 1971—which was also the year David Cassidy recorded "Cherish" (though it wouldn't be released until early the following year). He sold over one million copies and it made it to No. 1 on the Adult Contemporary chart.

The following year, in April 1972, The Association released its seventh studio album, *Waterbeds in Trinidad!*, our only album with Columbia (I'm not on it, since I wasn't in the band at the time). Ted shares, "We were trying to finish the album, we were out on Lake Michigan in Chicago and we were freezing, and Jim says, 'Why don't we call it *Waterbeds in Trinidad*?'—he said it to me bundled up in a coat and heavy sweater. It was so strange that it rang our bell. We worked with really fine studio cats and we performed very well vocally on the album—one of our best vocal recordings." Ted then recounts his two weeks in Trinidad in the early 1970s that he spent importing waterbeds with "...friends who weren't in good standing with the law. We went to Rat's house (in Trinidad) on this motorcycle and on the bottom floor there was a monkey chained up, throwing his poop on us. We got up to the third floor where Rat lived and he had women all over the place—he gave me the steel pan (drum) from his hands. You can't be in a gang without being in a band. We talked and hung out and snorted and smoked. We were stoned out of our minds for two weeks...I left the island, I walked into the airplane carrying a steel pan and so drunk on Brandy Alexanders..." he chuckles. "*Waterbeds in Trinidad!* to me was one thing and for the rest of the guys, it was just a funny name!"

The album was produced by Lewis Merenstein, perhaps best known then for producing *Astral Weeks* and *Moondance* for Van Morrison, both of which are ranked in *Rolling Stone*'s 2003 "500

Greatest Albums of All Time" and CNN's 2006 "The All-Time 100 Albums." If you include our greatest hits and our live album, *Waterbeds in Trinidad!* marked our ninth album. It ranked even lower than *Stop Your Motor*, at No. 194 on *Billboard*. Reviews like "the sound is pleasingly together, one of the traits of The Association"[155] didn't register. Our cover of the Lovin' Spoonful's "Darling Be Home Soon" got some traction for a hot minute, and I mean a minute, at No. 104 on the *Billboard* top singles chart.

Brian would die on August 2 that year. At the time of Brian's death, Jim's wife was pregnant, and Brian had told her, "If the baby's born on my birthday [September 8], I'll give you a hundred bucks." Jim's daughter was born at the end of that month, on August 29. Less than three weeks after Brian's death, The Association would play another concert at the RKO Orpheum in Davenport, Iowa, with an eight-member band, consisting of Ted, Terry, Larry, Jules, Jim, Richard Thompson (who had replaced me when I departed), Wolfgang Melz on bass guitar, and Maurice Miller on drums. "Playing before sell-out crowds of 2,500 for each of two performances...This 'super-group' from Los Angeles provided its distinctive sounds, definitely earmarked 'Association music,' with a blend of traditional favorites plus a couple of renditions from its new album, *Waterbeds in Trinidad!* The results were thoroughly entertaining and appreciated by the assemblage as the group was called back twice in the evening performance by thunderous ovations."[156]

I attended an Association recording session some time after I'd left, but there was something missing in the discipline of the group. The room was filled with wives and family members, which inevitably affected the work ethic, which in turn affected the performances. It wasn't the same.

After *Hexagram 16* fulfilled my creative soul but left little impression on my bank account, I turned to various other forms of

---

155   Morgan, Diane. "The Disc Seen." *The Press Democrat*. June 25, 1972.

156   Bergstrand, Tom. "Association Big Hit." *The Dispatch*. August 23, 1972.

musical endeavors—some of which involved putting bands together that didn't get much further past the effort of a publicity shot photo session or a couple of gigs at the various clubs in town. One of these, in early 1971, was called The Beachwood Rangers, consisting of me, Joe Lamanno, Bill Martin, Don Beck, Chester Anderson, and Warren Zevon, who would have an underground hit on his own in 1978 with "Werewolves of London." The Rangers' second lineup, a few months later, was me, Bill, Don, Dennis Conway, Gary Sherwood, and Scott Shelley. The name was *borrowed* from how friends of mine, including J. D. Souther, Bill Martin, and actor Harry Dean Stanton, referred to ourselves (as JD mentioned earlier) as The Beachwood Rangers—because at the time we all lived in Beachwood Canyon. The Beachwood Rangers group that I formed is not the group that sings with Linda Ronstadt in "Life is Like a Mountain Railway" on her 1970 *Silk Purse* album, nor is it the group of friends I had that called ourselves by that name; the band accompanying Linda on that song is called the Beechwood Rangers (note the different spelling) and comprised of Rodney Dillard, Bernie Leadon, and Harry Dean Stanton. You might be confused because Harry was part of the group of friends and another group that went by the same name with a different spelling, but what can I say? We clearly loved the name! Pat Colecchio represented us and we performed at The Ice House, UCLA, and once in Minneapolis, but that was about it. Another group was called Hollywood, and that was comprised of me, Steve Edwards, Scott Shelly (again), Gary Sherwood (again), Lee Mallory, and Michael Ney.

I did, however, enjoy some success in a music and comedy duo with my buddy Bill Martin. We actually did a bit we called "The Viking King," which was borrowed from a bit we did with The Association called "The Indian Bit," which involved me, the least American Indian-looking with my blue eyes and blond hair, speaking gibberish, and Brian giving an English translation. In the Viking version, I translated Bill's Nordic gibberish into English. I recently found an old flyer advertising our show at The Ice House:

Distressed and alarmed by recent reports of a possible "Laugh Gap" between the super powers, MARTIN & GIGUERE (pron: Mar-tin & Jig-air) have joined forces to ensure that America will never become the second funniest nation. Cleverly disguised as human beings, they operate out of their fortress-like Funny-Foam Geodesic Dome Home Drive-In Restaurant and Laboratory high in the hills overlooking the sleepy little hamlet of Los Angeles, California.

BILL MARTIN has performed with or written for Harry Nilsson, Linda Ronstadt, The Fifth Dimension, The Dillards, The Turtles, The Monkees and other endangered species. He has recorded a comedy album (you'll never find it) for Warner Bros., performed on Hoyt Axton's TV special last year that he also wrote for CBS and has written and performed countless radio and television commercials. Californians may currently see his furry face as the repulsive "Old Timer" on the Miller's Outpost TV spots. This year's credits also include materials for Larry Groce's "Junk Food Junkie" album and the hit comedy film "Tunnel Vision."

RUSS GIGUERE amuses himself by collecting precious metals (six Gold Records and one Platinum) as souvenirs of his five-year, eleven-million-record relationship as one of the original members of The Association. Russ also has a solo music album on Warner Bros. (you'll never find it either).

Cain & Abel...Sacco & Vanzetti...Leopold & Loeb...& Now...

Martin & Giguere

Not since Fred Astaire & Roy Rogers has such a sparkling new musical-comedy duo so captured America's heart!

Together they stand ready to add their mighty, bulging, steel-sinewed mass of yoks to our nation's vital comedy arsenal.

(Batteries not included.)

Bill Martin was one of the kindest humans on this planet—warm, funny, creative, sometimes outrageous, and a loyal friend. Life was never dull when Bill was around. Before "Martin & Giguere" he had also written songs that were recorded by The Monkees and Harry Nilsson. Nilsson even produced a comedy album, *Bill Martin's Concerto for Head Phones and Contra Buffoon in Asia Minor*, which Warner Bros. Records released in 1970. Bill voiced "The Rock Man" in Nilsson's animated TV film *The Point*, which aired on ABC in early 1971. One night in the 1980s, as he told it, Bill woke up in the middle of the night with a movie idea—Bigfoot and a human family in the Pacific Northwest. Working with his friend Ezra Rappaport, it became the feature film *Harry and the Hendersons*, starring John Lithgow. The face of Harry (Bigfoot) was based on Bill's face, down to the blue eyes. The Association never recorded any of Bill's songs but in the 1990s, we regularly sang his tune "Redstone" in concerts. Bill was also in demand as a voiceover actor in radio commercials, animated programs, and video games. He spent his last years with his wife Shari in beautiful Washington State—yes, the setting of *Harry and the Hendersons*—where he died in 2016. He was one of the best friends I ever had, and I miss him terribly.

In the beginning of the decade I spent not being in The Association, the rock and roll music landscape was changing, the band hadn't had any hits for a couple of years, and Brian was on a path of no return. He was still with the band, and he'd also crossed over into doing more voiceovers. According to Jordan Cole, Brian's eldest son, he did the voiceover for Mattel's Big Jim Camper.

As I'd already mentioned, Brian was unusual—he was smart, well read, articulate—but if you didn't know him, you might think he was pushing your buttons just to be a jerk or being weird for the sake of being weird. He was also a wordsmith. He turned the expression "she's built like a brick shithouse!" (slang for "she's sexy/has curves, etc.") into "she's built like a masonry defecating shelter." But the path of no return I refer to was about the drugs. Several of us witnessed firsthand his love of needles.

That's not to say I ever actually saw him shoot up—Jordan Cole, Brian's son, says, "...smack...it's a one-way street with a dead end. It changes you so much chemically inside that you're not going to be the same person even if you can somehow escape...brains work neurochemically, and when you introduce foreign chemistry into it, they rearrange the chemistry to fit it. They don't rearrange the chemistry back once you're done. And that influences personality..." The National Institute on Drug Abuse reports, "Repeated heroin use changes the physical structure and physiology of the brain, creating long-term imbalances in neuronal and hormonal systems that are not easily reversed. Studies have shown some deterioration of the brain's white matter due to heroin use, which may affect decision-making abilities, the ability to regulate behavior, and responses to stressful situations."

We all touched a lot of stuff back then, but smack is a nearly impossible path to steer away from once your wheels have touched down. Brian couldn't escape it. Danny Hutton threw Brian's needles down the sink; I shot down his remark about the healthy veins in my arms he wanted to get ahold of, but we couldn't help him.

According to Jordan, when Brian and his wife, Molly, separated around 1967, she moved with the kids—Jordan and his younger brother, Chandler—to Burbank. "Mom pretty much knew the marriage wasn't going to last. He was having affairs and loving the popularity and the fame and the fortune. Having such insecurities from his folks pretty much drove him. The same insecurities that cause musicians to seek adulation and limelight are the same ones that can cause them to self-destruct." Though Jordan was only ten at the time of his father's death and by that point living back in Portland,

Oregon, he's the only Cole child who remembers his father. He insists that all of his dad's behavior stemmed from insecurity at never being good enough—his parents had worshipped the ground Mike, Brian's UC Berkeley-educated lawyer older brother, walked on.

While I often think of Brian as being too smart for his own good, Jordan thinks of it as "too smart for somebody that insecure." He explains, "His family thought he wasn't near[ly] as good as his older brother. And they continued to think so until his band made it, and suddenly, they were so proud of him. And he knew that. He was extremely smart when it came to that kind of perception. He knew that they didn't really care about him, they liked his fame and fortune…that same insecurity that will sabotage is the same one that drives more public recognition. That is what insecure people seek—they seek attention. Somebody to let them know, 'You're okay. We like you!'…I've got Super 8 video footage of my dad visiting the family (without all of us)…They're all turning around, ignoring him."

If that's the case, it's sad. Lord knows everyone battles insecurities in life—who would have thought Brian's came directly from his family? Life came a bit full circle, though, when Jordan joined The Association on a December 1998 engagement on a cruise ship in Jamaica. Paul Holland, our bassist, couldn't do the gig, so Larry called Jordan up and asked,

"You want to do a show? I need a bass player." Jordan flew out sight unseen, no audition, nothing. He's self-taught—learned everything by ear. "Do you know the songs?" Larry asked. We were doing a full-hour set of our hits, and Jordan knew them all. Three months after that, Donni Gougeon, our keyboard player who sang so high only the dogs could hear him, retired from the band because his wife had some health problems and he wanted to be able to spend more time with her and help her out. Larry then called Jordan up again. "Would you like to play keyboards for the band permanently?"

Jordan remembers that the band liked to call me Old Razor Shorts. Jim was the first to call me that one morning because I was tired and cranky. Apparently it's also because I tell people my opinion before they ask for it; I have a reputation for knowing what I want and having no problem piping up. I'm sorry, is that a bad thing? I can't hold back what I think. I don't censor my thoughts. Life's too short and that never got anyone anywhere good. At least you always know where you stand with me.

Jordan still plays with the band. He even ad libs a bit at concerts. Jordan shares his rehearsed bit:

> The Association is defined as a group of people gathered together for a common cause. There is no one person that makes The Association. It is a group effort, it is a task that is too great for any one person. It requires everyone pushing and pulling and helping. It is not that some of the members are The Association, it is the sum of the members that make The Association. And it is a whole that is greater than the sum of all parts. And we like to call it "Whole Sum Music."

The apple doesn't fall far from the tree. Brian loved language and anything funny with a pun, or punny, was golden humor begging to be mined and an excellent way to evaluate the intelligence level of the company you were keeping: Did they follow the humor, did they "get it"? If they did, they passed your muster.

Larry told Jordan, "There's no cut too deep, no joke too cheap for this group." But Jordan took it a little far with this joke:

> What will make an Association reunion?
> *Six more needles.*

That was met with dead silence. Everyone had a bone to pick with Brian at some point in time, but heck, everyone had a bone to pick with me at one point in time. People get on your nerves. Some more than others. It's unavoidable, especially in a group of six to seven men with healthy egos.

On his second or third show Jordan ever did with us, we were in Detroit, and he remembers a fan asking, "So, is your dad still alive?"

Jordan quipped, "No, I'm just sitting in for him while he's dead."

I have to admit, that one would make his dad proud. As Paul Holland describes Jordan, "He's always saying, 'Well, I can't believe you laugh at my jokes, nobody else likes them!' He's got an incredible sense of humor, but it's very advanced, it's very intelligent. And not everybody gets him." When I hear that I think, *like father, like son.*

I stand by the fact that Brian was probably the most interesting of all of us—meaning he was more of a Renaissance man. Every guy had incredible wide-ranging musical chops, but Brian crossed over into other fields (acting, for one) with equal finesse that none of us could have competed in—he was a commanding presence. He was so unusual you couldn't *not* pay attention to him.

Brian had a third child, Jordan and Chandler's half-brother, Brant, with a woman from Texas. But he gave his gifts of gab and music to Jordan. According to Jordan, his family grew up in relative poverty after the death of Brian, and Molly struggled to make ends meet as a single mom. Jordan claims the family didn't receive its share of Brian's royalties from his death in 1972, all the way through to 2005—so over thirty years' worth of royalties.

Jordan says, "Ted was nice enough to make copies of every one of his receipts from '72 royalties. Considering his standing in the band, he wasn't as much of a music writer, so I figured he probably would be minimum. It comes to almost a quarter million dollars the band had split up, while me and Chandler and Brant were growing up in really tough neighborhoods.... That would be the whole total, to be split between me and my brothers. I could be off by $100,000, too."

Jordan says we all signed a document with Warner Bros. stating the monies should be split among the surviving members of the band—six ways, but it should have included Brian and been split seven ways. He also insists Pat Colecchio knew about it, even though, as he was dying of cancer, he told Jordan he didn't. Jordan says, "Two weeks before [he died] I had talked to him [Pat] about obtaining the royalties that we were never getting for all of the radio play and record sales and stuff like that."

Ted, who had to dig to the bottom of the situation with Jordan, insists: "I finally figured out that the royalties for Brian were sent to his brother, his estate manager (I found this out)—he sent the money for years and then the checks stopped. The checks went to the estate manager.... Checks were sent for six years and Michael Cole is the executor of the estate. Somebody got it. Anyway, I figured it all out and though I can't prove it, I left numerous messages on Michael Cole's phone, and he never returned any calls. He didn't want to get caught."

Knowing what Jordan said about his uncle, it's quite possibly true. And knowing that the band was hands off in our business affairs, particularly at that point and sometimes to the detriment of the band's financial health—from bad investments to, later, bad managers—makes it even more plausible. But no one, I repeat, no one in the group, no matter what, would have intentionally cut Brian or his family out of their fair share of royalties.

Jordan abandoned his pursuit—whether that's due to lack of financial means to hire a lawyer, which is what he claims, or because he realized his uncle had some responsibility in the matter, I don't know. I wish I could have been more involved in some of our decisions early on, but I was young and inexperienced in those matters. I got much better at it once I started handling the band's accounts myself in the past few years.

I saw Brian at his house on August 1, 1972, the day before he died, when he made that remark about wanting to shoot up my veins.

My veins remained unsullied. The morning after I saw him, Brian's girlfriend Linda called to tell me she couldn't wake him up or feel a heartbeat—she called me before she called anyone else. Brian had been speedballing—shooting heroin and then cocaine. It was later referred to as "John Belushi's disease." The newspapers reported, "Brian Cole, an original member of the Association, was found dead of a smack OD at his home last month…"[157] I told you how he used to tell me he wanted "It Didn't Look Deadly to Me" on his tombstone. It was just so stupid that he died, and so unnecessary. He was only twenty-nine years old, and had left behind three sons. When Linda called me, I got in my car and drove over to the house immediately and took three things: two personal phone books that would incriminate everyone he knew, most of whom had nothing to do with his bad habits, and an eleven-inch-wide wood-carved wall ornament of a winged anchor with a circle in the middle. I had given it to him for a boat he was planning on building—a hundred-foot trimaran for which he already had the blueprints. The boat never got built; the winged anchor hangs on my wall. And Brian will now be known as I forever call him—the Old Dead Guy, a nickname he would have relished.

  Brian Cole, may he rest in peace.

---

157 Lindsay, Sally. "Youth Beat." *Pottsville Republican*. September 16, 1972.

Then and Now...
(end of the 1970s)

BY THE TIME THE end of the 1970s rolled around, Presidents Nixon, Ford, and Carter had all revolved through the White House and the Vietnam War was over. My solo career had greeted the start of the decade with little fanfare, followed by the fast and furious fizzle of several other bands and musical endeavors. Don't act like you've heard of the Beachwood Rangers—I know you haven't! We were what they call a flash in the pan.

The one exception was the act with Bill Martin that I told you about. We had a little more staying power—we experienced great success in front of live audiences, performing our comedy act interspersed with original music. Bill played piano; I played guitar—one of Bill's original compositions was called "King Kong":

> *Who died for our sins?*
> *King Kong!*
> *He forgave us all when his back was against the wall.*
> *He forgave us all.*
> *The queen of hearts caught the king off guard.*
> *He hit the streets and he took it hard.*
> *Kong is long gone to Forest Lawn but his song lives on.*
> *Sing along, so long King.*
> *Sing along, so long Kong.*
> *Sing along, so long long gone King Kong.*
> *So long long gone Kong.*

I recently transferred some of the cassette tapes of our act and the two Bill Martin tunes I did on *Hexagram 16* as well as Bill Martin's tunes I did with other bands to CD, and I plan on releasing an album of these compiled works. There came a point about a year or year and a half in, where I knew we weren't going to make it to the next level. It wasn't until I left The Association that I realized the almost cosmic, for lack of a better word, work ethic that we had collectively, and just how hard that work ethic is to come by. I missed it—that automatic centering in on what had to be done. Talent is great—it's important and the first necessary ingredient, no doubt—but without that work ethic there's no way talent alone can propel you to the level necessary to sustain a career over years and through tough times. I took this work ethic for granted in The Association.

My friend Bernie Leadon of The Eagles remembers, "I left The Eagles in late '75. During that interim, I was in occasional touch with Russ. We still liked to go to the park and throw Frisbees—that was one of the exercises we enjoyed, so I would go to the park. But this one day, he said to me after I left The Eagles, 'Why did you leave?' I said, 'Well, it was personal differences, artistic differences, whatever,' and he goes basically, 'Well, that's too bad, because they were a great band.' And he kind of expressed regret that he'd left The Association. Because when you leave a band that's that big, it's kind of like leaving a pro sports team. Like leaving the NBA or NFL or something. You find that things are not quite the same when you leave," Bernie laughs, "in terms of career options."

As I mentioned, the band was limping along after disappointing album releases in the early part of the decade and still playing dates, but things were slowly disintegrating. Jerry Yester played with The Association at one point, which prompted Jim to rejoin briefly to play with his brother, but then Jerry and Richard Thompson allegedly trashed a hotel room one night and left the band after. I wasn't present, so I can't speak to the story and what all went down. You'll have to ask them what happened!

No matter what band I put together after *Hexagram 16*, I wasn't able to duplicate The Association's success. I think to some degree Jules experienced that with Joshua Fox, one of the best bands I ever heard. In Joshua Fox, Jules was on guitar, Tom Menifee on guitar, Dick Ellison on keyboards, Joe Lamanno on bass (who also played with me in the Beachwood Rangers and with The Association in the mid-1970s and later in 1983–84), and Mike Botts on drums, who would go on to be the drummer for Bread, which had thirteen songs on the *Billboard* Top 100 between 1970 and 1977. If you want to *do* music, to make it your life on a national or international level, you have to treat it like a baby and nurture it, day in and day out. (Remember, The Association rehearsed together five days per week for six months before we even went out in public.) There was no, "Oh, we'll get together when we have time, or maybe sometime next month when we have a gig on the calendar." We put in the time, rehearsing and polishing our sound, and the results speak for themselves. In many ways The Association was magical—it was the right group of talent coming together at the right time. We'd also been fortunate enough to have found the right fit in a manager with Pat Colecchio, who helped us steer our ship and land those gigs opening major venues to rock and roll around the country.

On a personal note, by 1979, I'd rotated through several relationships and one live-in girlfriend since my divorce from Birdie. My lovely daughter Jill was already ten going on eleven—I did get to enjoy more quality time with her once I left The Association. After *Hexagram 16*, The Beachwood Rangers, Hollywood, Martin & Giguere, and Bijou—a group I was in with Jules briefly in 1975—I gave up on music and spent four-plus years working as a carpenter doing construction and deconstruction and remodeling homes. (Big thanks to my seventh-grade woodshop teacher, to whom I owe my carpentry skills. *That* was a class I paid attention in.) In fact, most of the other carpenters I worked with were also musicians. John Merrill of The Peanut Butter Conspiracy worked with me on one of those jobs, and he was the go-to guy I called when I needed carpentry work done at my home (he gave me the special fellow musician discount rate). The construction company was owned by Lance Fent, a guitarist/singer for The Peanut Butter Conspiracy. Even Alan Brackett, bass player/singer/writer for the same band, worked for Lance's company. Alan has self-published a book, *Almost Famous*, about his life and experiences with Peanut Butter Conspiracy. Anyhow, my life's dream had been to make a living doing what I love—singing—and I'd done that. Pulling in six figures as part of a six-man (and sometimes seven-man) band at the height of my career with The Association was nothing to sneeze at, particularly at the time, and certainly more than I'd ever imagined.

But at the close of the decade, The Association was no longer together; the 1971 album *Stop Your Motor* had, as I mentioned, made it to an unimpressive No. 158 on the charts and was simultaneously the debut of keyboardist Richard Thompson, who had originally been brought onboard to replace me when I left in 1970. *Stop Your Motor* was also the end of The Association's collaboration with Warner Bros. In case you're wondering how the album got its name:

> Across the street from the clubhouse is where the picture
> for the cover of their most recent album was taken. "It's a
> gas station with signs saying, 'Stop Your Motor' and 'No
> Smoking,'" said Cole. "I liked that. But they didn't want to
> leave the 'No Smoking' sign on the album because it might
> offend the smokers. So we just used the 'Stop Your Motor'
> sign as the title of the album. We took a whole year to make
> 'Stop Your Motor.' That's ridiculous. It's too long. But we
> were getting our heads together.[158]

In that same article, Brian also spoke about the democratic voting process for which songs make it to an album. "We decide what songs we do—we make all our decisions by the democratic

---

158   Lane, Marilyn. "Rapping with The Association." *Quad-City Times*. Davenport, Iowa. August 18, 1971.

process—we vote. That way, fewer people are uptight. You know, it's funny. Usually the vote runs five to two or six to one, only rarely split four to three."

Reviews of *Stop Your Motor* were good, but they didn't help the charts.

> The Association is alive and kicking and for that the music world should be very thankful. True, the group has not had a smash like "Cherish" or "Windy" in recent years, but that doesn't mean they've gone sour. In fact, the group has progressed to the point where I believe they're several years ahead of pop music. With the emergence of soft rock, the Association should soon rise once again, and *Stop Your Motor* could be just the vehicle to do it...
>
> Somehow the Association is only remembered as a maker of yesterday's hits. Somehow with *Stop Your Motor*, I think that image will change. Buy it—and do yourself a favor.[159]

The San Bernardino County Sun disagreed, writing, "*Stop Your Motor* has the usually fine Association sound, but is lacking any really exciting material."[160] The following year, in April 1972, The Association went to Columbia to record and release *Waterbeds in Trinidad!* With producer Lewis Merenstein on board, and hot from his success with Van Morrison, it had all the makings of success on paper. One of the tracks, "Snow Queen," was written by the prolific and popular songwriting team Carole King and Gerry Goffin, but the fact is, none of the songs from *Stop Your Motor* or *Waterbeds in Trinidad!* are remembered or performed live in concert by The Association. Morrison's *Astral Weeks* had classical music, blues, jazz, and folk influence (not unlike The Association, Morrison refused to let others label him or give into their expectation to create hits in the same musical vein as "Brown Eyed Girl"), and his 1968 album is

159   Hazlett, Terry. "Disc Talk." *The Daily Notes*. July 16, 1971.

160   Mendoza, Henry. "'Stop Your Motor' Harmonious." *The San Bernardino County Sun*. July 28, 1971.

thought of as one of the first concept albums, or song cycle albums, where you are meant to sit down and have the auditory experience of every track, one after the other, so you can feel their progression and how they relate to each other—how all of the songs together tell a bigger story—rather than each song being a standalone composition.

But *Waterbeds in Trinidad!* performed even worse than *Stop Your Motor*, peaking at No. 194 on the chart. It was no *Astral Weeks*. The single released from it, a cover of the Lovin' Spoonful's "Darlin' Be Home Soon," didn't even break the Top 100. One review had this to say:

> *Waterbeds in Trinidad.* (Association, Columbia KC 31348); Rating: 2 ½ stars. Haven't progressed at all in the last four years. This is just a rehash of the same old thing. They could be a lot better if they had some better material and arrangements, plus a little motivation.[161]

The Baltimore Sun was kinder: "Nothing as catchy as 'Windy,' but relaxing, light listening."[162] But the band wasn't performing where it needed to be with record sales. The wind was going out of the sails. These albums failed to register, and on top of Brian's August 1972 death, it was the beginning of the end. Terry left, and while the band continued getting booked around the country, gigs were fewer than they'd been in our heyday. At concerts, the band promoted its (pre-1970) hits, but wasn't generating new material of any significance since new album recordings ceased after *Stop Your Motor* and *Waterbeds in Trinidad!*

So by 1977, the only original members still with the band were Jim and Ted. Jim left the band in 1972 when his daughter was born, and his brother Jerry Yester (of MFQ fame) replaced him for some time. Jim then rejoined the group in 1974 and for about nine months, both Jerry and Jim were in The Association (this was when Jerry allegedly trashed a hotel room with Richard Thompson). The Association did record a few singles with RCA in 1975—"One Sunday Morning" and

161   "Short Reviews." *The Post-Crescent.* Appleton, Wisconsin. July 23, 1972.

162   "County records." *The Baltimore Sun.* Baltimore, Maryland. November 5, 1972.

"Life is a Carnival"—to little fanfare. Jim then left the band again in 1977 when his father died and Ted held everything together for eight months before he gave up and used the opportunity to spend more time with his autistic son.

For a brief period, Ted leased the name of The Association to Rob Grill of the Grass Roots. This ultimately resulted in a few bands bogusly performing under our name (and sometimes even using a picture of Larry Ramos in the composite of the band's photos that would be up in the lobby of wherever they had a gig!), but we put a stop to that. And if you're wondering why *Larry*—in a group made up of mostly white men, Larry stood out and was more recognizable. I was once offered something like $1,000/gig to be in one of those Association wannabe bands. I politely declined—I had been a member of the real Association, why would I want to join the fake one?!

Meanwhile, the band members were, like me, picking up work where they could. For a short while, Jim opened an advertising agency with his army buddy, Jim Kirby. They called it Media Music. "We had a pretty good run of success, but we were underfunded, and there were so many big advertising companies in LA, we just couldn't compete."[163]

After he left in early 1973, Terry used his songwriting royalties to support himself and his family while devoting time to his passion: activism. In the early 1970s, that translated to him working for the Entertainment Industry for Peace and Justice and the Vietnam Information Project with his then wife, Judy. The Vietnam Information Project was dedicated to articulating "to the public a political point of view, or polarized point of view, or a radical point of view—we collected information in absolutely pure context— backing it up, presenting photographic evidence, and then going off to deliver lectures,"[164] Terry said.

Jules left the band in 1974 and began maximizing the precision optical instrumentation skills he'd gained in the Navy by building

---

163   Childs, Marti Smiley and March, Jeff. *Where Have All the Pop Stars Gone? Volume 1.* EditPros, 2011.

164   Ibid.

aircraft instruments, microfilm cameras, and viewers. At one point Jules worked at a company called Kinergetics, Inc., where he built small cryonics refrigerators that were used in infrared detectors. Jim also worked with Jules at Kinergetics for about a year in the seventies. Larry spent 1976–79 performing with his cousin Miles and his younger brother Del (who would join The Association many years later) in a trio act they called Homegrown where they played a variety of music, including blues and bluegrass. So you get that we were all scattered to the wind.

Musically speaking, in the music business in 1979, *Saturday Night Fever*, the soundtrack to the movie of the same name starring John Travolta, had been named Album of the Year at the Grammy Awards. The movie had made $74 million, just behind *Star Wars* and *Close Encounters of the Third Kind*. The album was on the *Billboard* charts for 120 weeks straight and No. 1 in the UK for eighteen weeks. It was the only movie soundtrack to ever have four No. 1 hits—"Stayin' Alive," "Night Fever," "How Deep Is Your Love," and "More Than a Woman"—all by the Bee Gees. Ultimately, it would sell over fifteen million copies. New York State had even declared one week in June the previous year "National Disco Week." Blockbuster movies like *Star Wars* and *Superman* released disco mixes of their soundtracks. *Dance Fever* and *Soul Train* were big hits on TV; even Mickey Mouse had an album, *Mickey Mouse Disco*, which went all the way to No. 35 on *Billboard*'s pop charts and was certified platinum not once but twice. Apparently people really needed to hear their "Zip-a-Dee-Doo-Dah," "It's a Small World," and "Chim Chim Cher-ee" with a disco beat. I've never actually been to a disco, so I can't say much about the scene, and some of the (real) disco music (not Mickey Mouse) was actually great rock 'n' roll—I happen to be a fan of the Bee Gees—but by the end of the decade, disco was on the decline in popularity. And when I say it was on the way out, I actually mean on its early evolutionary way toward what it morphed into: today's electronic, techno, and house music. So it's probably no surprise that in contrast, by the time it was 1979, we had a wave of nostalgia for music from decades prior creeping in.

The summer of 1979, a Chicago DJ named Steven Dahl was pissed. He'd lost his job at a radio station when it went all disco. He was so fed up, he'd taken up the sport of destroying disco records on the air. "Back in the day when we had turntables, I would drag the needle across the record and blow it up with a sound effect. And people liked that,"[165] he said. Dahl then created a Disco Demolition Night out of revenge toward his old radio station. If you brought your unwanted disco records to the Chicago White Sox/Detroit Tigers doubleheader at Comiskey Park on July 12, 1979, you could gain a reduced ninety-eight cents entry fee to the games and, in between the two games, watch all of your disco records get blown up. They expected the crowds to surge with five thousand more people than they'd usually get for a doubleheader. But something closer to fifty thousand people showed up, many of them tossing records around like Frisbees. (The Chicago White Sox promoters were probably ecstatic since they'd previously attracted just sixteen thousand fans per game.) The White Sox lost the first game and then as promised, Dahl, in a combat helmet and military jacket, led the crowd in a chant of "Disco sucks!" as a giant crate of records was pulled onto the field and blown up, leaving a crater in centerfield. The ball players then began warming up for their second game, but somebody rushed the field, and pandemonium ensued. Soon there were seven thousand people on the field, lighting things on fire and stealing the bases. The White Sox had to forfeit their second game.

Ironically, disco began as an underground movement. But with Studio 54 only allowing "the beautiful people" beyond the velvet rope, it evolved into something more sophisticated. Of that July 12, now known as "The Night Disco Died," Gloria Gaynor surmised, "I've always believed it was an economic decision—an idea created by someone whose economic bottom line was being adversely affected

---

165   John, Derek. "The Night Disco Died—Or Didn't." NPR. July 16, 2016.

by the popularity of disco music. So they got a mob mentality going." [166] Her theory has never been proven. But you get an idea how far the music pendulum swung from the early 1960s to the end of the 1970s.

The band members were living as six individuals and not in touch with one another often. Terry was working as a creative director at Motown Records. It was a job he hated with a passion. Ultimately, it was a job he would hold for only seven months. "It's not on my résumé, ever. It's like my year with the mafia. It was horrific. It gives me shudders. So totally antithetical to what I wanted my life to be about, but I was unemployed at the time. I was in the throes of my alcoholism, and it sounded like a place to hide out," he says, just to make the level of his loathing clear. It was nearing Christmas and Terry was working on a show for HBO called *One More Time: Music Then and Now*, a TV special featuring big acts from the past hosted by Mort Sahl. Well, everyone at work knew that Terry was the guy who wrote "Cherish." In Terry's words, "My whole name for forty-five years has been… 'I would like you to meet Terry Kirkman, he wrote "Cherish."' It haunts me, it changes the turf, it puts people on the spot. I haven't done it in thirty-two years, I've never sung it onstage by myself and it follows me around like a puppy you can't get rid of. Good, bad, indifferent, whatever, it's there." Anyhow, they knew Terry had been in The Association and wasted no time asking him to get the band back together and to be on the very show he was simply trying to make happen on the other (off-screen) side as part of his daily job.

"We'll give you five thousand dollars to put the band back together," the executives told him.

"I'm not interested," he said, waving them off.

"Do you think the band would be interested?" they asked.

"No," said Terry, shaking his head, not missing a beat. He called up all of the guys individually to make the offer. Every guy turned it down.

---

166   Sclafani, Tony. "When 'Disco Sucks!' echoed around the world." *Today*. July 10, 2009.

They then doubled the fee to $10,000, a nice chunk of change thirty-five years ago. Terry still waved it off, but his production partner, Spike Jones Jr., said, "You're not going to tell the other guys? You have guys working at a factory, and you're not going to tell the others they were offered $10,000 at Christmastime?" Framed like that, Terry rung all of us up and we agreed to tape the special. We only had to do something like five songs, and we could rehearse on the weekend and then tape the special—featuring Frankie Laine, the Shirelles, Sergio Mendes, and the Temptations at the Cocoanut Grove—on the weekend, to boot, so no one had to miss any work! *The Daily Utah Chronicle* reported in "Re-associated":

THE ASSOCIATION is reforming with all its original members (except the late Brian Cole): Terry Kirkman, Russ Giguere, Jules Alexander, Jim Yester, Ted Bluechel, Larry Ramos. One of the sixties' most successful groups (Cherish, Along Comes Mary) and one of the most effective vocal groups of any decade, the Association's original members have been pursuing solo careers for several years while an ersatz group calling itself The Association still tours the country. According to Jim Yester, "Ted Bluechel was the last to leave; he leased the name to that other outfit. We'll get him for that." Yester said they decided to regroup last Christmas when they reunited for a Home Box Office Artists of the sixties show. "It sounded so good, we decided to give it a shot." They're rehearsing now, with several labels anxious to hear the results. As for that other Association: "We'll have to work that out; we may have to end up calling ourselves the Original Association or something like that."[167]

The original band members hadn't all sung together since I'd left in 1970 (I'm not counting that time we sang with Judee Sill at the Troubadour because my replacement was also onstage at the time). But once we were back in that room together, it was as

167   "Out the Other..." *The Daily Utah Chronicle.* October 8, 1979.

though a day hadn't passed—the air in the room didn't move; the sound was glorious. "It was a one-shot, fantasy-filled reunion…and it just knocked us out,"[168] Terry described to one reporter. There were tears and there was laughter. After the taping was over, I went to the bar with Bob Shane of The Kingston Trio. We sat at a table drinking cocktails—the place had maybe twenty people in it—and Bob whipped out a joint, lit it, took a toke, and passed it to me. I took a toke. No one said a word. Pretty soon another couple across the room whipped out a joint and did the same, followed by another. It was still the seventies, and things were loose. (God, how I miss those times. Not necessarily the seventies, but the looseness.)

After we taped the HBO special, we all went back to our respective lives. It was a one-and-done thing. The show then aired in early 1979 and a few months later, a major talent agency called and told us they could book us all over the country. And just like that, The Association was looking at getting back together!

_____

168   "Harrah's brings back the 60s: the Association and the Turtles." *Reno Gazette-Journal*. September 29, 1983.

Happy Together
1979–1989

WITH AGENCY BOOKINGS IN hand, Terry convinced a relative to be a cosigner on a bank loan to get the band going again. The loan was something around $120,000. We were all doing our own thing—carpentry (that was me!), waterbed sales, optical design, and computer manufacturing—so it took a while to organize the logistics of getting up and running. We needed funds for equipment, clothes, crew, and rehearsal space, not to mention money to pay us a salary for leaving our jobs and for the time we needed to rehearse.

Larry, as I shared earlier, was still making music with his brother Del in the family trio Homegrown, and sometimes appearing as The Brothers Ramos & Cousin Miles. Years later, when Jim came onboard again, he had been working for a temp agency, "unloading semis, furniture factories, digging ditches, working in Christian CD factories." But as we were reforming in 1979–80, we also brought on a seventh member, Ric Ulsky, a bass singer on keyboards. Buzz began circulating: "With its fairly clean-cut look and relatively low-volume guitars, the band won widespread acceptance in venues not previously receptive to rock, appearing in numerous summer music festivals and TV shows."[169] We brought Pat Colecchio back onboard to manage us and got a deal with Elektra Records. Bones Howe produced our recording of "Dreamer."

> "It took quite a long time to get together again, because we were all in our different lifestyles and had different careers

---

169   Arar, Yardena. "The Association...one time reunion sounded too good to end." *Messenger-Inquirer*. February 20, 1981.

happening," says Alexander, the lead guitarist who turned to optical design.

"The TV show was two years ago and it's taken that long for us to get out of our previous obligations."

It also took that long to get a record deal. Although the records produced by the band in its twelve years together have sold in excess of twenty-five million copies worldwide—including a "Greatest Hits" album that is one of Warner Bros.' all-time bestsellers—the revived group's reception when it first approached record companies was not exactly enthusiastic.

"It was, 'Oh, they sound great, but...' And the 'buts' went into twenty different reasons why it wasn't going to happen," says Colecchio, who joined in a group interview at the band's garage-like rehearsal hall.

Colecchio says the reasons boiled down to "it was big ten years ago, but will the audience accept it now? Finally, Elektra-Asylum gave us a deal, and the irony of it all is that we're on the charts today."

The group's single, "Dreamer," is in fact being played on radio stations nationwide.[170]

There would be much talk of our "upcoming album" throughout the 1980s, but we were, once again, so busy touring that it didn't happen. "...We'd like to spend a little more time in the studio. We've got great material and the best group of musicians we've ever had. We're talking to a lot of people, and we're hoping the talk turns to ink soon,"[171] I told one reporter in 1987. We always referred to the tapes we made in the recording studio during that time as our "secret

170   Arar, Yardena. "The Association tries to make comeback after years of breakup." *Star Tribune*. May 10, 1981.

171   Edgar, Henry. "Hit parade: The Association's songs are timeless." *Daily Press*. May 5, 1987.

album." I have five of the tunes, but we're missing about five more. No one knows where those tapes are. Jim can't even remember if he gave them to Larry or me. I'm sure he gave them to Larry because if he gave them to me, I'd still have them!

We asked our agency to book us out of town in the beginning so we could work on the act, so our first concert once we were back together was at a convention for the Firefighters of America in Anchorage, Alaska, where we were on a triple bill with Paul Revere & the Raiders and Wolfman Jack. I love firefighters! Since Alaska was the only state we'd never performed in all the years we spent crisscrossing the country, it felt like we were coming full circle and it was meant to be. We would also return to Alaska five years later for the twenty-fifth anniversary of their statehood, where they had a number of lively events throughout the year, including the Eskimo Olympics, the Iditarod, the ever politically incorrect Fur Rendezvous Festival, and other general partying for its own sake, an Alaskan tradition. (It's cold up there and winter nights are long, making it an inevitable party state.)

Ted, who is rarely ever sick, fell seriously ill and couldn't make the dates in Alaska. So we hired Russ Levine, a drummer who had worked with the band in the late 1970s, to replace him for that date. With just one rehearsal, Russ filled in on drums and did a great job, too. He was dead-on; he had a great beat and innate sense of rhythm. He was paid well for the gig, but we always felt indebted to the boy. Two years later, we learned Levine was getting married in Cape Cod. We were on the road but realized we could make his wedding if we drove all night. We hatched a plan—to surprise him and his bride with a live rendition of "Never My Love." We got there about an hour before the ceremony, which was being held in the backyard of a gorgeous "salt box" house on a hill, with the Atlantic Ocean as a backdrop. We managed to stay out of his sight until the wedding began. As Russ Levine and his bride faced the minister, we snuck up behind them and when the minister finished, the unsuspecting couple turned around—and we sang "Never My Love" to them, accompanied by a single acoustic guitar!

We began logging many TV appearances, including *The John Davidson Show*, *The Mike Douglas Show*, *Tomorrow Coast to Coast with Tom Snyder*, *Dick Clark's Variety Show*, *Home*, and several *Solid Gold* shows, including their summer special, as well as radio and TV interviews. We were booked for symphony dates with the Atlanta Symphony, the Philadelphia Symphony, Wichita Falls Symphony, North Carolina Symphony, the Grand Junction Symphony, and many more.

We also began giving interviews to the press again. One of these interviews was broadcast during the 1980 Rose Bowl game in which the Los Angeles Rams played the Pittsburgh Steelers. Lucille Ball was also being interviewed, so viewership was especially high. J. D. Souther loves to tell the story about how he was watching the game that day while visiting his father in Texas. At halftime, he walked into the kitchen to make a sandwich and then swore he heard me laughing—from his father's living room (I am known for the loudness of my laugh). He dashed back in and saw it was true when he saw my face staring back at him—and he caught the rest of our interview on the tube.

Shortly after the band officially reunited, we headed to Dallas for a live appearance on *Ed McMahon and Company* with Showtime. We arrived by plane, and on our way from the airport to our hotel, we drove by the Playboy Club, which was advertising a concert by The Association. Imagine our surprise. We all looked at one another and shared a chuckle. Since we weren't scheduled to tape until the next day, several of us, including Pat Colecchio, went to the concert that night. When the lights went down, four guys walked onto the stage. Well, I'm sorry, but you can't do our harmonies and produce our sound with just a quartet—they are full-on six-part harmonies. In the middle of the show, Pat sent a note up to the stage saying, "Jules Alexander, Russ Giguere, Terry Kirkman, and Jim Yester are in the audience." We talked about the experience in interviews.

We've all heard of counterfeit coins, counterfeit watches, and even counterfeit Calvin Kleins. But counterfeit rock groups? Sounds ridiculous.

For members of the sixties supergroup The Association, however, phony rock bands are nothing to laugh at...

"It was strange hearing them do our songs," recall the members, "especially their personal introductions such as, 'Here's one of our biggest hits.'"[172]

I mean, these guys were up there talking as though they were the real deal! When they got Pat's note, we could see how embarrassed they were. They weren't necessarily bad, but they weren't very good, either. Pat sent around a Hawaiian lawyer—in other words, someone to talk to Rob Grill (best known for his band, the Grass Roots), who had leased the name from Ted, to deliver the message that he'd be wise to stop sending out groups posing as or calling themselves The Association any longer.

That next day in Dallas we taped *Ed McMahon and Company*. The episode The Association was on also featured Phyllis Diller, Richard Dawson, Shecky Greene, Jerry Lewis, Dinah Shore, Frank Gorshin, and Abbe Lane. Abbe Lane was a hoot and very easy on the eyes. When the cameras weren't turned on her, she asked, "Who do I have to fuck to get off this show?"

When we got back together, it was as though we had never parted; the crowds were big and loved us—in fact, we sounded better than ever. Money was being made, our calendars were full, and the phone was ringing off the hook. Booze flowed and the drugs—mostly cocaine and weed—were plentiful.

On a rare day off in New York City on July 10, 1981, the band took in a concert by The Temptations at the Savoy Club on West Forty-Fourth Street, a large venue that held over a thousand people (it opened in 1903 as the Hudson Theatre, the name it bears again

---

172   "Harrah's brings back the 60s: the Association and the Turtles." *Reno Gazette-Journal.* September 29, 1983.

today). The day before we had appeared on Tom Snyder's *Tomorrow Coast to Coast*. Anyhow, while we were at The Temptations concert, watching it from the balcony, this guy approaches me.

"Are you guys The Association?" he asks.

"Yes," I said.

"I love you guys—you're one of my favorite groups!" The man extended his hand and introduced himself as Paul Stanley. As in the Paul Stanley from KISS, one of the most famous rock bands of all time. As recently as 2017, Paul shared, "One of the songs that has been on repeat play in my dressing room while on tour is 'Everything That Touches You'...Love the counterpoint at the end between bass, vocals, horns and all!"

Pat Colecchio was with us for a year or so, but he left in 1981. "I don't care if you never go on the road, don't ask for thousands of dollars whenever the urge arises to satisfy your indulgences," he said. "Without the tours, the money well runs dry...Some are dipping in more than others. The tag I put on that declaration was that whatever extra money was asked for by any individual, every member was entitled to the like amount." Ted adds, "Some of the members had habits that they would be snorting so much coke that they needed money to buy more coke. When the individual needed an advance of ten grand, he would have to give that to everyone and we had to go back on the road. That was the vicious thing that killed us."

Pat had some differences with Terry, though I wasn't privy to them—none of us were. When Pat left, we needed a new manager and Terry connected us with a new guy, whom he'd met at a party. This is, at least, how I remember it, but Terry says Ted or Jules connected us with the bad manager, yet Ted and Jules say it wasn't them! Ah, the mystery of chasing down memories over thirty-five years old. Maybe with twenty-twenty hindsight no one wants to claim ownership over the decision we made to bring a new manager onboard. However, in the democratic process of The Association, we did all have to be on board with big decisions, so clearly the band collectively gave the green light to this new manager…however it was he came to us. (Incidentally, the manager says he learned about us from a Hollywood agent.) One story, so many points of view. The manager was a hotshot under-twenty-five sports agent looking to expand his client portfolio. I'm going to be a gentleman here, so let's just call him "bad manager" for these purposes. In 1984, a reporter wrote of this manager:

> When he received a call a few years back asking if he'd like to represent The Association, his response was, he says, "The association of what?"[173]

That says a lot right there. Not so much that he didn't know who we were at the time—okay, fine—but to say something like that to a reporter. Terry has a philosophy on representation: "My rule of thumb as a Hollywood veteran of TV, films, and radio…is that if you are really hurting and you are going to be a hard sell, the guy you want to get is either dumb enough or excited enough to sell you, but you don't want to get the guy who already has big acts, because you won't get enough attention." So I think the idea was that this new manager was young, he was up-and-coming and eager—since he was sharp and such a ballsy go-getter, we thought he'd be a good fit. People had already taken note of him as a force to be reckoned with: he "has clambered through the highly explosive world of big-time entertainment at a dizzying pace…It's a tale of a child who grew up hungry, itching to bust out of his clustered environment, eager to be somebody BIG. FAST." In that same article, the reporter interviews a colleague of the man who would become our manager and that colleague comments, "He was always a hustler, he did a very good job…But we had to teach him right from wrong…[he] would sell you the Brooklyn Bridge…is in it for the money and…is making a fortune."[174] Let it be known he would prove that he most certainly was not was taught right from wrong, or if he was, he just didn't care.

---

173   "Stars seek rights to 'Sally's saga.'" *Wisconsin State Journal.* January 13, 1984.

174   Feldman, Paul. "At 24, a show business mover and shaker." *The Record.* April 19, 1981.

The bad manager was not honest with us—in fact he stole money from us, and a lot of it—a million and a half by Terry's estimate—but it took years for us to realize it because our focus was, again, on the music, not the business. In the words of Mick Jagger, a musician's thinking is, "'Oh, I'm a creative person, I won't worry about this.' But that just doesn't work. Because everyone would just steal every penny you've got."[175] Our manager would say, "Hey, I got another deal for you, it pays this much." He was the middleman, and we never saw the original contracts for what he booked us on—this was in the days before email, so there was no electronic transparency. The manager would arbitrarily price out different rates for what we were getting paid at various concerts; they were all within a range of what we were used to, so we didn't question it, nor did we know he was skimming off the top. (Skimming is a kind description of what he was doing.) Terry says, "You'd just buy into it because you don't even know where you were. Where are you? I'm on the RV. I'm singing the same fucking songs I sang yesterday. What time do I get up? That's what happens on a tour like that." Our bad manager even screwed Pat Colecchio on monies owed to him for gigs he'd booked for us prior to his departure, but never paid up. "I had $160,000 of bookings coming up, all solidified at the William Morris Agency...of the $16,000 coming to me...I went to his office to pick up a measly $1,000. He said the group owed me the rest, never giving me the remainder of monies due me," Pat griped.

Jim shares, "I was kind of doing a lot of the business liaison stuff with [the bad manager] and I made the mistake of giving him my Amex number and he started putting the air flights on it and all of a sudden I had a $35,000 Amex bill!" Terry remembers storming up to the manager's office in New York after one of our gigs—we had probably been performing somewhere nearby, like the Catskills—and Terry confronted him about his stealing from the band, which the bad manager brazenly admitted to doing and declared there was nothing

---

175   Serwer, Andy. "Inside Rolling Stones Inc." *Fortune*, September 30, 2002.

that would stop him from continuing the same course of action. "I kept asking for original contracts," Terry remembers. "There weren't any—we were told how much we were going to be paid, and that was it...After I left the band [in 1984], I told them, I said this guy is killing you, he is painting you into a corner, you can't move."

That bad manager, however, was the individual responsible for putting together our very first Happy Together Tour in 1984. "I gave him the idea to do it," Terry continues. "I sat down with him...and I said, 'You can't sell us because at best we are a C-level act right now. Every time you pick up the phone you have to remind people who we are.' I said, 'Get a whole bunch of acts, put us all together, and put it into an event.' I didn't know the event would be with the Turtles."

In a 2012 book, that manager recalls:

I took a bunch of the agents to individual lunches and told them that I would split my 15-percent management fee with them in return for their working hard to book my band. Lo and behold, the next day, my phone started ringing off the hook with dates from the agents. "Is The Association available for two days at Bogart's in Cincinnati for fifteen grand?" "Can The Association do a gig at Summerfest, the yearly festival in Chicago, for $25,000?" Of course I said yes and yes! I called my buddy Mitchel Etess at the Grossinger's Hotel in the Catskills, and he booked the band on a Thursday night for five grand to help kick off a singles weekend at the hotel. Another agent called and offered me two days starting Friday afternoon at 4:00 p.m. at the Orange County Fair in Los Angeles.

With offers coming in this thick and fast, scheduling dates and travel was starting to get difficult. I called Terry Kirkman and Jim Yester, the band leaders at the time, to ask, with so many dates, who should give the final okay on which shows to take? Kirkman said, "Our old manager, Pat

Colecchio, did everything for us. It's your job to accept the dates," then hung up on me. I was on my own…

…By the end of the summer, The Association had grossed a million. I made nearly $100,000, and the agents made their money, too. But somehow, the band was left in debt. I couldn't understand how this had happened! I had worked so hard to make them the money, given them these great discount plane tickets, but still they had no money in the bank. I realized that I had pushed these guys too far. Making money wasn't the be-all and end-all—I had to take care of my artists as well.

The following October, The Association was on the same bill as Gary Puckett and the Union Gap, doing an oldies show with Chuck Berry at the Meadowlands Arena in New Jersey. Gary's song "Young Girl" was a favorite of mine growing up. I asked the members of The Association to introduce me to Gary because I wanted to sign him up for management. They told him about me, we had a meeting in my office, and the next thing I knew I was his manager. Again, I was very excited. I thought I was making great strides in the music business—but again, my agent friends told me that I was nuts. "You're representing the biggest athletes in the world… and you're spending your time managing these oldies acts!" But I didn't care. I liked these people. They were fun to listen to, and most of them were very nice.

After I signed Gary, I was approached by the Turtles, and I signed them, too. I was gathering all these great acts— now I needed to do something with them. So in 1984 I approached the William Morris Agency, and we came up with the idea of packaging these bands together, along with Spanky McFarlane of Spanky and Our Gang, and calling it the Happy Together Tour. The tour would feature four bands and a night of only hit songs.

Almost immediately, promoters started buying shows. Jules Belkin, who promoted the Ohio and Detroit markets, bought six shows. Arnie Granit, who promoted in Illinois, bought a bunch. Ron Delsener bought three shows for Jones Beach, the Garden State Arts Center, and the Pier in New York City. Ron always asked me to add on acts like Tommy James and the Shondells or Three Dog Night to enhance the package, and that way we could play to a bigger venue and sell more tickets. I have to credit him with some of this advice—some of the best I've received. He said that I have good ideas, but I should spend more money on big-name talent. I might have to pay more, but it would work. I will always feel indebted to him because he always believed in me and my projects.

In November of 1984 something great happened: The movie *The Big Chill* came out. All of a sudden, the whole country started getting nostalgic—and we started selling out shows. We decided to launch a summer tour and booked more than 125 gigs. A year later, I produced another version of the Happy Together Tour, adding on Gene Clark's Byrds, the Grass Roots with Rob Grill, and the Buckinghams ("Kind of a Drag" was the Buckinghams' hit song). This tour did another 125 dates and really helped relaunch some of these musicians' careers.[176]

Reading these words and knowing the truth of what actually happened make his blatant disregard for business ethics even more disgusting. I didn't think that was possible, but there you are.

The Turtles, helmed by Howard Kaylan and Mark Volman, had had a number of hits in the sixties, with "Happy Together" being their biggest. It hit No. 1 in February 1967, knocking The Beatles' "Penny Lane" out of its top slot. By far, however, my favorite song of

---

176 Fishof, David with Michael Levin. *Rock Your Business: What You and Your Company Can Learn From The Business of Rock and Roll.* BenBella Books, 2012.

theirs is "You Showed Me," which was released in December 1968. The first time I heard it, I was driving up Beachwood Drive to a friend's place. I walked up the stairs to the apartment and told them I had just heard a great tune by the Turtles. Gene Clark, a friend of mine, was there.

"I really like that song," I told him. "I think it's the best thing they (the Turtles) ever released."

"You really like that song?" Gene Clark asked me.

"Yes," I said.

"I wrote that song!"

Gene had written the song with Jimmy McGuinn when they were part of The Byrds. "You Showed Me" went all the way to No. 6 on the charts. Anyhow, on the Happy Together Tour, which was put together by that manager, we were also joined by Gary Puckett & The Union Gap and Spanky & Our Gang. Gary Puckett was known for "Young Girl," "Over You," "Woman Woman," and "Lady Willpower." "Young Girl" went all the way to No. 3 on *Billboard's* Hot 100. Elaine "Spanky" MacFarlane's best-known hits are "Like to Get to Know You," "Lazy Day," and "Sunday Will Never Be the Same," which hit No. 9 in the summer of 1967. In a review *The Philadelphia Daily News* wrote, "The Association was certainly the most successful... The Association epitomized the squeaky-clean sound and look of a hotel lounge band, the kind that wore matching tuxedos[177] and complimented the audience for being 'beautiful.'[178] So I could hardly believe the news, when one of the guys in this group died of a heroin overdose. It was comparable to discovering that Mickey Mouse was a junkie."[179]

Squeaky clean? That reporter didn't *really* know us. Craig Doerge (pronounced "dur-gee"), who is married to Judy Henske, told me a story about a time in the mid-1980s when he was on the road, playing

---

177   We never wore matching tuxedos. Tuxedos, yes, but not matching.

178   We've also never complimented the audience for being beautiful.

179   Takiff, Jonathan. "Live This Week! The Band/The Turtles/Gary Puckett/Spanky and our Gang." *Philadelphia Daily News*. July 27, 1984.

keyboards with Crosby, Stills & Nash. I actually gave Judy away at her wedding to Craig, her second husband (remember her first husband was Jerry Yester), an honor I did not take lightly, since her father had passed away and we had been great friends since I was sixteen. Anyhow, Craig and Crosby, Stills & Nash were picked up at the airport in a large white van (Craig thinks they were playing the Valley Forge Theatre in Pennsylvania—a theatre in the round). They asked the woman van driver if she usually met the entertainers at the airport.

"Yes," she said, "for a couple of years."

"Who's the biggest jerk you've ever picked up?" they asked her.

After much prodding she admitted it was Rodney Dangerfield, the comic.

Emboldened, they then asked, "Which is the *wildest* group you've ever picked up?"

"The Association," she revealed, without hesitation. "Especially that blond guy."

That would be me she was referring to! I laughed hard when Craig told me this story because I remembered being met at the airport by this same young lady, and the band was just laughing and having a good time. Bruce Pictor, who has been playing drums with us for thirty-four years, puts the unwritten band rule like this: "The Association had a standing rule for years because of past members' habits or what have you. There was no drinking or partying before showtime. And after the gig, that was your own time. Do what you're going to do. But pretty much no bleary eyes in the morning. We pushed that envelope like crazy."

The reviews were still great. "The Association took the stage, overwhelming the room with their exuberance and energy."[180] We were tapping into the wave of baby boomer nostalgia that is still very much alive today: "...the Association seems to retain the mellow appeal and soft melodies that may earn them a middle-of-the-road

---

180   Butkiewicz, Joe. "Woodlands show brings back the sounds of the '60s." *The Times Leader.* May 11, 1984.

listening audience."[181] And we still had what it takes. "The outstanding pop chorale group of the sixties still sings flawless harmony, still has its dense sound, and still shares its lead vocals among members…"[182] We were all now in our late thirties and forties and a little more… relaxed, you might say. "We've had as much or more fun [the second time around]. Everyone is just more graceful with each other. Everyone is older and wiser," I told a reporter in a phone interview. The article went on to mention, "The group does an average of 175 shows a year…It's a schedule that's 'healthy, but not killing.'"[183]

We played the Venetian Room of the San Francisco Fairmont Hotel twice, one of which was June 9–22, 1982. The Fairmont was and is a top-of-the-line hotel—the rooms, food, and staff are all aces. The Venetian Room, which had top-notch acoustics and sound system, was quite large. It had a huge kitchen and a carpeted hallway that went around the back and the other side. The other hallway was in the middle, going back to more hotel suites. It was our closing night, June 22, and Jules and I were walking around toward the back of the hall—we were wearing tuxedoes and looking good. Suddenly, a beautiful woman in a floor-length gown and diamond tiara with an entourage of ten or twelve people came around the corner. Jules and I stopped, bowed our heads toward her and smiled, and she smiled back as they passed. We continued on and did the show, which was magnificent (I really don't remember the show specifically, but all the shows we did in that room were wonderful—it was just one of those perfect places). And the lovely lady in the tiara? She was Queen Beatrix of the Netherlands, on her way to a dinner in her honor at the hotel. Jules and I remember it like it was yesterday—only at the Fairmont would you cross paths in the hall with actual royalty.

181   Walker, Charlie. "Fans turned on by Association." *The Morning News.* May 11, 1983.

182   Oermann, Robert K. "Sixties Nostalgia Brings Smiles to TPAC." *The Tennessean.* August 3, 1984.

183   Tancill, Karen B. "For The Association, second time is better." *The Journal Times.* August 21, 1986.

In 1985 we were invited to do the "Dodge Presents Legends for Liberty" Tour, a fifteen-day, thirteen-city tour through America's Heartland (Ohio, Illinois, Iowa, Indianapolis, and Michigan) with the Four Tops, Tommy James, Mark Lindsay, and the original Spirit featuring Jay Ferguson and Randy California. These days it's strange to think about an American car company sponsoring something that was billed as "the largest fundraiser on wheels."[184] *The Des Moines Register* wrote, "No matter how doleful the selection of a cause, the 8:00 p.m. September 11 concert at Veterans Memorial Auditorium here might be saved from the doldrums of entertainment-for-significant aid attempts by its solid lineup of artists."[185] We had done individual concerts with the Four Tops over the years, but actually touring with them was wonderful—they were gentlemen through and through and aptly named "The Tops."

The first time we began performing together, we did our version of "Walk Away Renee." Afterward, back in the dressing room, riding high on the adrenaline of our performance, somebody recalled that the Four Tops had had a hit with "Walk Away Renee" in 1967. And there we were, just taking it out from underneath their noses and including it in our own lineup. The band elected me to go to their dressing room and apologize.

"Gentlemen," I began, "you have had so many hits that we failed to remember 'Walk Away Renee' was just one in your impressive list of many."

"We like your version better," they told me. "We insist you keep doing it!"

What a class act all the way. I returned to the dressing room to share the news with the band. Bruce Pictor remembers, "Sometimes we had a day off, and we'd go barbecue at someone's house like the Four Tops...these guys are legends, and to be invited to their homes...it just was wild. Every now and again [on tour], you might

184   "'Liberty' tour coming to Indiana." *Municle Evening Press.* August 15, 1985.

185   Brune, Brett R. R. "The Fun Circuit." *The Des Moines Register.* August 1, 1985.

find one or more of them switching buses…you travel during the day. Sometimes we'd switch buses and somebody would ride with another group for a while and get to know them." On that tour, Bruce continues, "We're playing in an arena, there are about twenty thousand people there. In the middle of the arena, there's a backdrop…a scrim that separates the stage and there might be instrument cases in back of that and whatnot.…The Four Tops were onstage playing a song and me, Larry, and Del were doing the bunny hop to the song they were playing and while we were doing it backstage, we kind of got to the edge of the scrim and half the audience could see us and you could hear people laughing and applauding!"

By that time, Del was playing with us onstage. There was a while there when Del sang his part from the sound board. "He would be out in the house mixing the show and he would have a microphone out there and he would sing from the console, so he was part of the vocal ensemble, and it was very unique," Paul Holland shares. "People would come to see the singing sound guy. He was actually singing a necessary part in the vocals and also mixing the sound and he would usually have a headset on or an intercom handset or something to where he was calling spotlight cues as well. It was kind of interesting to watch him out there, singing, mixing, and talking with the spotlights at the same time. I don't know how he did that, but he made it work!"

On the Legends for Liberty Tour, all net profits were being donated to the Statue of Liberty Ellis Island Restoration Project. The promoter actually called me to offer The Association the fifteen-day, thirteen-city tour for something like $150,000 or $175,000. So I did what every loyal client would do. I said, "Sounds great, we can probably do that, but give our manager a call to go over the details." Soon thereafter, our bad manager calls us to offer the same tour, but for HALF THE FEE!

We had caught him in the act red-handed. We had suspected something was off, but now we had the proof. Terry had figured out prior to his departure that the bad manager was working with our agent to keep every third gig off the books to pocket the money. The bad manager even went so far as to try to loop Terry into forming a record company where they could do to other artists what he was doing to The Association. Sadly, this guy had—still has—deep pockets and a lot of lawyers. He's screwed over a lot of people, but he's still around, believe it or not, and this business is small enough that you don't want to badmouth anyone because it can rear up to bite you. We still do business with some of the concert promoters who've been booking us for thirty years, and you never know who is talking to whom or saying what. We simply want to make sure we are paid what we should be paid. But by catching him in the act, we were then able to walk away, stop working with managers, and begin working with an agency directly.

But that bad manager is the one who put together our original Happy Together Tour in 1984, where we performed with the Turtles, Spanky and Our Gang, and Gary Puckett. Each band would do something like a twenty-five-minute set, and at the end we'd all sing the Turtles hit song "Happy Together." The bands traveled in separate vehicles, but performed together—it was something like 140 concerts over eight months. We were riding the wave of the big resurgence in 1960s music after the disco backlash. The tour was lucrative and busy. Some people are built for the road, like me—I don't mind getting up early, and I'm always on time. For others, the basic demands of the road—you've got to get up early and you've got to be on time, coupled with the distance from home—are hard.

"Your nerves become frayed, you don't get the proper sleep," Bruce explains. "Tempers would flare and different people might call each other out and have a yelling or screaming match. But at the end of the day, you are performing with these people. You don't want to go onstage not feeling good about somebody, so you try and…get things talked out before you go onstage, because we're all full-grown men. Artists have egos, you know, it was something we needed to be aware of and over the years…because of situations like that I might have said or done something I regretted later, so the best policy then is to realize what you've done and apologize, correct the mistake, and get back to a level playing field because you've got work to do. Going onstage with somebody you're angry with or what have you just doesn't work. People can tell, you can feel it." Paul Holland, who first played with The Association in the late 1980s before taking a break and then coming back, shares, "It's a family, it's a very large family, and sometimes it's very dysfunctional, but it's an organization, it's a collective, a group of people that when we see each other, we're genuinely glad to see each other. We enjoy each other's company, we enjoy being around each other. For that short time that we're up onstage, we have so much fun."

It came to me in a dream that I was going to introduce Paul Holland as the only living son of Elvis. I would introduce him, and then we would play the opening to "Jailhouse Rock," so it became a thing we did. Sometimes people would even believe it! It was funny and it always got a reaction from the crowd. "Things would show up in the mail," Paul says, "and they were from Russ. Turns out they were serial-numbered Elvis collectibles. I have a pretty good stock of Elvis collectibles thanks to Russ. We can always count on Russ for fashion advice. Because he knew how to dress, how to keep himself up, and he was the front man of The Association—he drew everybody's attention because he was the good-looking personality onstage. If I ever needed clothing advice on how to dress or what to wear, I knew I could ask Russ and it would be good advice."

On the 1984 Happy Together Tour, the Turtles toured in a big white school bus that they called Gullfire, after the hang glider Kurt Russell flew in *Escape from New York*. The rest of us called it "the average white bus," a twist on/reference to the Average White Band, a Scottish funk and R&B band that was popular in the mid- to late 1970s. That bus just barely made it over the Rocky Mountains. Later they got a mobile home, like they should have in the first place! Gary Puckett's crew traveled in a large black van they named Black Beauty, but we were quick to dub it the "Puckett Bucket." Not everyone smoked, snorted, or drank, but those of us who did made up for the others. The Association toured in a large mobile home. The company that made the mobile home was named Georgie Boy—hence the nickname we gave our home on wheels, "The Death Ship Boy George." It had a giant king-sized bed in the back. In fact, it was such a mothership that Joe Lamanno, who had been a volunteer firefighter for fifteen years and played with us in the 1970s after Brian's death and then again during the Happy Together Tour, often took responsibility for driving it and developed a parking strategy: "I was used to driving fire engines, and I knew they could be intimidating. I parked it backward, because I didn't want to have to back it out at the end of the gig." The schedule, Joe recalls, was grueling, with maybe one day off every twelve to fourteen days, sometimes a two-day drive (though not often), and an overnight if a date happened to fall out. It was a dope-soaked tour. Jim missed out on the fun—he had left the band before the tour started to take care of family matters.

Gary Puckett was great onstage and had a large fan base. One time at a hotel, Howard Kaylan of the Turtles and I smelled marijuana and followed our noses 125 feet down the hall to a hotel room door. We knocked on the door, and a crew member answered.

"Aren't you going to share?" we asked.

"I haven't even smoked any yet," he told us. The weed was sitting on the table, no one was smoking it, and we had smelled it behind a closed door all the way down the hall! We were already stoned anyway.

"Let's go visit Gary's fans," Howard quipped. We continued our journey to the bar.

We did one show back east at Jones Beach in New York where they lined up five acts on the tour, adding Three Dog Night to the bill. I remember Cory Wells, one of the original band members, was arguing with Danny onstage about how he wanted to do the long version of "Eli's Coming." Danny tried to explain they were one of five acts and there was a time limit, but Cory didn't understand. That was the last time Cory played with them.

Cory had a heroin problem, which he finally overcame. We did a few concerts with him, including one in San Diego on the bay, when he was singing with Blood, Sweat & Tears. He is just so good. During one show back east in a large showroom at a casino/racetrack, I was talking with his bass player about how I was so impressed with his talent and how he was one of the few people I knew that had kicked smack. The bass player then told me he was Cory's son. I had no idea.

We did other gigs separate from the Happy Together Tour as well. I remember we played on a beach in Jacksonville, Florida, for one audience where we were on the bill with The Beach Boys, the Four Tops, and other acts, and even though it was bright daylight, you could not see the end of the crowd in front of us—they literally faded into infinity. For all I knew, the crowd went around the earth. Someone told me there were 125,000 people there. We sang the national anthem for Chicago Bears and Chicago Bulls games, and of course we performed several times at the Chicago Opera House and ChicagoFest. The first time we played ChicagoFest, we ran into our old pal Marty Nicosia again.

At the start of our performance in ChicagoFest, our sound was a disaster—we couldn't hear ourselves and the balance was off. I waved frantically to get the attention of the guy sitting behind the sound monitor, but he was too busy flirting with a girl. To our great surprise, along comes Marty. You'll recall we had first met him in the 1960s when we came to town to do a gig and our sound equipment decided to take another flight to another location and he saved our asses, all in the days before studio equipment rentals were a thing. Anyhow, during that performance, the flirting sound monitor man was about to get into it with Marty, who took over the board, but he backed down once he took in Marty's physically imposing presence and ponytail hanging down to his waist. Marty fixed our sound lickety-split. He remembers:

When they reformed the band, they came across me. I was a production manager for ChicagoFest on Navy Pier. They put barges up along the pier and set up bleachers [that] would face the barges, which were the stages; there was a country stage, an oldies rock stage, a new wave stage—ten or twelve different categories. It was also a food festival. Toward the front there were two 25,000-seat stages. One was for the popular rock bands of the day, (like) John Mellencamp, Cheap Trick, and the other side was Aretha Franklin... You'd pay one fee of six dollars, and get in and have food and music all day.

Here came the guys, playing on the oldies stage. I was busy with the main stage up front—I arranged for someone to cover my stage so I could go see them perform. They didn't have time for sound check, but with all those vocals, you have to be able to hear everyone so your voices can blend— they were brilliant at it...I got up there and I could see in their faces, they had panic. In the monitors they listened to, the mix was wrong and they couldn't hear what was going on. I heard it walking up and knew something wasn't right...I shoved the engineer out of the way and got the mix right in about one minute and it was off and running! This was one of the last nights of the festival."

"We've got to get together," we told Marty following the performance. "We have a road manager we can't stand, you've *got* to come out with us!" We hired him on the spot.

"[So] I went out on the road as their tour manager," Marty shares. "It was great—I'd heard them through their whole career and they really were sounding fantastic."

There was another time in the Happy Together Tour where we nearly missed our cue for the big finale where all the bands sang "Happy Together"—we'd gone to a room upstairs to get stoned, but Peter Zale (keyboardist for the Turtles) heard those first few telltale notes of the finale, and we all ran down the stairs and made it onto the stage just in time for all of the bands to sing their snippet of one of their most beloved songs before we all launched into a group rendition of "Happy Together." We also did a show at the San Diego Wild Animal Park—they had a hillside where the audience sat and at the bottom of the hill was a large mobile stage they rolled in, with a sound system and lights, and the dressing rooms. And right behind that were giraffes, elephants, and rhinos meandering through what appeared to be an African-like plain with lakes and hills in the distance. My mom and sisters came to that show. I remember that the sunset over the scene was spectacular and I gave thanks onstage to the Wild Animal Park and God. When the Happy Together Tour performed at the New Orleans Zoo, I asked the audience for a moment of complete silence, just so we could listen to the animals. The animals—dare I say it—went ape, reacting to the music.

Before that same show in New Orleans, one of the crew members went to score some weed. He had found a guy who said he could help him.

"Let me see if my connection is in," the guy told the crew member.

He led him down the street, went through the door to check with his connection, and then returned to report back to the crew member: "Yeah, he's in."

The crew member gave him the money for the weed and the guy went back through the door to pay him and get the product. The minutes ticked by and the guy didn't return. Eventually, the crew member opened the door, and behind the door was nothing.

There was another time that we arrived in New Orleans during Mardi Gras, but we were so tired from touring that everyone just went to sleep. Nobody even went out. And we were known to be major partiers!

The tour was a blast—but people couldn't sustain the lifestyle for various reasons, many of them having to do with family—though in Terry's case, by 1984 he was drinking and snorting cocaine in excess, so he left to get sober and clean. In his own words, "I'm drinking again and I'm snorting cocaine and I'm probably dying inside and we're on the road probably 250 days of the year. I walked out and said I'm never ever going to get involved with the music business ever again...I was probably so crazy and so abhorrent that everybody said, 'What are we going to do about the *Terry* problem?'"

Speaking about the band, Joe Lammano comments, "When they were aligned and everything was rosy, it was really rosy, because it was dynamic times six. The lows were lower, but the highs were higher. I liked that they came from the folk scene—they talked in between songs and they had that sense of entertainment."

The fact that our manager was stealing from us is what convinced Terry that it was time to get out. Everybody left—Ric Ulsky (I'm not sure why he left), Terry to get sober, and Ted to spend more time with his autistic son again. Some people just can't take the pressures on the road. It's hard; it leads to excess. So by the last chunk of that first Happy Together Tour dates, the only original band members remaining were Larry, Jules, and me.

"What are we going to do about all this debt?" Larry, Jules, and I asked Terry and Ted as they left.

We still owed the bank more than six figures for the loan we'd taken out to get the band going again. Larry, Jules, and I agreed to take on the debt in exchange for taking ownership of the band's name, which everyone considered a fair trade on both sides. We signed the paperwork and then paid off the debt in a little over a year. When Jules then left the band in 1989 (I think he left the band for a woman he met during one of our cruise ship engagements; it was a relationship that then fizzled out very quickly), it was just Larry and me, so we shared ownership of the band and use of the name, and then when Larry died in 2014, ownership was left to me.

Anyhow, squared away legally after Ric, Terry, and Ted left one after the other on the 1984 Happy Together Tour, we embarked upon more epic touring, musically speaking and...party-wise.

Bruce, who joined us in 1985 after an audition in Los Angeles, recalls, "When I first joined, we were doing 250 one-nighters a year. Flying in and out—I remember one time I swear we went from… Memphis to Alaska and then we flew from Alaska to Florida and then I think we went to San Juan, Puerto Rico, and then back to New Orleans. And that's night after night, no days off."

The enthusiastic audience reception never wavered. We played the Grand Ole Opry many times. On one occasion, Bruce remembers that the sound engineer told him that we received the first full-house standing ovation he'd seen in his seven years. When we played Dubuque, Iowa, again for the first time since 1966, we asked if anybody in the crowd remembered being present for that 1966 concert where we played outdoors at the top of a parking ramp. And lo and behold, there were people present who remembered. We also continued breaking audience attendance records, including one at Disney World in 1985, which was the first performance for which Bruce joined us. "So many that there were people who trampled their landscaping," says Bruce. "It was a record crowd. It was a sea of people. I remember driving into Disney World, I had my cassette tape and headphones still on, still listening to the songs, going over my vocal parts." Donni Gougeon remembers, "In one and a half years, we did fourteen cruises."

Larry once joked in an interview, "The reason the other three original members aren't with us is because they can't take the road. Only the strong survive on the road…We're basically a bunch of gypsies. We're on the road two hundred days a year, mostly flying."[186] And by the end of the 1980s, the only original members remaining in the band were me and Larry. We had added additional talented guys to the band's roster, some of whom had also played with us after Brian's death during the years the band was active in the 1970s. To date, there have been over forty members of The Association.

---

186   Drabyk, Beth V. "BLAST from the PAST." *Florida Today*. July 5, 1985.

Donni Gougeon auditioned for the band and would go on to tour with us during Dick Clark's 1989 American Bandstand tour, where the Drifters was the band representing the 1950s, The Association the 1960s, the Guess Who the 1970s, and the Spinners the 1980s. The tour also included live dancers who would dance along to the hits from each decade. One of the Drifters, "who at that time had been on the road for about forty years, said it was the toughest tour they had ever been on," Bruce says. To me, this tour was not difficult—it was just another tour. Incidentally, it had been Pat Colecchio who convinced Dick Clark to dedicate an entire episode of "A Very Special American Bandstand" to music from The Association.

Donni would get his passport stamped any chance he got—even at the zoo. "When I joined...I learned really fast how intricate the harmonies were." Donni also recounts a trip north on I-95, heading for a concert in New Hampshire, when the cops pulled them over to search for drugs, with the help of some dogs. At that point we were traveling in two white Cadillacs and a white Chrysler convertible (which was Bruce's and my personal vehicle for the summer), and the rest of the bands on that tour and the crew were in a bus. We were on the road, clocking over twenty-seven thousand miles that summer, and I wasn't going to spend it with a roof over my head, so we rented a set of wheels where if I wanted to, I could roll the top down. "The cops thought we were a caravan of dope dealers," Donni remembers, and when the dog pawed at the hubcap of the Cadillac, "they took the hubcaps [off]. It was really ridiculous. Luckily, they didn't go under the spare tire [of the convertible]—Russ had a half a pound of weed there! They searched my wife's luggage, and then they let us go. The bus went by and they all waved at us!" He also fondly recalls performing with us at the 1990 Academy of Songwriters Fifth Annual Salute to the American Songwriter, where Dick and Don Addrisi were honored.

I had scored that weed on the road. I carried weed on me all the way up until the end of the 1980s. While working at a fair

(I think it was the Minnesota State Fair) in the late 1980s, where we had an afternoon show and a night show, we went back to the motel between shows. I was smoking a small amount of weed, but the rooms had transoms above the doors and I forgot to close mine. Someone smelled it—it was a strong, pungent type that a lot of people call "skunk weed"—and called the police, and I was busted by two plainclothes policemen. I sat on the bed with my hands cuffed behind my back.

"What do we do now?" I asked the policeman.

"We'll head to the station and you'll pay a fine," one of them told me.

"Couldn't I just write a check here?" I asked, thinking that would be easier.

"Fine," they said.

"Can you please kindly remove the handcuffs so I can write the check?"

They removed the cuffs, I wrote the check—a couple hundred dollars at most, and they left. I straightened the room—and *never* carried weed on the road again. I haven't done cocaine in a little over twenty years. Maybe ten years ago, a friend of mine called and asked, "Do you know where I can get half a gram of coke?" I told him, "I haven't seen coke in ten years—I really wouldn't know where to get it!" There are other band members who got busted for drugs on the road, but those are their stories to share.

Donni remembers that during one of the gigs where he played with us at a nightclub in a hotel, Jules had gone to the hospital, so Larry and I had to count the money at the end of the night. This wasn't something that we typically had to do, but in this type of venue, we did. "Larry asked Russ to come up and count the money and at the end of the night, the lady turned to Larry and said, 'You're the most arrogant son of a bitch I've ever met.' Then she turned to Russ and she said, 'You, too.' We just laughed our asses off."

David Jackson played with us when we toured the Philippines. He recalls, "Last time we played…we were treated like kings, and a bottle of the best Philippines rum was one dollar." To our surprise, we had a huge fan following, in particular for our song, "No Fair At All" (from our *Renaissance* album), which didn't see that much airplay on American music charts. "The group was once asked to play a song which they 'didn't know was a hit' in the Philippines. Their audience was so disappointed to learn the song was not a part of the band's repertoire; following the tour, the members of the group made it a point to relearn it."[187] We couldn't play the song at their request because we hadn't done it in decades. We made sure to relearn it so we could play it on our next tour there. I loved playing in the Philippines because at breakfast time, there would be ten different juice options. I would always pick something I'd never heard of before. I also love how much Filipinos appreciate great food. The first time we went there, we went to a restaurant with giant clamshells coming out of the walls, with water running into them. Every dish they brought us was outstanding.

"I have never seen men eat with such gusto," our host said.

On one of those trips, Manila was decked out in pink-and-white decorations for Valentine's Day.

"The Filipinos are such horny devils," Larry explained.

"What do you mean?" I asked.

"Well," he said, "they have to get a Valentine's Day gift for their wife, their lover, their mistress, *and* their mother!"

"*My* favorite story," David Jackson shares, "is walking into the Smart Araneta Coliseum[188] in Quezon City outside Manila for sound check, (where it was) boiling hot and damp. [We] got out of the cars, and Russ clapped his hands and it reverberated for two and a half minutes and Russ said, 'That's the sound of rock and roll.'...All of rock and roll started in gymnasiums and high schools and huge, cavernous places, and that's the sound of rock and roll! So perfect,

---

187   Spotlight Central. "'Just like it was the '60s!' The Association LIVE! at The Newton Theatre!" *Medium.* January 26, 2017.

188   This is where Muhammad Ali fought Joe Frazier in the "Thrilla in Manila" on October 1, 1975. Ali won, 2-1.

so clear!" He's right. Before there were ever concerts in stadiums, there were concerts in high school and college auditoriums.

No matter who revolved through the ranks of The Association lineup, the quality of the music did not suffer. We always welcome the musical talents of our contributors. Bob Werner, who played with us first in the mid-1990s for forty to fifty shows and later for something close to three hundred shows between 1999 and 2008, says, "(The Association) always gave us full credit for being part of the group, and we all felt that way for sure." Bob was actually offered a job with the band in 1975—he was a recording engineer and Jim Yester called to offer him a job doing sound. "Bob Werner?" Jim said into the phone. "This is Sargent Taylor from the New York Sherriff County Department. We have some reports of some obscene things going on in your apartment..." Jim joked before offering him a spot in the band. Bob turned it down, but he kept in touch. He owned a music store in Orange County where Larry and Del were customers, and Paul Holland was an employee. Paul would start playing with us in 1988 when we borrowed his keyboard for a recording. About life on the road, Paul shares, "I always say living out of a suitcase is okay if you have the right suitcase. Along the way I've learned things like how to make a grilled cheese sandwich with a travel iron. And how to heat up a pizza or some wings with a cardboard box, a towel, and a blow dryer."

Dick Clark's *American Bandstand* television show had done much to further popular music in the country. "*Bandstand* was one of the first nationwide platforms for rock."[189] Sadly, 1989 was to be the same year the television program ended, when Dick refused ABC's request to reduce the hour length of the show; it was moved to the USA Network with a different host and promptly faltered. The tour, however, did very well. And even though by 1989 we'd been around for twenty-five years, The Association was still answering the same questions.

---

189   Browne, David. "Dick Clark Remembered." *Rolling Stone.* May 10, 2012.

'Is it about marijuana?'

"Everybody always asks, 'Is it about marijuana, is it about marijuana?" said Russ Giguere, the group's only remaining founding member…. "I think it's about everything that was going on then—all the social changes that were going on, all of the feelings."

"But I can tell you when we first heard the song, we didn't know what the hell it was about. Here's the way we heard the song: [former guitarist] Jules [Alexander] cut the demo, and he brought it back to the house where four of us lived. He said, 'Check this song out!' He put the song on and everybody said 'Great tune, let's do it!'"

"And then we asked 'Well, what does it say?' Jules said, 'I don't know, I can't understand the words: we'll work it out as we do it.'"

"People hear what they want to hear, and they interpret what they want to interpret—but that's what art is supposed to be."[190]

And so we continued doing what we do best—making music!

---

190   Lannert, John. "American bandstand tour: Spinner, Drifters, Guess Who join with Association." *The Palm Beach Post.* July 7, 1989.

Never My Love
1990–(I wrote *"never,"* didn't I?)

As we entered the last decade of the twentieth century, The Association continued riding high with hundreds of concerts per year—some of them unusual gigs, and the crowds kept returning. In 1994, in one of those unusual gigs, we spent the summer performing outside Yosemite National Park in the town of Oakhurst in a short-lived venture named "SierraLand," a "new family entertainment complex in the musical tradition of Branson, Mo…the spacious thousand-seat theater offers daily shows including lunch or dinner and an Artisan Fair."[191] The New Christy Minstrels even reformed with some of the original members—Barry McGuire, Dolan Ellis, Art Podell, Paul Potash, Jackie Miller, Gayle Caldwell, Clarence Treat, Ann White, Karen Gunderson, and our own Larry Ramos—to perform there.

Two businessmen had a huge tent erected to serve as the complex's performance area, including one large stage, a smaller stage, a great sound system, and an elaborate light system. A large shop sold souvenir shirts and cigarettes, and a bunch of smaller shops offered soft drinks, ice cream, and local crafts. They even had a gold-panning operation set up for the kids.

The Christys called themselves "The Mountain Minstrels" and The Association was the opening act. Dolan was "Arizona's Official State Balladeer" so he would occasionally have to leave Oakhurst and return to Arizona for a state function, and I'd fill in for him in the Christys. I had to train for this because even though I knew most of their songs, I had to learn to sing and play a few from scratch.

---

191   "Snapshots: Sierraland." *The San Bernadino County Sun.* August 28, 1994.

Larry and Del's cousin, Miles Unite (pronounced "you-nee-tee"), a big fan of Doug Dillard, was brought on as one of the Minstrels' backup band members on banjo. The Association's Donni Gougeon (keyboards), Del Ramos (bass), and Bruce Pictor (drums) also played background on a small stage next to the main one. By the end of the summer, SierraLand had folded, an experience that could fill another book entirely.

Every so often at meet and greets, a devoted fan would pass me a copy of *Hexagram 16* and ask for my John Hancock. Like The Association Admiration Aggregation taught us all those years ago, you answer to your fans—they are the audience that keeps you alive.

And still I was giving those interviews, this time with the "wise" perspective of someone in his sixties.

...[the] Association, the folk-rock band of that name has sold seventy million or more albums since its 1965 debut...

One of the two original members, Russ Giguere, discussed the latest.

How would you describe Association music?

At the time, I thought we were just another rock 'n' roll band, but now when I look back, it's this weird sort of art rock 'n' roll. It's very hard to bag it. We definitely did some good ol' rock 'n' roll, and we did some ballads, and some of that other stuff was strictly art. So I can't really classify it.[192]

Before the September 11, 2001, terrorist attacks, the last concert we'd performed in New York was at the World Trade Center in 1994, the year after the first terrorist attack there, when a bomb exploded. There was a series of noon concerts in the plaza, at the foot of the twin towers, and people came down to a comfortable area with tables, chairs, and trees. We were always thrilled to be in New York and always did great shows. At 6:00 a.m. Los Angeles time, on 9/11/01,

---

192   Locey, Bill. "Harmonic Staying Power: As the Association nears 90 million records sold, its sound is still sweet." *Los Angeles Times*. September 1, 2000.

I turned on the TV and was stunned to see one of the twin towers on fire after being struck by a plane just minutes before. When the second plane deliberately flew into the other tower, I instinctively knew that this was a heartless, gutless attack by soulless assassins on thousands of my innocent brothers and sisters. I expected the death toll to be ten times worse and was grateful for the rescues by the first responders, and the inspirational acts of so many of the people in the buildings. My tears continued for a long time and turned to rage as I went from being a pacifist peace creep to a warmonger.

We played concerts that were already on the books for the remainder of 2001, but after 9/11 we went five or six months with no additional bookings. I don't know if there was any reasoning behind this, or it was just an emotional response, but the dates just weren't there. Eventually, the bookings picked back up. We did countless cruises in addition to our standard concert venues, and when we finally worked New York again a couple of years later, it was at the Rainbow Room at Rockefeller Center with the Coasters, at a birthday party for a very wealthy man, and the work picked up from there.

Our music still gets airplay; a few years ago "Never My Love" was used in a commercial, and we made money on that. In 2006 we sang a medley of "Cherish"/"Windy" with Barry Manilow on his CD *The Greatest Songs of the Sixties*. The *Los Angeles Times* wrote, "He even enlists The Association, the choral group whose 1967 hit 'Windy' turned hippie femininity into something worthy of a *Good Housekeeping* seal, for a medley-blending hit that hit with the group's 'Cherish,' from the previous year. The pairing produces a marvelous sonic wreck, a hyper-arranged mishmash that merges a painfully sad song with a demonically perky one, ultimately eliminating coherent feeling altogether."[193]

Ouch! Remember, a reviewer is one person's opinion in a world of many. Bob Werner calls Larry and me "road dogs forever," but in January 2014, I retired from performing with The Association,

---

193   Powers, Ann. "Music for the rocker: Rod Stewart and Barry Manilow rework rock history into something lulling and safe." *Los Angeles Times*. November 4, 2006.

though I still do the books (accounting) and work with the agency for the bookings. When I retired, I wrote a long letter that was published on The Association's official website, mostly talking about my recent health issues and the death of important people in my life—from my mother to Noma, Penny, and Birdie, to Paul Revere of the Raiders, to Doug Dillard, and finally to Larry:

> ...Then there's Larry Ramos...He had a heart attack at the end of September 2011 after returning home from the road. This of course was quite unexpected and a tragic turn of events, especially for his wife and ninety-year-old mother who both lived with him in Idaho. He had a large family, friends and of course the group. We brought in Godfrey Townsend; singer, guitarist and leader of the band for the 2011 Happy Together Tour for dates Larry couldn't make.
>
> Larry came back with the band after he was feeling stronger. Larry was a real dyed-in-the-wool trouper, the road had been a major part of his life for many years. After he was feeling better he did some shows with us, but later had more problems so we called Jules and he said he would come into the band for a month or so. A few days later, Larry took another turn for the worse and Jules rejoined the band at my request. Larry would come on the road with us when he could. He felt we couldn't afford to tour with seven guys, but as far as I was concerned, Jules brought 110 percent to the band—Jim and the rest of the guys loved it, so we did it.
>
> A while later, Larry told me he had three months to live. He was right. April 30, 2014 he was gone. His passing was made easier by his attitude toward it. Still, it was a great loss!...

In January 2014, I retired from the group. After Noma was gone, everything became difficult. I increased my tobacco smoking and it had a negative effect on my voice. I could still hit the notes, but not with the quality I felt was necessary for The Association.

As to my physical condition, in August 2014, I had a biopsy and was diagnosed with prostate cancer. In October, I began ten weeks of forty-two radiation treatments, which ended December 16. This was radiation, not chemotherapy. I also had a head-to-toe bone scan to determine if I had bone cancer; I do not. I have been asked if I had radiation burns; I do not. The therapy was very precise, in fact it's called Accu-Beam.

I am somewhat of a recluse; I socialize some. My dog Annie (she's half-Yorkie and half-Maltese) is twelve years old and eleven pounds; she takes me for walks five times a day. We walk in the hills; around the block; at one of the many parks nearby and sometimes just down the street.

Everything has changed. I still drink, but every week or two. I eat a pie a week and have dessert with every meal; a nutritional shake every day (used by most people as a meal replacement, I use it as a supplement) all to keep my weight up. Generally I eat like a big ol' pig. My urologist tells me my PSA test came back ZERO, so the radiology seems to have worked. Being bathed with invisible rays was somewhat debilitating, but I'm improving. I'm on hormones and yes, I have hot flashes. I take Flomax. Jim used to joke about how now when we talk about taking drugs, it's most likely Flomax.

The Association features: Jim Yester; tenor/rhythm guitar, Jules Alexander; tenor/lead guitar—both original members; Del Ramos; baritone/bass (Larry's brother), our drummer since 1985; Bruce Pictor, baritone; Jordan Cole, keyboard/guitar/recorder; tenor-bass (Brian Cole's son); and of course our newest member Paul Holland, tenor-baritone/guitar. Paul is an excellent singer, musician, and human. Paul was with us for years (starting in the 1980s). Larry and I thought highly of him.

The group sounds great and is still one of the best vocal & rock and roll bands on the planet.

Good art.

God bless us everyone.

Love,

Russ

I'm no longer on hormones. I omitted one of the paragraphs that appeared in the original letter because I said we went with a new agent. We did, but as it turns out this man was not a licensed agent. One year, he booked us just ten dates for the entire year.

"The group can't exist on just ten concerts a year," I told him.

"You need to economize," he told me.

The next day, we went with Paradise Artists and are now doing great. I soon learned that this former "agent" of ours was a thief and a liar. I have proof that he took $11,500 off the top—and that's just one date.

I'm no longer performing with the band, but I do see them play live every time they're local, and I'm still talking to all the guys, as with Larry gone, I'm the only owner of the band still alive! So I'm still running the show, saying yes to the concerts, and making sure all is fair and everyone is getting paid—all that business stuff I never thought I would be doing in a million years. Bruce recently shared, "I enjoy the personnel of the group right now. There are very few arguments, everybody's a little older on the tour, and we have a great time. Larry and Russ, when they ran the group—they're pretty much polar opposites in their approach to life and the way things should be run, and with Russell at the helm now, he lets us do our thing. There's nobody telling us what to do, which wasn't always the case. We go out and we're comfortable and we have fun and it's just as good as it ever was."

In January 2014, *Goldmine* also inducted us into their Hall of Fame:

> This six-man band from California released two[194] of the most played songs in the history of recorded music. That both were slow love songs paints a distorted picture of what The Association was capable of. And while some discredit them because session musicians participated in some of their output, those who had the good fortune to hear them live in their prime will attest to their proficiency, both instrumentally and vocally.[195]

Writing this book has taken a few years to put together—I figured I'd be dead by the time it came out. But it has been a great experience for me. I've read so much over the years about the group that is just flat-out lies and untruths that I felt compelled to set the record straight. The opinions in this book are not all mine, but they are all real.

On my seventy-fifth birthday in October 2018, I was at the mechanic, getting my brakes done. While washing my hands in the bathroom, I looked in the mirror and discovered an inch-long ear hair sticking out. I hope there's more to growing old than this. But maybe not!

You know, some bands make it, and some bands don't. We were fortunate to be one of the ones that did. And that's a huge reason why I wanted to share my story with you—because I know that even after I'm long gone, the music, our legacy, will live on. What's the reason why some make it and some don't? Much of that has to do with talent and quality of the product (music), a strong work ethic, and perseverance. A lot of it also has to do with the mix of attitudes and personalities, and the gambles the people you trust (agents, managers, bookkeepers, record producers) take on the decisions

194   Incorrect! We released *three* of the most played songs in the history of recorded music: "Never My Love," "Cherish," and "Windy."

195   Goldmine's Hall of Fame Inductees. Vol. 1. January 30, 2014.

they make: Which record should you release first? Which record should you release second? How long should you wait? How often and where should you tour? How do you depart from what you're "known" for?

Ultimately, it's a combination of all of the above. Every guy in the band or crew who traveled with us will have his theories or his private opinions of the other members. "Over that many years," Marty shares, "there was a lot of baggage everyone was carrying with them—this guy can't stand this guy—there were big issues between a couple of them. Somebody had no business ever drinking at all and if they did, the rest of the band was pissed because he was a jerk the next day, or somebody would get high and somebody else didn't like that. But they were very professional when it came to showtime. Getting drunk or getting high, that was after showtime." Well, now, that last part is also true. We didn't mix the pleasure of... *extracurriculars*...with the pleasure of performing.

But in the end, all it really boils down to is the lasting power of the beauty of the music. That's all you're left with—it's what you remember and take with you—it's what keeps us going and keeps people coming back.

Whenever I did a concert, I didn't really want to *think*—it's best just to *be*. The sound and our monitors should always be perfect, and they usually were. When you can't hear everything onstage, you can't get a proper vocal blend. Even when it's wrong in the stage monitors (and this is the hard part) onstage, you have to make it sound right for the audience. This is when you use knowledge, balls, and, dammit, *thought*. I hate to think of it!

But when it's perfect, it's heaven, and *that's* always worth going for. In the nineties, I remember we were performing at Disney World and signing autographs after a show. A mom and her ten-year-old daughter approached us in the autograph line and as I was signing, the little girl asked me, "What's it like to be onstage and make such beautiful music?"

"In all my years," I told her, "I've never been asked that question." I then thought for a moment. "You know how you feel when you're riding in a car with the radio on and your favorite song is playing and you're singing along and everything is perfect? That's it—only *you're* making the music."

I once saw a TV show on John Philip Sousa—who I feel had the first "supergroup"—and he told his band something like, "Always do the music perfectly. You never know when someone will be hearing it for the first time." I'm paraphrasing what I heard, but you get the idea. That's the magic I felt every single time I performed with The Association.

And that's what I'll always *cherish*.

The Association...by the Numbers

To date, The Association has:
sold more than 70 million records

and with:
6 gold records
1 platinum record (2 times over)
7 Grammy nominations
1 Golden Globe nomination

7 Top 40 Hits:
"Along Comes Mary"—#7
"Cherish"—#1
"Never My Love"—#1
"Windy"—#1
"Everything That Touches You"—#10
"Pandora's Golden Heebie Jeebies"—#35
"Time for Livin'"—#39

and

3 of their songs listed as the most played BMI-licensed
songs of the twentieth century:
"Never My Love"—#2
"Cherish"—#22
"Windy"—#61

the honor of:
opening the 1967 Monterey Pop Festival

the first rock and roll band to play:
Cocoanut Grove

Greek Theater

Tanglewood Music Festival

Blossom Musical Festival

Ravinia Park

...to name just a few...

Somewhere in a city or town near you...
The Association is still rocking out in concerts played for
their fans

and The Association remains...
Unnecessary

like

Water

Sleep

Food

and

Love.[196]

---

196   The original slogan as printed on buttons worn proudly by members of the Association Admiration Aggregation (AAA).

THE ASSOCIATION IS UNNECESSARY
like
WATER
SLEEP
FOOD
and LOVE

BMI Top 100 Songs of the Twentieth Century

1. "You've Lost That Lovin' Feelin'," Barry Mann, Phil Spector, & Cynthia Weil
2. **"Never My Love," Donald & Richard Addrisi**
3. "Yesterday," John Lennon & Paul McCartney
4. "Stand By Me," Ben E. King, Jerry Leiber, & Mike Stoller
5. "Can't Take My Eyes Off of You," Bob Crewe & Bob Gaudio
6. "Sitting on the Dock of the Bay," Steve Cropper & Otis Redding
7. "Mrs. Robinson," Paul Simon
8. "Baby, I Need Your Loving," Lamont Dozier, Brian Holland, & Eddie Holland
9. "Rhythm of the Rain," John Gummoe
10. "Georgia on My Mind," Hoagy Carmichael & Stuart Gorrell
11. "Killing Me Softly with His Song," Charles Fox & Norman Gimbel
12. "More," Marcello Ciorciolini, Norman Newell, Nino Oliviero, & Riz Ortolani
13. "I Will Always Love You," Dolly Parton
14. "When a Man Loves a Woman," Calvin Lewis & Andrew J. Wright
15. "Every Breath You Take," Sting
16. "Gentle on My Mind," John Hartford
17. "Something," George Harrison
18. "Sounds of Silence," Paul Simon
19. "Bridge Over Troubled Water," Paul Simon
20. "By the Time I Get to Phoenix," Jimmy Webb

21. "Angel of the Morning," Chip Taylor
22. **"Cherish," Terry Kirkman**
23. "You Can't Hurry Love," Lamont Dozier, Brian Holland, & Eddie Holland
24. "Proud Mary," John Fogerty
25. "Sunny," Bobby Hebb
26. "Oh, Pretty Woman," William Dees & Roy Orbison
27. "Everybody's Talkin'," Fred Neil
28. "I Heard It Through the Grapevine," Barrett Strong & Norman Whitfield
29. "Goin' Out of My Head," Teddy Randazzo & Bobby Weinstein
30. "Suspicious Minds," Mark James
31. "Scarborough Fair," Art Garfunkel & Paul Simon
32. "Traces," Buddy Buie, J. R. Cobb, & Emory Gordy
33. "All I Have to Do Is Dream," Boudleaux Bryant
34. "Only You," Ande Rand & Buck Ram
35. "Canadian Sunset," Norman Gimbel & Eddie Heywood
36. "Oh Girl," Eugene Record
37. "Your Song," Elton John & Bernie Taupin
38. "How Sweet It Is (To Be Loved By You)," Lamont Dozier, Brian Holland, & Eddie Holland
39. "(Your Love Has Lifted Me) Higher and Higher," Gary Jackson, Raynard Miner, & Carl William Smith
40. "I Can't Stop Loving You," Don Gibson
41. "Wind Beneath My Wings," Larry Henley & Jeff Silbar
42. "Michelle," John Lennon & Paul McCartney
43. "Up, Up and Away," Jimmy Webb
44. "Happy Together," Garry Bonner & Alan Gordon
45. "On Broadway," Jerry Leiber, Barry Mann, Mike Stoller, & Cynthia Weil
46. "Twilight Time," Al Nevins, Morty Nevins, & Buck Ram
47. "Strangers in the Night," Bert Kaempfert, Charles Singleton, & Eddie Snyder

48. "Breaking Up Is Hard to Do," Howard Greenfield & Neil Sedaka
49. "Save the Last Dance for Me," Doc Pomus & Mort Shuman
50. "For the Good Times," Kris Kristofferson
51. "We've Only Just Begun," Roger Nichols & Paul Williams
52. "What a Wonderful World," Lou Adler, Herb Alpert, & Sam Cooke
53. "Snowbird," Gene MacLellan
54. "Everlasting Love," Buzz Cason & Mac Gayden
55. "My Special Angel," Jimmy Duncan
56. "The Most Beautiful Girl," Rory Bourke, Billy Sherrill, & Norro Wilson
57. "Brown Eyed Girl," Van Morrison
58. "The Girl from Ipanema," Vinicius DeMoraes, Norman Gimbel, & Antonio Carlos Jobim
59. "My Cherie Amour," Sylvia Moy, Henry Cosby, & Stevie Wonder
60. "Always on My Mind," Wayne Carson, Johnny Christopher, & Mark James
61. **"Windy," Ruthann Friedman**
62. "If You Don't Know Me by Now," Kenneth Gamble & Leon Huff
63. "Margaritaville," Jimmy Buffett
64. "Spanish Eyes," Bert Kaempfert, Charles Singleton, & Eddie Snyder
65. "Daydream Believer," John Stewart
66. "Daniel," Elton John and Bernie Taupin
67. "Take It Easy," Glenn Frey & Jackson Browne
68. "Let Your Love Flow," Larry Williams
69. "The Rose," Amanda McBroom
70. "The Heart of the Matter," Don Henley, J. D. Souther, & Mike Campbell
71. "Don't Be Cruel," Otis Blackwell & Elvis Presley
72. "Listen to the Music," Tom Johnston
73. "A Groovy Kind of Love," Carole Bayer Sager & Toni Wine
74. "Crying," Joe Melson & Roy Orbison

75. "Put a Little Love In Your Heart," Jackie DeShannon, Jimmy
    Holiday, & Randy Myers
76. "Don't Let the Sun Go Down on Me," Elton John & Bernie Taupin
77. "Help Me Make It Through the Night," Kris Kristofferson
78. "Best of My Love," Glenn Frey, Don Henley, & J. D. Souther
79. "The Letter," Wayne Carson
80. "Dreams," Stevie Nicks
81. "Mr. Bojangles," Jerry Jeff Walker
82. "Fire and Rain," James Taylor
83. "Then You Can Tell Me Goodbye," John D. Loudermilk
84. "Hooked on a Feeling," Mark James
85. "Blue Bayou," Joe Melson & Roy Orbison
86. "Born Free," John Barry & Don Black
87. "Release Me, Eddie Miller," Dub Williams & Robert Yount
88. "It's Just a Matter of Time," Brook Benton, Belford Hendricks,
    & Clyde Otis
89. "Let It Be," John Lennon & Paul McCartney
90. "I'd Really Love to See You Tonight," Parker McGee
91. "(I Can't Get No) Satisfaction," Mick Jagger & Keith Richards
92. "Up on the Roof," Gerry Goffin & Carole King
93. "Layla," Eric Clapton & Jim Gordon
94. "I Honestly Love You," Peter Allen & Jeff Barry
95. "California Girls," Mike Love & Brian Wilson
96. "Imagine," John Lennon
97. "You Send Me," Sam Cooke
98. "How Deep Is Your Love," Barry, Maurice, & Robin Gibb
99. "I Never Promised You a Rose Garden," Joe South
100. "Sometimes When We Touch," Barry Mann & Dan Hill

Bonus Appendix

Other bands and acts The Association has performed with live on the same bill (1965–present)

Symbols
The 5th Dimension

A
America
Nancy Ames
The Animals
Frankie Avalon

B
Baja Marimba Band
Chuck Berry
Beach Boys
Big Brother and The Holding Company /Janis Joplin
Les Brown and His Band of Renown
Oscar Brown Jr.
Debbie Boone
The Box Tops
Buffalo Springfield
The Buckinghams
The Byrds

C
Canned Heat
Ray Charles
The Chiffons

Petula Clark
The Committee
The Cowsills
Norm Crosby

D
Bo Diddley
The Dillards
The Dixie Cups
Dr. Hook & The Medicine Show

F
Lola Falana
The Four Tops
Aretha Franklin
Annette Funicello

G
Gary Lewis & the Playboys
Gary Puckett and The Union Gap
Crystal Gayle
Lesley Gore
The Grass Roots
The Grateful Dead
The Guess Who

H
Richie Havens
Jimi Hendrix
Herman's Hermits
Al Hirt
Bob Hope

I
Janis Ian

Marty Ingels
The Irish Rovers

J
Wolfman Jack
Jay and The Americans
Jefferson Airplane

K
B. B. King

L
The Lettermen
Jerry Lee Lewis
Mark Lindsay
Little Anthony and the Imperials
Little Eva
Little Richard
Los Piccolinos
The Lovin' Spoonful

M
Miriam Makeba
The Mamas and the Papas
Martha & the Vandellas
Hugh Masekela
Mitch Ryder and The Detroit Wheels
The Mob
Moby Grape
The Modern Folk Quartet
Wes Montgomery

N
Rick Nelson
The Nelson Riddle Orchestra

The Nitty Gritty Dirt Band
Peter Noone

O
Donald O'Connor

P
Paul Revere & The Raiders
Pat Paulsen
Peter & Gordon

Q
Quicksilver Messenger Service

R
The Rascals
Lou Rawls
Otis Redding
Debbie Reynolds
The Righteous Brothers
Johnny Rivers
The Rolling Stones
Linda Ronstadt

S
The Shangri-Las
Ravi Shankar
The Shirelles
Judee Sill
Simon & Garfunkel
Frank Sinatra
Sir Douglas Quintet
Sly and the Family Stone
The Smothers Brothers
David (Troy) Somerville

Sopwith Camel
Spanky & Our Gang
The Spinners
Spirit
Dusty Springfield
Frank Stallone
Connie Stevens
Strawberry Alarm Clock
The Supremes

T
B. J. Thomas
Three Dog Night
Tommy James and the Shondells
The Turtles

W
The Who
Mason Williams
Flip Wilson

Index

NOTE: The abbreviation *f.* following a page number indicates a graphic or photo.

"Maggie and Jiggs"—Mom and Dad—were married on February 16, 1942.

The father I never knew, Russell Henry Giguere, Sr., Chief Pharmacist's Mate of the USS Plymouth.

A traveling photographer took this shot of me on his pony in San Diego, at our house on Marlboro Street near University Ave.

Left: With my half-siblings Judy Beisner and Nancy and Tyson Bilyue in San Diego on Easter Sunday 1956.

Right: My original business card as Light and Sound Technician and Hootenanny Coordinator at The Ice House.

Delight

RUSS GIGUERE
LIGHT & SOUND TECHNIC
HOOTENANNY CO-ORDINA

BE PEACEFUL DURING SHOWS

Left: This image ran with the Sept. 6, 1963, Los Angeles Times story on the Pasadena Junior Bachelors Party at The Ice House.

Nelson Tiffany

Above: The Men before I joined. Back row, l-r: Harvey Gerst, Terry Kirkman, Ted Bluechel, Nyles Brown, Bob Page, Mike Whalen. Front row: Gary Jules Alexander, Howard Wilcox, Steven Cohen, Brian Cole, and Steve Stapenhorst.

Right: Me at eighteen, when I was a dental supply shipping clerk. I usually wore a shirt.

Andy Williams takes the lead and sings his favorite Association song, "Changes," (music/lyrics by Jules) with us on The Andy Williams Show *in 1966.*

George Burns and Carol Channing attended our opening show at The Cocoanut Grove *in September 1967. We were the first rock and roll band to play the venue.*

This was our first formal shot taken by Steven Poster on the south wall of the exterior of the Los Angeles County Museum of Art.

Henry Diltz

Playing wiffle football with The Lovin' Spoonful band and crew while on tour. Left to right: our sound man, Steve Nelson; Terry Kirkman; me; Steve Boone; Ted Bluechel; Zal Yanovsky; a crew member.

Malcolm Lubliner

"What do the handcuffs mean, Brian?"

Photos from our tour of Texas in 1967, after Larry Ramos joined the band.

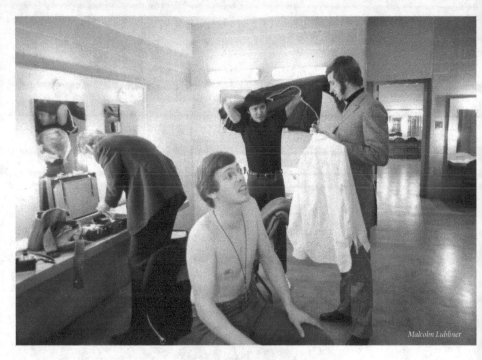

"I think I'll wear a shirt." Jim, me, Larry, and Terry before a show.

Oinking at the airport before taking off again. Me, Brian, and Jim.

Me, Ted, Larry, Jim, Brian, and Terry goofing off in a Texas park.

Larry and I at the iconic Hollywood Bowl on November 19, 1967.

During a live taping for a talk show in Antwerp, Belgium, on our 1968 European Tour, Brian and I were inspired to begin doing these high kicks at the end of "Windy."

Henry Diltz

This is from a photo session for our 1969 Stonehenge album. Jim and Ted (shirtless) are wearing $20 gold pieces around their necks, which we all had. I still have mine.

My first solo band, the original Beachwood Rangers, included left to right: the soon to be famous Warren Zevon, Bill Martin (playing my guitar here), me, and Don Beck, who played banjo and guitar.

My band Hollywood in the early 1970s. Back row: Lee Mallory (guitar), Gary Sherwood (bass), Steve Edwards (guitar). Front: Michael Ney (drums), me (guitar, lead vocals), Scott Shelley (guitar and keyboards).

Rock photographer Linda Eastman (later Mrs. Paul McCartney) took this shot inside Terry Kirkman's house below the Hollywood sign. Our manager Pat Colecchio is seated at the bottom of the stairs.

I joined Jules's band, Bijou, in the 1970s. Clockwise from top left: Kit Lane, Jules Alexander, Michael Williams, me, Carol Hunter, Tony Greco, and sisters Alex Sliwin and Joan Sliwin.

Henry Diltz

With our manager, Pat Colecchio, at CBS in April 1969. I loved this man.

The multitalented Bill Martin and I worked as a comedy duo, Martin & Giguere, for a couple of years in the mid-1970s. Bill was one of the most creative, kindest, funniest, and off-the-wall people I've ever known.

When the band reformed in 1980, we added Ric Ulsky (far left) on keyboards and singing bass because The Old Dead Guy (Brian) was no longer available.

A band line-up from the 2000s. Clockwise from the top left: Jordan Cole (Brian's son), Del Ramos (Larry's brother), Bruce Pictor, Larry Ramos, Jim Yester, and me.

Henry Diltz

Henry Diltz

The current lineup of The Association since 2014. Front row, left to right: Jules Alexander, Jim Yester, Del Ramos. Back row: Paul Holland, Jordan Cole, Bruce Pictor.

*Me onstage in the 1990s—I think! My daughter gave me
the black onyx bolo tie for my birthday.*

Printed in the USA
CPSIA information can be obtained
at www.ICGtesting.com
JSHW031208030124
54720JS00002B/5